Communications
in Computer and Information Science 409

Borworn Papasratorn   Nipon Charoenkitkarn
Vajirasak Vanijja   Vithida Chongsuphajaisiddhi (Eds.)

Advances in Information Technology

6th International Conference, IAIT 2013
Bangkok, Thailand, December 12-13, 2013
Proceedings

Springer

Volume Editors

Borworn Papasratorn
Nipon Charoenkitkarn
Vajirasak Vanijja
Vithida Chongsuphajaisiddhi

King Mongkut's University of Technology Thonburi
School of Information Technology
126 Pracha-U-Thit Rd.
Bangmod, Thungkru, Bangkok 10140, Thailand
E-mail: {borworn; nipon; vachee; vithida}@sit.kmutt.ac.th

ISSN 1865-0929   e-ISSN 1865-0937
ISBN 978-3-319-03782-0   e-ISBN 978-3-319-03783-7
DOI 10.1007/978-3-319-03783-7
Springer Cham Heidelberg New York Dordrecht London

Library of Congress Control Number: 2013951793

CR Subject Classification (1998): H.3, I.2, C.2, H.5, I.4, I.5, H.2.8, H.4

Typesetting: Camera-ready by author, data conversion by Scientific Publishing Services, Chennai, India

Printed on acid-free paper

Springer is part of Springer Science+Business Media (www.springer.com)

Preface

It is true that information technology (IT) provides new opportunities for humanity. Today, IT promises not only to improve our business, but also the effectiveness of learning and health care. IT accelerates the global integration of social and economic activities, leading to new applications for the improvement of life quality. It also offers several opportunities to any community to leapfrog to the future with advanced economic and social development. In view of this, IAIT 2013 focused on the effective deployment of IT. IAIT 2013 aimed at not only fostering the awareness and appreciation of the advances in technology , but also at assisting IT professionals to develop strategies to deploy the current and future technology for the benefit of mankind.

One special aspect of IAIT, which is not always found in large international conference, is its friendly atmosphere giving experts, scholars, and industrialists the chance to exchange research ideas, research finding, best practice, and challenges related to the deployment of IT. For years, IAIT has shown that informal discussion can lead to new ideas and fruitful collaboration. There are 56 papers submitted to the review process. There are 23 papers from 13 countries are accepted and published in the proceedings.

Many thanks go to all authors for their submissions and everyone who participated in this year's event. Our thanks also go to the many people who helped make this conference happen, including our Advisory Committee, keynote speakers, and the editorial team at Springer.

We hope that IAIT will continue to be a forum for the stimulating exchange of ideas to enable us to build future IT applications that surpass what we can currently envision.

October 2013   Borworn Papasratorn

Organization

IAIT2013 was organized by the School of Information Technology, King Mongkut's University of Technology Thonburi.

Executive Committee

Honorary Chairs

Borworn Papasratorn, Thailand
Roland Traunmuller, Austria

Program Chairs

Hironori Nakajo, Japan
Kittichai Lavangnananda, Thailand
Prutikrai Mahatanankoon, USA
Wichian Chutimaskul, Thailand

Advisory Committee

A. Min Tjoa, Austria
Gerald Quirchmayr, Austria
James H. Kauffman, USA
Joaquin Vila-Ruiz, USA
Jonathan H. Chan, Thailand
Keiichi Kaneko, Japan
Mark Chignell, Canada
Nipon Charoenkitkarn, Thailand
Pascal Bouvry, Luxembourg
Sung-Bae Cho, Korea
Wichian Chutimaskul, Thailand
Yannick Le Moullec, Denmark

Organizing Committee

Vajirasak Vanijja, Thailand
Vithida Chongsuphajaisiddhi, Thailand
Suree Funilkul, Thailand
Ekapong Jungcharoensukying, Thailand

Program Committee

C. Arpnikanondt

L. Boongasame

P. Bouvry

J.H. Chan

N. Charoenkitkarn

Y. Chen

M. Chignell

L.P. Chin

S. Cho

V. Chongsuphajaisiddhi

H. Chu

N. Churcher

W. Chutimaskul

A. Delis

S. Eriksen

S. Funilkul

Osama Halabi

C. Haruechaiyasak

A.N. Hidayanto

M. Jeremy

A. Kamiya

K. Kaneko

J.H. Kauffman

K. Lavangnananda

Y. Le Moullec

K. Lertwachara

H. Marzi

F. Masaru

J. Millard

P. Mongkolnam

T. Neligwa

A.A. Niknafs

C. Nukoolkit

B. Papasratorn

A. Piyatumrong

M. Plaisent

K. Porkaew

N. Premasathian

G. Quirchmayr

O. Rojanapornpun

K. Sandhu

Y. Sato

T. Soorapanth

A. Srivihok

G. Stylianou

U. Supasitthimethee

M. Suzuki

W. Tangkuptanon

S. Thainimit

A.M. Tjoa

V. Vanijja

K. Vibhatavanij

J. Vila-Ruiz

S. Wangpipatwong

T. Wangpipatwong

N. Waraporn

B. Watanapa

L. Wilson

F. Yang

C.C. Yu

Table of Contents

Mining Top-k Frequent/Regular Patterns Based on User-Given Trade-Off between Frequency and Regularity

Komate Amphawan[1,*] and Philippe Lenca[2]

[1] CIL, Faculty of Informatics, Burapha University, Chonburi 20131, Thailand
`komate@gmail.com`
[2] Institut Telecom, Telecom Bretagne, UMR CNRS 6285 Lab-STICC, France
`philippe.lenca@telecom-bretagne.eu`

Abstract. Frequent-Regular pattern mining has been introduced to extract interesting patterns based on their occurrence behavior. This approach considers the terms of frequency and regularity to determine significant of patterns under user-given support and regularity thresholds. However, it is well-known that setting of thresholds to discover the most interesting results is a very difficult task and it is more reasonable to avoid specifying the suitable thresholds by letting users assign only simple parameters. In this paper, we introduce an alternative approach, called *Top-k frequent/regular pattern mining based on weights of interests*, which allows users to assign two simple parameters: (*i*) a weight of interest on frequency/regularity and (*ii*) a number of desired patterns. To mine patterns, we propose an efficient single-pass algorithm, *TFRP-Mine*, to quickly mine patterns with frequent/regular appearance. Experimental results show that our approach can effectively and efficiently discover the valuable patterns that meet the users' interest.

Keywords: Association rule, Frequent patterns, Top-k frequent patterns, Frequent-regular itemset, Top-k frequent regular patterns.

1 Introduction

The frequent pattern mining problem, introduced in [1], plays a major role in many data mining tasks that aim to find interesting patterns from databases. Many efficient algorithms have been proposed for a large category of patterns. Excellent surveys can be found in [2, 3]. Roughly speaking, a pattern X is called frequent if its support is no less than a given minimal absolute support threshold where the support of X is the number of its occurrences in the database (support is also often considered from relative frequency point of view with a minimal frequency threshold). Obviously, frequent pattern mining gives an important role to occurrence frequency.

---

* Corresponding author.

B. Papasratorn et al. (Eds.): IAIT 2013, CCIS 409, pp. 1–12, 2013.

However, the occurrence behavior of patterns (*i.e.* whether a pattern occurs regularly, irregularly, or mostly in a specific time interval) may also be an important criteria in various applications (*e.g.* retail marketing [4], stock marketing [5], elderly daily habits' monitoring [6], etc.). The frequent-regular pattern mining problem thus also consider the maximum interval at which a pattern occurs (or disappears) in the database. To mine frequent-regular patterns, the users have to assign two parameters: (*i*) support and (*ii*) regularity thresholds. However, it is well-known that it is not an obvious task. If the support threshold is too large, then there may be only a small number of results or even no result. In that case, the user may have to fix a smaller threshold and do the mining again. If the threshold is too small, then there may be too many results for the users. Thus, asking the number of desired outputs is considered easier and mining top-k patterns has become a very popular task (see for example [7–13]).

The problem of top-k frequent-regular patterns mining was introduced in [14] and enhanced in [15, 16]. It aims at mining the k patterns with highest support that occur regularly (the users has to specify a regularity threshold and the number k of desired results). Moreover, frequent-regular patterns mining was extended in several manners (e.g. on incremental transactional databases [17], on data stream [18], for both frequent and rare items [19], with maximum items' support constraints [20]).

However, all approaches mentioned above need to specify an appropriate value of regularity threshold to discover results. In the same way as the support threshold, if the regularity threshold is set too small, there may be only few regular patterns or even no patterns. On the other hand, there may be too many patterns with a large regularity threshold. We thus propose a trade-off between support and regularity. Indeed, the user may also be interested by a mix between frequency and regularity. The trade-off can simply be tuned with a weight parameter. According to his preferences the user may then choose to focus more or less on frequency and/or regularity.

The rest of this paper is organized as follows. Sections 2 introduce the top-k frequent-regular patterns mining problem. Section 3 extend the problem to top-k frequent-regular pattern under user-given weights of interest. The proposed *TFRP-Mine* algorithm is described in details in Section 4. Section 5 reports the experimental study. Finally, we conclude the paper in Section 6.

2   Notations on Top-k Frequent-Regular Patterns Mining

Let $I = \{i_1, i_2, \ldots, i_n\}$ be a set of items. A set $X \subseteq I$ is called a pattern (itemset), or a k-pattern when it contains k items. A transaction database $TDB = \{t_1, t_2, \ldots, t_m\}$ is a set of m transactions which each transaction $t_q = (tid, Y)$ is a tuple containing: (*i*) a unique transaction identifier, $tid = q$, and (*ii*) Y is a set of items. If $X \subseteq Y$, then X occurs in t_q, denoted as t_q^X. We define $T^X = \{t_p^X, \ldots, t_q^X\}$ $(1 \leq p \leq q \leq m)$, as the set, called *tidset*, of all *ordered* *tids* in which X appears. The support (frequency) of a pattern X, denoted as $s^X = |T^X|$, is also defined as the number of *tids* (transactions) that contain X.

To measure the regularity of occurrence of X (as described in [5]), let t_p^X and t_q^X be any two consecutive *tids* in T^X. The regularity between the two consecutive *tids*, *i.e.* the number of *tids* not containing X between t_p^X and t_q^X, can be expressed as $rtt_q^X = t_q^X - t_p^X$. In addition, for the first and the last occurrences of X, their regularities are also regarded as (i) the first regularity is the number of *tids* not containing X before its first appearance, $fr^X = t_1^X$, and (ii) the last regularity is the number of *tids* not containing X from the last occurrence of X to the end of database, $lr^X = |TDB| - t_{|T^X|}^X$. Based on the regularity values mentioned above, we can define the total regularity of X as follows:

Definition 1. *The regularity of X is the maximum number of tids (transactions) that X disappears from database which can be defined as,*

$$r^X = max(fr^X, rtt_2^X, rtt_3^X, \ldots, rtt_{|T^X|}^X, lr^X)$$

From the regularity of X, we can guarantee that X will appear at least once in every set of r^X consecutive transactions. The problem of frequent-regular pattern mining is thus to discover patterns that frequently and regularly appear in a database. However, frequent-regular patterns mining still suffer from setting of appropriate thresholds [14]. Hence, the *Top-k frequent-regular pattern mining* [14] was proposed to avoid the difficulties of setting an appropriate support threshold by allowing users to control the number of patterns to be mined. It can be defined as follows:

Definition 2. *A pattern X is called a top-k frequent-regular pattern if (i) its regularity is no greater than a user-given regularity threshold σ_r and (ii) there exist no more than $k-1$ patterns whose support is higher than that of X.*

The users have thus to specify only the number k of desired patterns and a regularity threshold σ_r to obtain the k regular patterns with highest support. However, it can be still difficult to specify a proper regularity threshold.

3 Defining of the User-Given Weights of Interest on Support/Regularity

We here introduce an alternative approach, called *Top-k frequent/regular pattern mining based on user-given weight of interest*, to discover patterns by alleviating difficulties of setting the appropriate thresholds. This approach requires users to specify two simple parameters: (i) the number of desired patterns (k) and (ii) a weight indicated users' interest on frequency/support(λ) or regularity(ϕ) (the users can identify only one or both weights in range $[0, 1]$; the summation of the two weights is equal to 1). This lets the users to express their interest on the support and/or regularity measures. We thus define the following notations/definitions for our approach.

Definition 3. *Let* $\lambda \in [0,1]$ *be the weight of support given by a user; the weight of regularity is then* $\phi = 1 - \lambda$. *On the other hands, if the user gives weight of regularity,* $\phi \in [0,1]$, *the weight of support is* $\lambda = 1 - \phi$.

With the user-given weights of interest on support/regularity values, we then define the *support-regularity value* of the patterns to measure their interestingness based on weights of interest under the support and regularity constraints.

Definition 4. *Let the weights of interest be* λ *and* ϕ. *The value of support-regularity of a pattern* X *is defined as* $sr^X = (\lambda)(s^X) - (\phi)(r^X)$.

The *support-regularity* of any pattern is in $[-m, m]$ where m is the number of transactions. Patterns with high support and low regularity will have high *support-regularity*. Otherwise, the value of *support-regularity* depends on user-given weights. If user gives high weight of support λ (weight of regularity ϕ will be low), the patterns with high support and high regularity will have the *support-regularity* greater than that of patterns with low support and low regularity. Lastly, patterns with low support and high regularity will absolutely have low *support-regularity value*. We can thus define the the top-k frequent-regular pattern mining problem under user-given weights of interest as follow.

Definition 5. *A pattern* X *is called a top-k frequent/regular pattern based on under-given trade-off between frequency and regularity if there exist no more than* $k - 1$ *patterns whose support-regularity values are greater than that of* X.

The top-k frequent/regular patterns mining problem is to discover the k patterns whith highest support-regularity values from transactional databases under two user-given parameters: (i) weight of interest on support λ or regularity ϕ, and (ii) the number of expected output k.

4   Mining Top-k Frequent/Regular Patterns Mining under User-Given Weights of Interest

We here introduce an efficient algorithm, *TFRP-Mine*, for mining top-k frequent/regular patterns based on user-given weights of interest. It consists of two steps: (i) *TFRP-Initialization (TFRP-I)* captures the database content with only one database scan (patterns (items or itemsets), their support, regularity, support-regularity) into a top-k list, and (ii) *TFRP-Mining (TFRP-M)* that quickly discovers the desired patterns from the top-k list.

TFRP-Initialization (TFRP-I). *TFRP-I* builds the top-k list which is simply a linked-list associated with a hash table (for efficient updating). Each entry of the top-k list contains five informations: pattern (item or itemset) I, support s^I, regularity r^I, support-regularity value sr^I and a set of transaction-ids (tidset) T^I where pattern I occurs in database.

To construct the top-k list, *TFRP-I* first creates the hash table for all single items. Subsequently, each transaction of the database is sequentially scanned and then each item in the transaction is regarded. For each item, the top-k list is accessed once via the hash table to seek the entry of the item. If the entry does not exist, a new entry for the item is created with its support, regularity, and tidset. Otherwise, its information is updated. The scanning step is repeated until the last transaction of the database. After all scanning, the regularity and support-regularity value of each item in the top-k list are calculated. Finally, all entries in the top-k list are sorted by descending order of support-regularity values and the entries after the kth entry are eliminated (they cannot belong to the result).

Following definition 4 we can notice that the support-regularity value has the downward-closure property (i.e. any superset of a low support-regularity pattern is also a low support-regularity pattern). Thus, the support-regularity measure can be used to prune the supersets of low support-regularity value during the mining process.

TFRP-Mining (TFRP-M, see Algorithm 1). *TFRP-M* applies a best-first search strategy to pairs of patterns with highest support-regularity values first to the lowest ones, since two patterns with high support-regularity values tend to frequently and/or regularity appear together in database. However, even if the the two consider patterns do not frequently and/or regularity appear together, the performance of applying the best-first search is still acceptable. It will consider at most $O(k^2)$ pairs of patterns to mine the complete set of top-k frequent regular patterns. To mine patterns, two patterns in the top-k list are joined to generate a new pattern if they meet the following constraints: (i) they have the same number of items, and (ii) they have the same prefix (i.e. each item from both patterns is the same, except only the last item). These two constraints can help to reduce the redundancy of regarding pairs of patterns. Whenever both patterns satisfy the above constraints, their sets of transaction-ids(tidsets) are sequentially intersected and collected in order to calculate support, regularity, and support-regularity value of the new generated pattern. If the support-regularity value of the new pattern is greater than that of the kth pattern then it is inserted at its place into the top-k list and the kth element is removed from the top-k list. Joining and intersection steps are repeated for all pairs of patterns in the top-k list.

Table 1. A transactional database

Transaction-id	items	Transaction-id	items
1	a b c d	6	a e
2	a c d	7	a b c
3	a b d	8	b c d e
4	b c d e	9	a b d e
5	a b c e	10	a e

Example of TFRP-Mine. Let consider the database with 10 transactions of Table 1. Suppose our task is to find the top-5 frequent/regular patterns under weight of interest on support $\lambda = 0.4(40\%)$ (to save space the hash table is not presented).

Algorithm 1. *TFRP-Mining (TFRP-M)*

Input:
- Top-k list
- The number of desired result (k)
- The weights of interest on support (λ) and regularity (ϕ)

Output:
- Top-k regular/frequent patterns

for each pattern X in the top-k list **do**
  for each pattern Y in the top-k list ($X \neq Y$) **do**
    if X and Y satisfy the two joining constraints (mentioned above) **then**
      • merge patterns X and Y to be the pattern $Z = \{i_1^X, \ldots, i_{|X|}^X, i_{|Y|}^Y\}$
      • initialize values of Z, $r^Z = 0$, $s^Z = 0$ and $T^Z = \{\}$

      for each t_p in T^X and t_q in T^Y (where $p \in [1, |T^X|]$ and $q \in [1, |T^Y|]$) **do**
        if $t_p = t_q$ **then**
          • calculate rtt_j^Z by t_p (where j is the number of tids in T^Z)
          • add the support s^Z by 1
          • collect t_p as the last tid of T^Z

      • calculate regularity of Z, $r^Z = max(fr^Z, rtt_2^Z, rtt_3^Z, \ldots, rtt_{|T^Z|}^Z, lr^Z)$
      • calculate support-regularity value of Z, $sr^Z = (\lambda)(s^Z) - (\phi)(r^Z)$

      if $sr^Z \geq sr^K$ (where K is the current k^{th} pattern in the top-k list) **then**
        • remove k^{th} entry and then insert the pattern Z into top-k list (with its values: r^Z, s^Z, sr^Z and T^Z)

TFRP-I first creates the hash table and calculates the weight of interest on regularity, $\phi = 0.6$. As shown in Fig. 1(a), the entries for items a, b, c and d are created by reading the first transaction t_1. Their supports, regularities and tidsets are initialized to be 1, 1 and $\{1\}$, respectively. Next, transaction $t_2 = \{a, c, d\}$ is read and the support of items a, c and d are increased to 2 whereas their tidsets are updated to $\{1, 2\}$. With the scanning of transaction $t_3 = \{a, b, d\}$, the supports and the tidsets of items a, b and d are adjusted as shown in Fig. 1(b), and so on for transactions t_4 to t_{10}. After scanning the entire database, the regularity and the support-regularity value of each item in the top-k list are calculated using Definition 1 and Definition 4. Finally, the top-k list is sorted by descending order of the support-regularity value. As illustrated in Fig. 1(c), the final top-k list, is composed of five entries (each entry consists of *item, support, regularity, support-regularity value, and tidset.*

To mine patterns with the best-first search strategy, item b is first joined with item a since they have highest support-regularity values. Consequently, their tidsets, T^a and T^b, are sequentially intersected to compute $s^{ab} = 5$, $r^{ab} = 2$ and $sr^{ab} = (0.4)(5) - (0.6)(2) = 0.8$ and $T^{ab} = \{1, 3, 5, 7, 9\}$ (transactions id where ab occurs). By comparing sr^{ab} with that of the $k^{th}(5^{th})$ pattern, $sr^e = -0.6$, *TFRP-M* removes pattern e and then inserts pattern ab into the top-k list

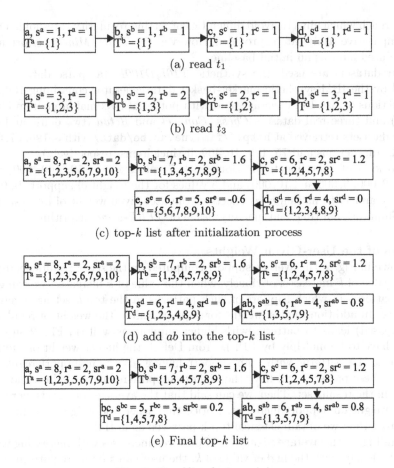

(a) read t_1

(b) read t_3

(c) top-k list after initialization process

(d) add ab into the top-k list

(e) Final top-k list

Fig. 1. Top-k list during mining

(see Fig. 1(d)). Next, the pattern c is merged with a and b. After joining and intersecting steps, we get the $s^{ac} = 4, r^{ac} = 3, sr^{ac} = -0.2$ and $T^{ac} = \{1, 2, 5, 7\}$ for the pattern ac. Since the support-regularity value sr^{ac} is less than that of d (the current k^{th} pattern), pattern ac is not added into the top-k list and then ac is eliminated from the mining process. For the pattern bc, its support, regularity, support-regularity value and tidset are $s^{bc} = 5, r^{bc} = 3, sr^{bc} = 0.2$, and $T^{bc} = \{1, 4, 5, 7, 8\}$. With the investigation of sr^{bc} with sr^d, the pattern d is removed and the pattern bc is inserted into the top-k list. *TFRP-M* proceeds the remaining patterns in the top-k list with the same manner and we finally obtain the k patterns with highest support-regularity values as illustrated in Fig. 1(e).

5   Performance Evaluation

We here report some experimental studies done to investigate the performance of the proposed *TFRP-Mine* algorithm. From the best of our knowledge, there is no approach which aims to avoid difficulties of setting regularity threshold. Thus, no comparative study can be provided. However, the *TFRP-Mine*'s performance can be used later as an initial baseline.

Four datasets are used: the synthetic *T10I4D100K* (a sparse dataset generated by the IBM synthetic market-basket data generator containing $100,000$ transactions of size 10 in average, and with potential maximal large itemsets of size 4) and three real datasets *Chess, Connect* and *Retail* (two dense and one sparse datasets retrieved at http://fimi.ua.ac.be/data/ with $3,196$, $67,557$, $88,122$ transactions and 75, 129, $16,469$ distinct items, respectively).

Two kind of experiments are done with 7 values for k (50, 100, 200, 500, $1,000$, $2,000$, $5,000$ and $10,000$) and 5 values for the weight of support (0, 0.25, 0.5, 0.75 and 1) to measure: (i) effects of the user-given weight of interest, and (ii) computational time and memory usage of *TFRP-Mine* algorithm.

Effects of the User-Given Weights

As shown in Fig. 2, the average support computed on the set of results decreases as the value of k increases: obviously, when the value of k increases, we can gain more patterns in which support of such patterns in the top-k set are likely to decrease. In addition, higher weight for support value (the weight of regularity is decreased) leads to patterns with higher support as well (in Fig. 2 support values have to be multiply by 10^3;). From Def. 4, the higher weight of support will cause the patterns with high support having also high support-regularity values. These patterns will have the highest support-regularity values and thus will be in the results set. Then, we can said that the average support is increased as the weight on support increases. Notice that when the weight of support is equal to 1 then we obtain classical top-k patterns as in [14].

From Fig. 3, the average regularity of patterns increases with increasing value of k. Obviously, with the higher value of k, the user can gain more patterns with less frequency and/or high regularity values. Moreover, the average regularity also increases with the increasing of weight of support. In this case, there may be patterns with frequently appearance that have a large gap of disappear included in the set of results (*i.e.* the new included patterns may appear frequently at the beginning and then disappear for a long time (this will cause patterns have high regularities). Another case is the case that new patterns disappear for a long time at the beginning and then frequently occur in database. From these situations, we can claim that with the higher value of k and higher value of weight on support, we will gain more patterns with more irregularly occurrence.

Computational Time and Memory Usage

Fig. 4 shows the runtime on the four datasets. Obviously, runtime increases with k. Runtime also increases with the weight of support. This is due to the fact that *TFRP-Mine* then needs more time to collecting and intersecting larger tidset for each pattern. However, we can see from the figure that even with very low support weight (*i.e.* the results may have low support and/or low regularity), *TFRP-Mine* is efficient.

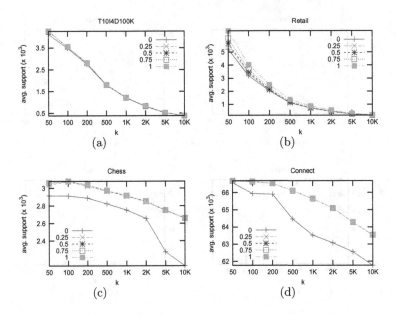

Fig. 2. Average support of results from TFRP-Mine

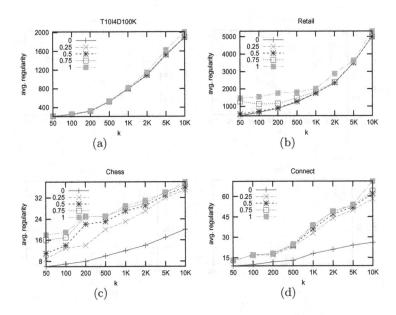

Fig. 3. Average regularity of results from TFRP-Mine

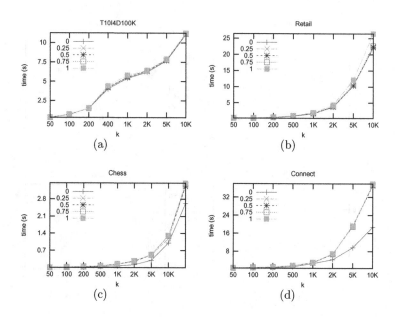

Fig. 4. Computational time of TFRP-Mine

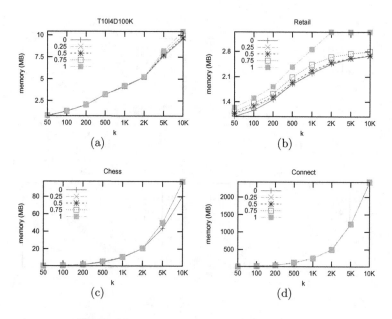

Fig. 5. Memory consumption of TFRP-Mine

The investigation of memory consumption is presented Fig. 5. It increases with k (obviously). It increases also with the weight of support. This is due to the fact that *TFRP-Mine* then needs to collect more tids in main memory to compute the support, regularity and support-regularity values of patterns.

As a whole when compared to classical top-k patterns mining as described in [14] *i.e.* when weight of support is equal to 1 in each figures one can notice that *TFRP-Mine* is very competitive: performance are slightly degraded and *TFRP-Mine* offers more flexibility between frequency and regularity.

6   Conclusion

Regular patterns and top-k regular patterns have recently attracted attention. Mining frequent and regular patterns require a support and a regularity thresholds. However, it is well-known that setting these thresholds is not easy. We thus propose to mine top-k regular/frequent patterns with one weight to balance between frequency and regularity depending on the user interest and the number k of desired patterns. This allows also to balance between the two criteria in comparison with the classical approach that requires two strict thresholds. An efficient single-pass algorithm, *TFRP-Mine*, is proposed. Experiments show that it can discover a wide range of patterns with low, middle and high value of supports and regularities.

References

1. Agrawal, R., Imielinski, T., Swami, A.N.: Mining association rules between sets of items in large databases. In: Proceedings of the 1993 ACM SIGMOD International Conference on Management of Data, Washington, D.C., May 26-28, pp. 207–216 (1993)
2. Goethals, B.: Frequent set mining. In: The Data Mining and Knowledge Discovery Handbook, pp. 377–397. Springer (2005)
3. Han, J., Cheng, H., Xin, D., Yan, X.: Frequent pattern mining: current status and future directions. Data Min. Knowl. Discov. 15(1), 55–86 (2007)
4. Chang, J.: Mining weighted sequential patterns in a sequence database with a time-interval weight. Knowledge Based Systems 24(1), 1–9 (2011)
5. Tanbeer, S.K., Ahmed, C.F., Jeong, B.-S., Lee, Y.-K.: Discovering periodic-frequent patterns in transactional databases. In: Theeramunkong, T., Kijsirikul, B., Cercone, N., Ho, T.-B. (eds.) PAKDD 2009. LNCS, vol. 5476, pp. 242–253. Springer, Heidelberg (2009)
6. Heierman, E.O., Youngblood, G.M., Cook, D.J.: Mining temporal sequences to discover interesting patterns. In: KDD Workshop on Mining Temporal and Sequential Data (2004)
7. Fu, A.W.-C., Kwong, R.W.-W., Tang, J.: Mining N-most Interesting Itemsets. In: Ohsuga, S., Raś, Z.W. (eds.) ISMIS 2000. LNCS (LNAI), vol. 1932, pp. 59–67. Springer, Heidelberg (2000)
8. Wang, J., Han, J., Lu, Y., Tzvetkov, P.: Tfp: an efficient algorithm for mining top-k frequent closed itemsets. Proceeding of the IEEE Transactions on Knowledge and Data Engineering 17, 652–664 (2005)

9. Yang, B., Huang, H., Wu, Z.: Topsis: Finding top-k significant n-itemsets in sliding windows adaptively. Knowl.-Based Syst. 21(6), 443–449 (2008)

10. Li, H.F.: Mining top-k maximal reference sequences from streaming web click-sequences with a damped sliding window. Expert Systems with Applications 36(8), 11304–11311 (2009)

11. Ke, Y., Cheng, J., Yu, J.X.: Top-k correlative graph mining. SDM, 1038–1049 (2009)

12. Webb, G.I.: Filtered-top-k association discovery. Wiley Interdisciplinary Reviews: Data Mining and Knowledge Discovery 1(3), 183–192 (2011)

13. Fournier-Viger, P., Tseng, V.S.: Tns: mining top-k non-redundant sequential rules. In: Shin, S.Y., Maldonado, J.C. (eds.) SAC, pp. 164–166. ACM (2013)

14. Amphawan, K., Lenca, P., Surarerks, A.: Mining top-k periodic-frequent patterns without support threshold. In: IAIT 2009. CCIS, vol. 55, pp. 18–29. Springer, Heidelberg (2009)

15. Amphawan, K., Lenca, P., Surarerks, A.: Efficient mining top-k regular-frequent itemset using compressed tidsets. In: Cao, L., Huang, J.Z., Bailey, J., Koh, Y.S., Luo, J. (eds.) PAKDD Workshops 2011. LNCS, vol. 7104, pp. 124–135. Springer, Heidelberg (2012)

16. Amphawan, K., Lenca, P., Surarerks, A.: Mining top-k regular-frequent itemsets using database partitioning and support estimation. Expert Systems with Applications 39(2), 1924–1936 (2012)

17. Tanbeer, S.K., Ahmed, C.F., Jeong, B.S.: Mining regular patterns in incremental transactional databases. In: Int. Asia-Pacific Web Conference, pp. 375–377. IEEE Computer Society (2010)

18. Tanbeer, S.K., Ahmed, C.F., Jeong, B.S.: Mining regular patterns in data streams. In: Kitagawa, H., Ishikawa, Y., Li, Q., Watanabe, C. (eds.) DASFAA 2010. LNCS, vol. 5981, pp. 399–413. Springer, Heidelberg (2010)

19. Surana, A., Kiran, R.U., Reddy, P.K.: An efficient approach to mine periodic-frequent patterns in transactional databases. In: Cao, L., Huang, J.Z., Bailey, J., Koh, Y.S., Luo, J. (eds.) PAKDD Workshops 2011. LNCS, vol. 7104, pp. 254–266. Springer, Heidelberg (2012)

20. Kiran, R.U., Reddy, P.K.: Mining periodic-frequent patterns with maximum items' support constraints. In: Proceedings of the Third Annual ACM Bangalore Conference, COMPUTE 2010, pp. 1–8 (2010)

Cross-Media Analysis for Communication during Natural Disasters

Gerhard Backfried[1,2], Johannes Göllner[5], Gerald Quirchmayr[2], Karin Rainer[3],
Gert Kienast[4], Georg Thallinger[4], Christian Schmidt[1], Mark Pfeiffer[1],
Christian Meurers[5], and Andreas Peer[5]

[1] SAIL LABS Technology AG, Vienna, Austria
[2] University of Vienna, Multimedia Information Systems Research Group, Vienna, Austria
[3] INSET Research & Advisory, Vienna, Austria
[4] Joanneum Research, Inst. for Information and Communication Technologies, Graz, Austria
[5] National Defence Academy, Dept. of Central Documentation, Austrian MoD, Vienna, Austria

Abstract. In this paper we describe the role of media in the context of natural disasters. Traditional media have a long history in covering disasters and will continue to be a major provider of information in the future. In recent years, however there has been a significant change: information about natural disasters has increasingly been disseminated on a large scale on social media platforms. These media are typically faster but may be less reliable. They provide additional and complementary angles on events and, combined with traditional media, provide a wider spectrum of coverage. We argue that cross-media information combined with multi-lingual data provides huge opportunities for first-responders and decision makers to gain improved situational awareness allowing for improved disaster relief, support, mitigation and resilience measures.

Keywords: disaster communication, multimedia processing, social media, situational awareness.

1 Introduction

Traditional media have a long history in covering disasters and crises. They are a major provider of information in times of disasters and will without a doubt remain so in the future. As recent natural (and man-made) disasters have shown, social media have become a new vehicle to provide additional useful insights into events as they unfold. They combine with traditional media in various ways sparking off initial coverage, amplifying information or providing different and unfiltered angles. Together they produce a wide spectrum of coverage of an event and lead to significantly improved situational awareness for decision makers and planners [1], [2]. The boundaries between social media and traditional media have become increasingly blurred as news providers use social media as alternative and additive channels. For example, 8 out of the 10 most active Twitter users reporting on an earthquake in Chile in 2010 [3] were found to be directly related to mass-media. Likewise, TV stations receive input about storm damage which is then broadcast immediately on TV [4]. In other cases,

B. Papasratorn et al. (Eds.): IAIT 2013, CCIS 409, pp. 13–22, 2013.

such as the Queensland floods [5] social media even became a main source for mainstream media. As helpful as all this combined information may potentially be to disaster relief organizations, it usually comes in multiple formats, multiple languages, immense amounts, across multiple media, is generally unstructured and inhomogeneous and also attributed with different levels of reliability and trust. Whereas in this paper we focus on incoming information, clearly many aspects regarding the integration of social media and traditional media equally apply to outgoing information, communication between first-responders and the affected population as well as among themselves.

2   Media in Disaster Communication

For large portions of the population traditional media, such as TV, radio and websources remain a major source of information even today. Depending on the infrastructure and social factors, they may still even form the primary source of information. Under certain conditions, official and traditional channels may not be readily accessible or only be able (or willing) to provide partial information. Nevertheless, these media form an integral part of the spectrum of sources used to obtain situational awareness in times of crises and disaster and will continue to do so in the future.

With the advent of social media, the way people communicate, search for and receive information has undergone a radical transformation. Not only have social media changed the way people communicate in their day-to-day lives, but also - and increasingly so - during emergencies and crises. Effectively it can already be assumed, that in many cases a part of the population will indeed turn to social media during crises [6].[1] Particularly micro-blogging systems like Twitter play an increasingly important role in this respect and form a new way to disseminate and receive information [5], [7]. Social media lend themselves to two-way communication, allowing data to be gathered as well as distributed. This type of communication is valuable to first responders because it allows them to not only receive information, observations, opinions and emotions from individuals who experience the incident or crisis first hand, but also allows them to send out important disaster-related information, critical updates, clarifications or corrections to each other and to the persons who need it most. Activities of affected persons are not limited to mere communication and observation but also involve active participation at the disaster site to perform specific tasks relevant for immediate support, relief activities, preventive on-site tasks or additional fact-finding. In terms of situational awareness, data from social media have to be combined, reconciled and contrasted with information from traditional sources to arrive at a more complete picture of an event.

For decades, communities have been relying on specific groups to assist in times of disaster. But the present day communications environment with its new and increased expectations has changed the game, not just for first responders, but also for

---

[1]   It should be noted, though, that in a broad spectrum of societies, large social groups are still far from being able to participate in this form of communication due to limited economic/technical access, education or gender.

the general public [9]. (Near) Real-time communication/information, personal involvement, reliable, critically-challenged and -questioned sources, as well as multimedia content are common requirements and assets of currently shared information. The technology is constantly evolving which results in people having even higher expectations of first responders but also vice-versa. Affected persons may indeed expect authorities to respond quickly to information provided via social media [4]. There remains no doubt that the impact of social media on crisis communication is already significant and will only continue to grow in significance in the years to come.

Even though social media may sometimes not be regarded as the actual drivers of news [10], they can certainly be viewed as amplifiers and often play a time-critical role in the development and communication of events. In certain settings, they may actually be the first medium on which an event is reported about and form the spark for coverage on other, more traditional media channels. On other occasions, professional journalists may still be the first ones to report. In a study comparing trending hash-tags on Twitter and headlines on CNN it was found that in approximately 50% of the cases CNN was ahead of Twitter [11]. Regarding professional sources, a large portion of the activity on social media may simply be re-emitting content which is available via other channels (such as feeds from the same source). Both, professionals as well as numerous individuals (citizens) may provide further insight on and add different angles to events already covered by traditional media. Including them and following the information provided by links within them allows for increased coverage and better and extended contrast across sources and media. Social media may add valuable dimensions like detailed micro-perspectives and (near) real time images of dynamically changing situations to a complex, already multi-lingual, multi-source, multi-media environment. In addition, they might provide unfiltered information, in contrast to official or commercial sources, whose coverage may be biased in different ways. Social media, particularly the links mentioned in them, can be regarded as a gateway and amplifier to yet more relevant news-sites covering similar or identical topics. An increased amount of links may point to certain types and stages of events and serves as an indicator of the amount of external information included in communication [12]. Particularly in this context, social media may act as information brokers and broadcasters [4], [10]. Regarding the quality, veracity and trustworthiness of the retrieved data, the frequency by itself is usually no reliable indicator. However, re-tweeting behavior can serve as an indicator of whether or not a tweet's content can be trusted [13]. Linking tweets to traditional media can likewise be envisioned to serve this purpose.

3   Existing Work, Case-Studies and Technology

The first decade of the 2000s witnessed the birth of a number of social media platforms. These have been adopted on a wide scale and are being used by increasingly large portions of the population for personal and professional purposes. They have changed the digital landscape immensely and in a lasting way and produced new online social- and communication behaviors. Clearly, there are regional and cultural differences in the popularity and accessibility of individual platforms and the way users embrace them. However, some large networks - above all Facebook - have managed to dominate increasingly large regions of the globe and continue to extend their reach, establishing the de facto standard across many countries.

Social media platforms may roughly be classified into the following categories:

- Social Networks (e.g. Facebook, LinkedIn, Google+, Odnoklassniki,...)
- Micro-Blogging (e.g. Twitter, Weibo,...)
- Photo-Sharing (e.g Flickr, Instagram,...)
- Video-Sharing (e.g. YouTube)
- Bookmarking (e.g. Delicious, StumbleUpon,..)
- Social News (e.g. Digg, Reddit,...)
- Discussion Forums
- Incident-related platforms (e.g. Ushahidi, Crisis-Tracker,...)

These platforms target different user-groups, environments and objectives and offer different sets of features and functionalities. Many of them involve the process of sharing textual and/or multi-media data and the possibility to establish links and communication threads between them and/or the involved persons and entities. Some of them, like Ushahidi involve crowd-sourcing or activist-mapping. The nature of these platforms ranges from purely commercial ventures to open-source projects.

Since their respective time of introduction, social media have also been used to collect and disseminate information about natural disasters. Not all platforms and services lend themselves to a natural and direct use within disaster communication. Platforms like Twitter or Facebook, allowing to disseminate snippets of information in realtime to a selected or general public and allowing users to comment and enrich information have found wide adoption during crises and disasters. Photo-sharing services, being fed by an increasing amount of mobile devices have been used as targets for linking of information across media. Web sites and RSS-feeds are used for similar purposes in addition to providing a separate source in their own right. Linking between the different media, e.g. including links to video in tweets or mentioning Facebook accounts on TV has become a common way of communicating and referencing information.

Since 2004, several disasters have been investigated in the context of social media and crises. Figure 1 depicts some of the platforms and their respective years of launch along with a set of natural disasters which have been investigated using social media as information sources.

Examples of investigated disasters are the South East Queensland floods of 2011 where social media played a central role in crisis communication. During this disaster, the Queensland Police Service used Twitter (@QPSMedia) to communicate with affected people [5]. Social media have likewise played important roles during and following the earthquakes in New Zealand [14], Haiti [15], Chile [3], and the US [13], grassfires [13], hurricanes Katrina [19] Ike, Gustav [10] and Sandy [19], [25], typhoons in the Philippines and floods in Brazil [17]. Their role in the floods in central Europe in May and June 2013 is being investigated in the QuOIMA project [18].

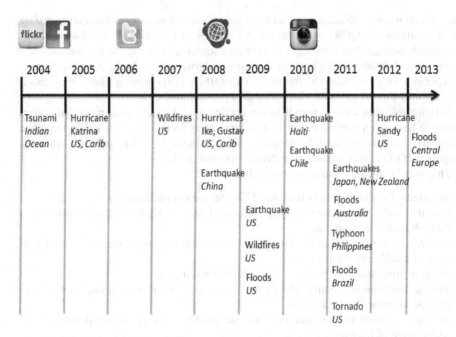

Fig. 1. Social media platforms and research on their use in natural disasters

Other disasters during the same period of time, such as the winter storm in the US in 2010 known as *Snowmageddon*, the wildfires in Russia in the same year, several floods, landslides, earthquakes or droughts in Africa, South-East Asia or Central America were almost certainly also covered by social media platforms. However, no research on their particular role and the extent to which they were used in these events seems to have been carried out thus far.

Reference [7] provides an overview of social media in the context of crisis information. They find that media – traditional as well as social – form an important source for sending out and retrieving information about different aspects of a crisis or disaster. In particular they examine various approaches and channels which can be used for dissemination of crisis-relevant information. [3], [10] and [11] elaborate on the structure and types of communication which emerge on Twitter, [4] does so particularly for the crisis-case. [19] provides an overview of social media in the disaster context using a set of case spotlights covering specific events. [5] provides an in-depth and comprehensive overview of how social media played a role during the 2011 Queensland floods. [8] focuses on the connection between Twitter and TV from the point of view of how to combine social network interaction with programming. [11] provides a brief overview of existing and potential future uses of social media in disasters. Relatively little attention seems to have been paid to the actual use of language in the context of social media and natural disasters: [3] and [19] deal with this topic to some extent.

Numerous research projects aim at improving the effectiveness of communication and alerting during crises. For example, in the EU FP7 Alert4All [20], the screening of new media (SNM) tool [7] serves to enhance situational awareness using opinions and emotions found in on-line web content and social media. MASSCRISCOM [21] takes social media into account as an emerging means of mass communication during crisis situations. At QCRI in Qatar, the AIDR project [22] aims at developing semi-automated mechanisms, combined with crowd-sourcing, to form the foundations of a Twitter-based dashboard for analytical purposes during crises. In the Austrian Security Research Program KIRAS, the project QuOIMA [18]) aims at combining cross-media, multi-lingual analysis with visual analytics methods.

It is notable that most research in connecting social media with natural disasters seems to have been carried out in - or at least been focusing on - a single language (English), a single medium (text) and a single source (Twitter) only. In addition, roughly half of the investigated disasters concerned the US.

This may be attributed to a number of factors:

— the affected population may have used Twitter for communication
— internationally visible target organizations of such systems operate primarily in English speaking countries
— researchers are limited in the languages they focus on, sometimes ruling out portions of a collected data set
— research programs may prefer to fund particular setups
— natural language processing (NLP) tools may exist only for a limited set of languages, in particular for English
— automatic speech recognition may not be available for particular domains (and wider range of languages)
— visual processing technology may not be available for a particular domain
— data sets may have been collected by entities in the English speaking world
— data sets are available for a single medium only (no parallel corpora across different media)
— data may simply be accessible more easily for certain platforms than for others, particularly for Twitter (privacy and legal concerns naturally play a strong role)

4   Media Requirements of First Responders

Since social media were not created from the start with first responders in mind, but rather for the general public to simply connect and share their thoughts and emotions with friends and family, certain limitations exist for first responders in the context of disaster communication. New ways to systematically incorporate and integrate social media and the related technology into disaster communication and combine them with traditional media form current areas of research and development. Technologies, which are not purely based on textual input, such as speech recognition or visual processing form natural extensions of current systems, augmenting, extending and complementing existing sources which currently remain largely untapped. Clustering methods for data across media – e.g. multiple video clips of almost identical content - are required for navigating large amounts of data and presenting them in an efficient and manageable way. The speed and granularity of reporting across the different kinds of media need to be balanced against the requirement of obtaining reliable information. A combination of social media (fast but not less reliable), traditional media (slow but more reliable) and background material provided by official and governmental organizations (slow but more reliable) has to be balanced and structured flexibly to allow for different setups and foci during the different stages of a disaster. Information provided in several languages may have to be consolidated along the way, especially in international and cross-border settings of crises.

Fusing these diverse, mixed and complementary sources of information and allowing decision makers – and the public - to make sense of a large and inhomogeneous body of data is of utmost importance to first responders and their coordinating organizations. Access to data from different modalities just minutes after they have been published should allow users to perform various types of visualization and analysis activities by connecting and inter-linking information from different sources and media. The early detection of structures and patterns of communication as well as of perceived incidents are required to allow authorities to react earlier, swifter and more adequately in situations of crisis or disaster. It enables them to position vital assets adequately in order to minimize impact, speed up recovery and rebuilding efforts and even anticipate critical events before escalation.

Figure 2 depicts a generic 5-phases model developed at the National Defence Academy of the Austrian MoD [23]. First responders can benefit in all phases by the combined processing of data across media and languages and their underlying patterns of communication in a unified, fused manner.

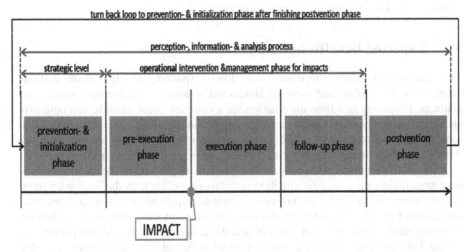

Fig. 2. 5-phases disaster model

According to the above model first responders face different challenges and requirements in crisis and disaster communication depending on the management / leadership level (strategic, operational etc.) as well as the phases themselves. On the strategic level first responders should have the ability to use the results of media fusion for analytical tasks to identify communication patterns and to link them to particular disaster phases. Emerging risks could be identified more quickly and reliably and the behavior of the affected population interpreted, monitored and influenced more effectively. On the operational level first responders require a large amount of information to understand the local requirements and tasks and to gain insights about emerging risks and possible threats to the population. The combination of media sources could help to improve shared situational awareness beyond organizational limitations which may exist between the different first responder organizations.

Additionally first responders require complex (semi-) automated analysis and visualization tools and techniques to complement and support their decision making processes. The technologies involved have to be multi-lingual and have to provide cross- and multi-media analysis facilities to ensure access to a large variety of diverse media and information sources. Accessibility and persistence of information has to be guaranteed for later justification of actions or decisions taken or not taken. Visual analysis is required to tap into the growing number of photographic and video-content collected and uploaded to social media sites. These documents do not exist in a vacuum but rather form a complex network with textual and audio-data available across different media. The combinations of these modalities can serve as the base for a holistic approach of disaster communication and management. A combined system may also serve as a platform for first responders to share awareness, coordinate the operation, capitalize on synergy effects and synchronize their forces in a theater of operation. It cannot be stressed enough, that all methods and technologies should not be designed to replace people but to help decision makers to handle the increasing flood of information and fulfill their tasks in a more efficient way. Technological advances have to be accompanied by the establishment of best practices that enhance the goals of communication in crisis and disaster situations [4].

5   Expected Benefits and Approach

As stated in [24], monitoring information flows – spanning multiple media and languages – will establish and increase situational awareness for decision makers and planners. Obtaining real-time information, as a complex event unfolds, can help officials determine where people are; arrange mitigation measures, assess concerned persons' needs, and alert citizens and first responders to changing conditions and new threats and allow them to target their relief-measures more precisely and timely.

Analysis of communication content and -patterns might lead to the identification of structures indicating a specific situation or crisis-phase, such as the follow-up phase already having started. This in turn could result in improved and more targeted communication towards to affected population. Few or no models seem to exist thus far, capturing such communication patterns and deducing operation relevant parameters. Figure 3 depicts a schematic overview of which different types and sources of information and their interrelationship could be identified and combined into a unified analysis model for disaster communication.

References from one medium linking to information in other media could be collected, followed and put into perspective for analysis. This is envisioned to take place in a unified framework, thus allowing to capitalize on the combination- and fusion capabilities of the system. Textual, audio as well as visual information and cues could be combined to arrive at a more complete picture. Multi-lingual information might add different angles and aspects not visible within a single medium or source. Media clips recorded around a number of key locations during a disasters are typically uploaded multiple times to different platforms leading to (near-) duplicate information. Being able to detect and interconnect such items, link them to other media and group them more adequately for navigation might reduce the workload of first responders significantly. Verification and completion of information or the detection of inconsistencies and rumors might be possible by combining the different sources and media. However, in all of these processes human intervention is expected to occur and eventually also be required to some extent. This is in line with an architecture aiming to support rather than to replace human operators. From a practical point of view, it is a strategic advantage for decision makers sending in first responders to know how a situation is developing. This forms an essential input for team configuration and mission preparation.

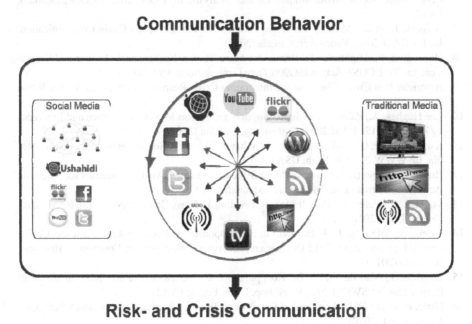

Fig. 3. Cross-media communication model

The authors are actively engaged and cooperating with first responders in creating such a unified model fulfilling the above identified requirements to the largest extent possible. These requirements as well as the models and technologies involved are being refined as new disasters strike and insights are gained. With the help and support of first-responders, assumptions are verified against real-life environments and checked with regard to their real-world applicability and integration into best practices.

References

1. Kwang-Hoong, L., Mei-Li, L.: The Fukushima Nuclear Crisis Reemphasized the Need for Improved Risk Communication and Better Use of Social Media. Health Physics 103(3), 307–310
2. Tyshchuk, Y., et al.: Social Media & Warning Response Impacts in Extreme Events: Results from a Naturally Occuring Experiment. In: 2012 45th International Conference on System Science (HICSS), vol. 818 (2012)

3. Mendoza, M., Poblete, B., Castillo, C.: Twitter Under Crisis: Can we trust what we RT? In: SOMA 2010, Washington, D.C., USA (2010)

4. Holmes, W.: Crisis Communication and Social Media: Advantages, Disadvantages and Best Practices, Univ. of Tennessee, CCISymposium, Knowville, USA (2011)

5. Bruns, A., Burgess, J., Crawford, K., Shaw, F.: #qldfloods and @QPSMedia: Crisis Communication on Twitter in the 2011 South East Queensland Floods. ARC Centre of Excellence for Creative Industries and Innovation, Brisbane (2012)

6. Johansson, F., Brynielsson, J., Narganes Quijano, M.: Estimating Citizen Alertness in Crises using Social Media Monitoring and Analysis. In: EISIC 2012, Odense, Denmark (2012)

7. Nilsson, J., et al.: Making use of New Media for Pan-European Crisis Communication. In: ISCRAM 2012, Vancouver, Canada (2012)

8. Harrington, S., Highfield, T., Bruns, A.: More Than a Backchannel: Twitter and Television. In: 2012 COST Action ISO906 Transforming Audiences (2012)

9. American Red Cross, The Case for Integrating Crisis Response with Social Media, White Paper (2010)

10. Lee Hughes, A., Palen, L.: Twitter Adoption and Use in Mass Convergence and Emergency Events. In: ISCRAM 2009, Gothenburg, Sweden (2009)

11. Kwak, H., Lee, C., Park, H., Moon, S.: What is Twitter, A Social Network or A News Media. In: WWW 2010, Raleigh, USA (2010)

12. Bruns, A., Stieglitz, S.: Towards More Systematic Twitter Analysis: Metrics for Tweeting Activities. Journal of Social Research Methodology (2013)

13. Starbird, K., Palen, L.: Pass It On?: Retweeting in Mass Emergency. In: ISCRAM 2010, Seattle, USA (2010)

14. Bruns, A., Burgess, J.: Local and Global Responses to Disaster: #eqnz and the Christchurch Earthquake. In: 2012 Disaster and Emergency Management Conference, Brisbane, Australia (2012)

15. Dugdale, J., Van de Walle, B., Koeppinghoff, C.: Social Media and SMS in the Haiti Earthquake. In: SWDM 2012 Workshop, Lyon, France (2012)

16. Earle, P., et al.: OMG Earthquake! Can Twitter Improve Earthquake Response? Electronic Seismologist (2010)

17. Nagar, S., Aaditeshwar, S., Joshi, A.: Characterization of Social Media Response to Natural Disasters. In: SWDM 2012 Workshop, Lyon, France (2012)

18. Backfried, G., Göllner, J., Quirchmayr, G., et al.: Integration of Media Sources for Situation Analysis in the Different Phases of Disaster Management. In: EISIC 2013, Uppsala, Sweden (2013)

19. Faustino, J.D., Liu, B., Jin, Y.: Social Media During Disasters: A Review of the Knowledge Base and Gaps, Final Report to Human Factors/Behavioral Sciences Division, U.S. Department of Homeland Security, College Park, USA (2012)

20. Alert4all (August 30, 2013), http://www.alert4all.eu

21. MASSCRISCOM (August 30, 2013), http://www.masscriscom.eu

22. AIDR (August 30, 2013), http://www.qcri.qa

23. KIRAS-Antrag: Modellbildungs- und simulationsgestützte Entscheidungsunterstützung in der Last-Mile-Katastrophenbewältigung (LMK-MUSE), S. 18 (February 28, 2013)

24. Lindsay, B.: Social Media and Disasters: Current Uses, Future Options, and Policy Considerations, Congressional Research Service (2011)

25. DHS Report, Lessons Learned: Social Media and Hurricane Sandy (August 30, 2013), https://communities.firstresponder.gov/DHS_VSMWG_Lessons_Learned _Social_Media_and_Hurricane_Sandy_Formatted_June_2013_FINAL.pdf

An Intelligent Cloud Cache Replacement Scheme

Thepparit Banditwattanawong[1] and Putchong Uthayopas[2]

[1] Information Science Institute of Sripathum University, Bangkok, Thailand
thepparit.ba@spu.ac.th
[2] Computer Engineering Department, Kasetsart University, Bangkok, Thailand

Abstract. Cloud computing services heavily relies on data networks. The continuous and rapid growth of data in external private clouds accelerates downstream network-bandwidth saturation and public cloud data-out overspends. Client-side cloud caching is a solution. This paper presents the core mechanism of the cloud caching, called i-Cloud cache replacement policy. Simulation results showed that 1) i-Cloud could deliver stable performances and outperformed three well-known cache replacement policies in all standard performance metrics against almost all workloads, 2) i-Cloud could attain optimal hit and byte-hit ratios without sacrificing one to the other, 3) i-Cloud did not give performance minima if properly trained, 4) i-Cloud could perform well for longer runs than its training periods, and 5) in terms of scalability and economy, i-Cloud is suitable for small cache sizes whereas nonintelligent-mode i-Cloud suffices larger cache sizes and the realization of responsive cloud services.

Keywords: Cloud cache replacement policy, Artificial neural network, Workload adaptive, Cost-saving ratio, Window size.

1 Introduction

Scalability, economy and responsiveness are the principal requirements of cloud computing services. In presently digital cultures, data has been proliferating in various formats such as instant messaging texts, high definition images and voices, massively streaming videos and SaaS applications. Not only WWW contents but also big data such as social media and archive of videos gathered via ubiquitous information-sensing devices have been hosted on cloud and being shared in a distributed fashion in unprecedented volume, variety and velocity. These will lead to several problems from a consumer standpoint including the downstream bandwidth saturation of network connection between external cloud and consumer premise, increases in external private-cloud data-out charge imposed by public cloud provider (such as [2], [10] and [11]) and long-delayed cloud service responsiveness. One solution to these problems is allocating more organizational budget for long-term network bandwidth investment. With this solution however, cloud economy is questionable. Instead, improving both cloud scalability, economy and service responsiveness simultaneously can be attained by deploying client-side cloud cache system, which is located in or nearby the

B. Papasratorn et al. (Eds.): IAIT 2013, CCIS 409, pp. 23–34, 2013.
© Springer International Publishing Switzerland 2013

consumer premise. The deployment scenario of a shared cloud cache is that HTTP requests sent from end users to external private cloud are proxied by a cloud cache, which in turn replies with the valid copies of the requested digital-content objects either from its local storage (i.e., cache hits) or by downloading updated copies from the cloud (i.e., cache misses).

Cloud caches basically inherit the capabilities of traditional forward web caching proxies since cloud data is also delivered by using the same set of HTTP/TCP/IP protocol stacks as in WWW. Unavoidably, the limitation of web caching is also inherited that is caching entire remote data in local cache to serve future requests is not economically plausible, thus cache replacement policy is also mandatory for cloud caches as in web caching proxies.

As an early attempt in the new field of client-side shared cloud caching, this paper presents a novel intelligent cloud cache replacement policy, i-Cloud (named so for its intended application domain), along with technical and economical performance results and significant findings based on real HTTP traces.

2   Related Works

We have investigated an extensive number of nonintelligent web cache replacement policies [12] as summarized in our previous work [6]. NNPCR [9] and its extension, NNPCR-2 [14], apply artificial neural networks to rate object cacheability. A lower rating score represents a better choice for replacement. The networks were supervised to learn cacheable patterns from valid HTTP status codes and object sizes not bigger than administrator-specified threshold. The perceptrons' inputs are frequency, recency and size. Intelligent long-term cache removal algorithm based on adaptive neuro-fuzzy inference system (ANFIS) [1] takes access frequency, recency, object size and downloading latency as the inputs of a trained ANFIS to dictate noncacheable objects. In training ANFIS, objects requested again at later point in specific time are considered cacheable. The oldest noncacheable object is removed first. Intelligent web caching using artificial neural network and particle swarm optimization algorithm [15] trained the network to keep slow downloading, big and frequently accessed objects in cache. Adaptive web cache predictor [16] utilizes artificial neural network and sliding windows to find whether objects will be re-accessed at least certain times within the certain number of accesses following a current one. The network learns inputs: type of object, number of previous hits, relative access frequency, object size and downloading latency. In training phase, objects reaccessed at least certain times within forward-looking window are most likely re-accessed. To recap, no explicit policy aims for cloud computing paradigm for two main reasons. First, those policies evict big objects to optimize hit rates rather than byte-hit and delay-saving ratios, which are important to the scalability of cloud-transport infrastructures and the responsiveness of cloud computing services. Second, they are not optimized for public cloud data-out charges, thus neither improve cloud consumer-side economy nor support the uses of hybrid clouds.

This paper proposes a significant improvement of our previous work Cloud policy [6], [7], [8] by enlisting an artificial neural network. A result is i-Cloud cache replacement policy, which can adapt itself intelligently to changing work-load to maintain superior performances. New trace-driven simulations have been conducted in comparison with three well-known strategies, LRU, GDSF and LFUDA [12], which are all supported by popular Squid caching proxy to evaluate this fully developed policy.

3   Performance Metrics

To understand the rest of this paper, it is important to revisit the definitions of standard performance metrics for web caching [4], [12]. For an object i, $byte-hit$ $ratio$ $=$ $\sum_{i=1}^{n} s_i h_i / \sum_{i=1}^{n} s_i r_i$, $delay-saving$ $ratio$ $=$ $\sum_{i=1}^{n} l_i h_i / \sum_{i=1}^{n} l_i r_i$ and hit $rate$ $=$ $\sum_{i=1}^{n} h_i / \sum_{i=1}^{n} r_i$ where s_i is the size of i, h_i is how many times a valid copy of i is fetched from cache, r_i is the total number of requests to i, and l_i is the loading latency of i from cloud. In addition to the standard metrics, a new metric, cost-saving ratio, originally proposed in [6], was also used to capture the economical performances of our studied policies. The metric measures how much money can be saved by serving the valid copies of requested objects from cache. It is expressed as follows. Given an object i,

$$cost-saving\ ratio = \frac{\sum_{i=1}^{n} c_i s_i h_i}{\sum_{i=1}^{n} c_i s_i r_i} \tag{1}$$

where c_i is the data-out charge rate or monetary cost for loading i from cloud. This metric is particularly useful for hybrid cloud where organization employs multiple cloud providers, which charge data-outs based on different pricings.

4   A Proposed Cloud Cache Replacement Policy

As justified in Section 1, the design goals of i-Cloud are cloud scalability, economy and responsiveness that are realized by optimizing byte-hit, cost-saving and delay-saving ratios, respectively. Hit rate has become less important (explained in [6], [7] and [8]) since these days with globally available large-bandwidth network infrastructures, it is perceived that loading remote small objects is fast as if they were fetched from user locality.

Table 1 presents the pseudo code of i-Cloud algorithm in details. The main principle behind the scene of i-Cloud is contemporaneous proximity [5]. i-Cloud quantifies a profit associated with each object inside the cluster by using Eq.(2). Given an object i,

$$profit_i = s_i\ c_i\ l_i\ f_i\ TTL_i \tag{2}$$

where s_i is the size of i, c_i is data-out charge rate for loading i, l_i is latency for loading i, f_i is the access frequency of i, and TTL_i is the remaining lifespan of i. An object with least profit is evicted first from cache. This object eviction process is repeated on the next least profitable objects in the cluster until gaining enough room in cache that fits the required cache space.

Table 1. i-Cloud algorithm

Algorithm: i-Cloud

input variables:

      cd /*cache database (recency-keyed min-priority queue)*/;

      ws /*window size*/;

      rs /*required cache space*/;

local variables:

      ecd /*empty cache database (recency-keyed min-priority queue)*/;

      oc /*an object cluster of least-recently-used (lru) objects

             (profit-keyed min-priority queue of evictable objects)*/;

      co /*a candidate object to be included in a cluster*/;

      $ts \leftarrow 0$ /*total size of ws objects initialized to zero*/;

      eo /*an evicted object*/;

      $c \leftarrow 0$ /*counter for objects in a cluster initialized to zero*/;

begin

      if $cd.getTotalNumberOfObjects() < ws$

      then $ws \leftarrow cd.getTotalNumberOfObjects()$;

      $ecd \leftarrow cd$;

      do

            $co \leftarrow ecd.removeLeastRecentlyUsedObject()$;

            $ts \leftarrow ts + co.getSize()$;

            $oc.addObject(co)$;

            $c \leftarrow c + 1$;

      while $(c < ws) \lor (ts < rs)$;

      do

            $eo \leftarrow oc.removeMinProfitObject()$;

            $cd.evict(eo)$;

      while $cd.getFreeSpace() < rs$;

return $cd.getFreeSpace()$;

Table 2. Window-size parameter values

	BO				NY			
Cache size (% of	15 days		31 days		15 days		30 days	
the first 15 days)	ws_o	ws_w	ws_o	ws_w	ws_o	ws_w	ws_o	ws_w
10	500	25,000	8,000	35,000	2,000	100	1,000	60,000
20	1,300	40,000	8,000	60,000	5,000	100	8,000	100
30	100	60,000	8,000	5,000	500	80,000	3,500	100

4.1 Window Size Parameter

A significant parameter influencing all performance aspects of i-Cloud is window size (ws in Table 1). Our previous works, [7] and [8], have determined both optimal window sizes (ws_o) and worst window sizes (ws_w) for simulations by extensively trial-and-error experiments as shown in Table 2. Using the uniform cost model [8], each optimal window size had been tuned towards a maximum

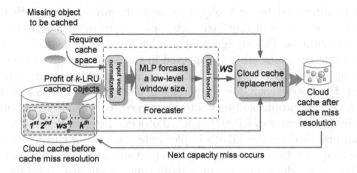

Fig. 1. Conceptual framework of i-Cloud cache replacement policy

byte-hit ratio for each certain trace and cache size. Optimal window sizes yielded byte-hit performance maxima, whereas worst window sizes produced byte-hit performance minima and had been tuned towards minimum byte-hit ratios based on the uniform cost model.

4.2 Forecaster Module

The effective selection method of window size is needed to approach optimal window sizes and to avoid the worst ones. As the optimal window sizes varied from one input HTTP trace and cache size to another. Therefore, i-Cloud must be aware of changing workload to adapt its window size properly. We have thus proposed i-Cloud based on an artificial neural network, in particular, a multilayer feedforward neural network or multilayer perceptron (MLP).

Fig. 1 demonstrates the conceptual framework of i-Cloud. It consists of two main processing modules, forecaster and cloud cache replacement. They operate as follows. When a capacity miss (i.e., a request for an object that was in a cache but has been since purged, thus cache eviction is required to serve the request [3]) takes place, the vector of k lru cached objects' profits together with a required cache space are fed into the forecaster to forcast a near-optimal window size. During this stage, each input vector is passed internally into the input vector normalization process then the normalized vector is presented to the MLP component to forecast a low-level window size. Such a low-level window size is later denormalized by the distal teacher component [13] to obtain an actual (potentially near-optimal) window size. The actual window size is subsequently presented to the cloud cache replacement module, which follows i-Cloud algorithm (Table 1).

MLP structure prescribes the number of layers and nodes to be placed in each layer of the MLP. Our goal is to find the smallest structure possible since too large MLP learns training set well but is unable to generalize [13]. We have designed the MLP structure based on the following guidelines.

- The appropriate number of input nodes were determined by two lessons learned from our previous studies [6], [7], [8]. First, both current cache state, which is influenced by past object request stream together with total allocated cache size, and required cache space were main factors to window size optimizations. This design guideline has been implemented as shown in Fig. 1: a current cache state is captured in the form of a profit vector while a missing object size is used to indicate a minimum required cache space. Second, the optimal window sizes ranged between 100 and 8,000 meaning that the lowest profitable objects to be purged from cache were potentially found inside a cluster of 8,000 lru cached objects. Leveraging this fact simplifies and practicalizes the MLP's implementation since a current cache state can be snapshot by examining only the part of cache database rather than the whole one, which can be much more time consuming. However, to give chance for any unveiled maximum values of optimal window sizes, we chose 10,000 (i.e., k in Fig. 1) lru cached objects to represent each current cache state to be examined by the MLP. Thus, the total number of input nodes is 10,002 including a required cache space node and a bias one.

– It is guided in [13] that some continuous functions cannot be approximated accurately by single-hidden-layer MLP whereas two hidden layers are sufficient to approximate any desired bounded continuous function, which is also the case of i-Cloud. Moreover, the hidden layers are usually kept at approximately the same size to ease training.

– The output layer necessitates a single node to deliver an estimated low-level window size.

Several structures were experimented in an effort based on these guidelines. We finally came out at a minimal structure that can be expressed in the conventional notation of 10,002/2/2/1, which means 10,002 input nodes, two hidden layers with two nodes each, and a single output node. All the nodes are fully-connected between two adjacent layers, except a bias node is connected to all noninput ones.

A complete input vector presented to the MLP is denoted as

$$X = < 1, p_1, p_2, ..., p_{10,000}, rs > \qquad (3)$$

where p_i (i=1 to 10,0000) is the profit of ith lru object and rs is a required cache space. Notice that the bias is set to a constant activation 1. Every link connecting node j to node i has an associated weight w_{ij}.

Learning Phase. Besides the MLP structure, to obtain the complete MLP mandates the appropriate set of weights on all node-connecting links. This has been done by means of supervised learning with a distal teacher and backpropagation [13]. We used mean squared error as an objective function. Our MLP learns patterns inherent in caching state history. Each input pattern is organized into a training vector of the form X (Eq.(3)) and was generated every time capacity miss occurs during the i-Cloud simulation of a certain trace, cache size and respective optimal window size. The result of each simulation is a number of input patterns, which were contained inside a training data set. We prepared four different training data sets shown in Table 3. All patterns within the same training data set were associated with a single target window

Table 3. Characteristics of training data sets

Training data set	Size (patterns)	Original trace and cache size	Target window size
BO15D10%	54,639	15-day BO 10%	500
BO15D30%	42,636	15-day BO 30%	100
NY15D10%	62,607	15-day NY 10%	2,000
NY15D20%	31,420	15-day NY 20%	5,000

size (i.e., an optimal window size in Table 2) because i-Cloud was found to give a successful performance results when using a fixed window size per trace as substantiated by [6], [7] and [8].

The input vector normalization and distal teacher components portrayed in Fig. 1 also contributed to the successful learnings of the MLPs. We normalized every element value within each input vector except the bias constant by the following formula, which has been derived from max-min linear scaling.

$$v' = 2v/10^{14} - 1 \tag{4}$$

where v' is the normalized value of a range [-1, 1] and v is an actual value.

Because the MLP outputted a low-level window size of [0.0, 1.0] via sigmoid function, to achieve desired window sizes requires the distal teacher to denormalize the low-level window size. A distal teacher function used was a linear scaling:

$$y' = 10000y \tag{5}$$

where y is an MLP output, 10000 is a maximum optimal window size, and y' is a denormalized output to obtain an actual window size of [0, 10,000]. Note that too small value of actual window size tended to be increased later by i-Cloud as coded in Table 1 to be able to fit a required cache space.

Validation Phase. We provided 12 validation data sets to evaluate the performance of the forecaster module. During validation phase, each validation data set was forward propagated through an MLP, and the generalization ability of each MLP was assessed by measuring errors on separate validation data sets. We used mean absolute error (MAE) = $\frac{1}{P}\sum_p | d_p - y_p |$, which is easy to interpret, as a measure of error made by an MLP. Fig. 2 presents MAE for each pair of training and validation data sets. Notice that there is no graph bar reported for identical training and validation sets that an MLP had seen during training. One should not translate window sizes generated by the MLPs with high MAEs as inefficient window sizes since they might be local maxima (i.e., near-optimal window sizes giving i-Cloud good caching performances). For this reason, MAE was not our concentration but only used to guide overall i-Cloud performance evaluation as described next. The MLPs of lowest accumulative MAEs from both user communities, BO15D10% and NY15D10%, were selected with hopes that they would give near-optimal window sizes instead of local or global minima. Each of both selected MLPs was deployed into the forecaster module to measure i-Cloud's overall caching performances.

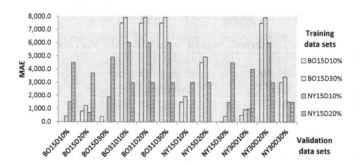

Fig. 2. MAE for each pair of training and validation sets

Table 4. Forecaster algorithm

Algorithm: Forecaster

input variables:

  cd /*cache database (recency-keyed min-priority queue)*/;

  rs /*required cache space*/;

  w_{ij} /*inter-node connection weight*/;

local variables:

  ecd /*empty cache database*/;

  ip /*MLP's input node*/;

  i, j /*node indices where j is on preceding layer of i*/;

  temp /*temporary object*/;

  l /*layer index*/;

  u_i /*weighted sum*/;

  y_i /*output activation*/;

begin

  $ecd \overset{1...10000}{\longleftarrow} cd$; /* duplicating 10,000 lru objects */

  /* Read a current cache state into 10,002 input nodes */

  $ip_0 \leftarrow 1$; /* bias constant */

  for *j*=1 to 10000 **do**

   $temp \leftarrow ecd.removeLeastRecentlyUsedObject()$;

   $ip_j \leftarrow temp.getProfit()$;

  $ip_{10001} \leftarrow rs$;

  /* Normalize inputs except bias node based on Eq.(4) */

  for *j*=1 to 10001 **do**

   $ip_j \leftarrow 2\ ip_j\ /\ 10^{14} - 1$;

  /* Propagate the inputs forward to compute an output */

  for each *noninput layer ℓ* **do**

   for each *node i in ℓ* **do**

    $u_i \leftarrow \sum_j w_{ij} ip_j$;

    $y_i \leftarrow sigmoid(u_i)$;

  /* Denormalize the output based on Eq.(5) */

  $y_{10006} \leftarrow 10000\ y_{10006}$;

return y_{10006}; /*return window size*/

The algorithm of this module is shown in Table 4. The output of this algorithm, window size, is the input of i-Cloud algorithm (Table 1).

4.3   Algorithmic Practicality

Because the total number of cached objects (N) can be increasingly large at runtime. It is necessary to conduct the algorithmic practicality analysis of both modules in Fig. 1. As for the time complexity analysis of i-Cloud algorithm (Table 1), the statements that take significant part in processing time are: replicating cd into ecd takes O(NlogN); the first $do-while$ loop takes O(NlogN) as the window size can be set via the preceding $if-then$ statement to as many as N and removing each object from ecd is O(logN) just like adding each object into oc; the second $do-while$ loop has the worst-case running time of O(NlogN) because the number of evicted objects is bounded by N, while removing each object from oc takes O(logN) and deleting an object from cd is O(logN). The other statements are all identically O(1). Therefore, the algorithm is O(NlogN).

Regarding the time complexity of the forecaster algorithm (Table 4): copying 10,000 lru objects from cd to ecd takes O(logN), the first for loop takes O(logN) to remove lru object from cd, while the other statements are all identically O(1). Thus, the algorithm is O(logN).

Since the cloud cache replacement and forecaster modules are sequentially connected as shown in Fig. 1, i-Cloud algorithm is totally O(NlogN) + O(logN) equal to O(NlogN). In other words, i-Cloud strategy can be implemented.

5   Performance Evaluation

We have evaluated the i-Cloud modules (Fig. 1) as a whole by HTTP trace-driven simulations based on four preprocessed traces 15-day and 31-day BO trace and 15-day and 30-day NY traces. (The preprocessing details can be found in [8].) The traces supplied the values of most i-Cloud parameters declared in Eq.(2) excluding c_i, which can be ignored here since we used uniform cost model (meaning that cost-saving ratio is absolutely equal to byte-hit ratio). Four configurations of window sizes have been used for comparisons as follows.

- Configuration 1: i-Cloud deployed the BO15D10%-learning forecaster to obtain dynamic window sizes intelligently.
- Configuration 2: i-Cloud engaged the NY15D10%-learning forecaster to obtain dynamic window sizes intelligently.
- Configuration 3: i-Cloud operated in a nonintelligent mode (the forecaster module was disabled; this trimmed setting is actually comparable to our previous work Cloud policy [6], [7], [8]); and for each certain trace and each size, a respective *static optimal window size* (i.e., ws_o in Table 2) was preconfigured into the cloud cache replacement module. This configuration demonstrated the static optimal performance of i-Cloud.
- Configuration 4: nonintelligent-mode i-Cloud used *static worst window size* (ws_w in Table 2) to demonstrate the static worst performance of i-Cloud.
- Configuration 5: nonintelligent-mode i-Cloud utilized a static window size of 5,000 (which is the interposing value of the possible range of window sizes generated by the forecaster module) to represent performance baselines.

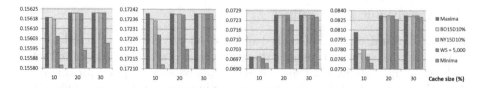

Fig. 3. Comparative byte-hit and cost-saving ratios of i-Cloud based on 15-day BO, 31-day BO, 15-day NY and 30-day NY traces, respectively

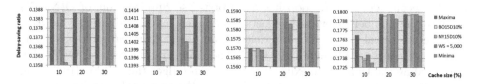

Fig. 4. Comparative delay-saving ratios of i-Cloud based on 15-day BO, 31-day BO, 15-day NY and 30-day NY traces, respectively

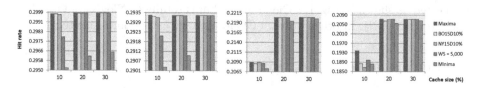

Fig. 5. Comparative hit rates of i-Cloud based on 15-day BO, 31-day BO, 15-day NY and 30-day NY traces, respectively

The results can be discussed as follows. For byte-hit and cost-saving ratios in Fig. 3, i-Cloud tended to perform well for user communities where i-Cloud had learned their workloads: i-Cloud with BO15D10%-learning forecaster (configuration 1) performed against 15-day and 31-day BO traces slightly better than with NY15D10%-learning forecaster (configuration 2), while NY15D10%-learning forecaster served the NY workloads better than BO15D10%-learning forecaster.

In many cases of byte-hit and cost-saving performances, the forecaster modules of configurations 1 and 2 profited i-Cloud to outperform the nonintelligent mode of configuration 5, especially at small allocated cache size 10%. This means that small relative cache sizes like 10% (e.g., a cache size deployed by data-intense organization tend to be deemed small relative to its entire cloud-hosted data) tend to benefit more from i-Cloud than larger cache sizes. For larger cache sizes, nonintelligent-mode i-Cloud (which has lower overhead than i-Cloud with MLP equipped) using a moderate window size (configuration 5) seems to be enough. This allows consumers to choose i-Cloud's operational mode that best suits their available resources.

For delay-saving ratio in Fig. 4, dynamic window sizes produced by configurations 1 and 2 did not give significant performance improvement beyond the static window size produced by using configuration 5 regardless of cache sizes. This can be translated that nonintelligent-mode i-Cloud is simply enough for improving cloud service responsiveness.

In all performance metrics, the forecaster modules did not cause i-Cloud's performance minima except hit rate, resulted from the 30-day NY trace and 10% cache size and configuration 2, in Fig. 5. This can be translated that the forecaster could produce a series of dynamic window sizes resulting in even lower hit rate than using the static worst window size of configuration 4. This was probably because the forecasters were trained against target window sizes, specifically tuned for byte-hit performance rather than hit rate. This finding implied that, first, to perform well in which metric requires that the forecaster be trained against target window size concentrating on that metric as well, and second, training the forecaster module appropriately is not so trivial task that using any arbitrary static window size can replace the forecaster for comparable performances.

By superimposing the graphs presented in our previous work [8] (not repeated here due to paper space limitation), it was found that i-Cloud with the forecaster modules surpassed LRU, GDSF and LFUDA in all cases in byte-hit, cost-saving and delay-saving metrics and in almost all cases in hit metric. For 20% and 30% cache sizes, i-Cloud performances also stabilized almost up to those of the infinite cache sizes. This convinces users the basic benefits to obtain from i-Cloud.

Finally, by considering one-month-based results, we can see that although the forecasters had learned merely half-month data sets, they could delivered very close to performance maxima over the long running periods of one months. This convinces users that i-Cloud would not degrade easily for long-term deployment.

6   Conclusions

This paper presents i-Cloud cache replacement policy that is capable of improving off-premise private cloud scalability, economy and responsiveness. The artificial neural network module of i-Cloud successfully enabled automatic workload adaptation to retain superior performances and also helped avoid performance minima when properly trained. This simplifies i-Cloud deployment regardless of target user communities.

Acknowledgments. This research is financially supported by Thailand's Office of the Higher Education Commission, Thailand Research Fund, and Sripatum university (grant MRG5580114). The authors also thank Duane Wessels, National Science Foundation (grants NCR-9616602 and NCR-9521745) and the National Laboratory for Applied Network Research for the new trace data used in this study.

References

1. Ali, W., Shamsuddin, S.M.: Intelligent client-side web caching scheme based on least recently used algorithm and neuro-fuzzy system. In: Proceedings of the 6th International Symposium on Neural Networks (2009)
2. Amazon.com, Inc.: Amazon web services (August 8, 2013), http://aws.amazon.com/s3/
3. Arlitt, M., Friedrich, R., Jin, T.: Performance evaluation of web proxy cache replacement policies. Perform. Eval. 39(1-4), 149–164 (2000)
4. Balamash, A., Krunz, M.: An overview of web caching replacement algorithms. IEEE Communications Surveys Tutorials 6(2), 44–56 (2004)
5. Banditwattanawong, T., Hidaka, S., Washizaki, H., Maruyama, K.: Optimization of program loading by object class clustering. IEEJ Trans. Elec. Electron. Eng. 1(4), xiii–xiv (2006)
6. Banditwattanawong, T.: From web cache to cloud cache. In: Li, R., Cao, J., Bourgeois, J. (eds.) GPC 2012. LNCS, vol. 7296, pp. 1–15. Springer, Heidelberg (2012)
7. Banditwattanawong, T., Uthayopas, P.: Cloud cache replacement policy: new performances and findings. In: 1st International Conference on Annual PSU Phuket, PSU PIC 2012 (2013)
8. Banditwattanawong, T., Uthayopas, P.: Improving cloud scalability, economy and responsiveness with client-side cloud cache. In: 10th International Conference on Electrical Engineering/Electronics, Computer, Telecommunications and Information Technology, ECTI-CON 2013 (2013)
9. Cobb, J., ElAarag, H.: Web proxy cache replacement scheme based on back-propagation neural network. J. Syst. Softw. 81(9), 1539–1558 (2008)
10. Google Inc.: Google app engine (August 8, 2013), http://developers.google.com/appengine/
11. Microsoft: Windows azure (August 8, 2013), http://www.windowsazure.com/
12. Podlipnig, S., Böszörmenyi, L.: A survey of web cache replacement strategies. ACM Comput. Surv. 35(4), 374–398 (2003)
13. Reed, R.D., Marks, R.J.: Neural Smithing: Supervised Learning in Feedforward Artificial Neural Networks. MIT Press, Cambridge (1998)
14. Romano, S., ElAarag, H.: A neural network proxy cache replacement strategy and its implementation in the squid proxy server. Neural Comput. Appl. 20(1), 59–78 (2011)
15. Sulaiman, S., Shamsuddin, S., Forkan, F., Abraham, A.: Intelligent web caching using neurocomputing and particle swarm optimization algorithm. In: Second Asia International Conference on Modeling Simulation, pp. 642–647 (2008)
16. Tian, W., Choi, B., Phoha, V.V.: An adaptive web cache access predictor using neural network. In: Proceedings of the 15th Intl. Conf. on Industrial and Engineering Applications of Artificial Intelligence and Expert Systems (2002)

Exploring Video Steganography for Hiding Images Based on Similar Lifting Wavelet Coefficients

Kornkanok Churin, Jitdumrong Preechasuk, and Chantana Chantrapornchai

Department of Computing, Faculty of Science, Silpakorn University
Nakhon Pathom, Thailand
ctana@su.ac.th

Abstract. This stegaphography is the science that attempts to hide the secret information through the cover media. It considers the combination of various issues such as security, privacy etc. This paper interests in the video steganography method, where the image is hidden in a video file. The approach uses the intensity features together with the lifting multiple discrete wavelet transform. The approach contains two steps. First, we bring the secret image and cover video file to transform using lifting based multi-level wavelet transform. Then we find the positions with the similar values from both secret image and video. The key idea is the finding of the position with the "same" or "similar" coefficients. We embed the image coefficients in those frame positions. In the experiments, we explore the efficiency of the method using various wavelet transforms with random coefficient and similar coefficient selections. The experiments also consider the different payload image size in the video file. For all the results, the proposed approach with similar coefficients and lifting multi-level wavelet transform has a better PSNR for all the test cases.

Keywords: Video Steganography, Lifting Wavelet, Multi-Level Wavelet Transform, Intensity.

1 Introduction

Multimedia content protection has recently become an important issue because of insufficient cognizance of intellectual property. Steganography is one possible method to protect digital assets, and the technology of steganography has extended its applications from copyright protection to content indexing, secret communication, fingerprinting, and many others. The steganography techniques are classified based on the cover media and secret message type. The possible secret message types are text, images and audios while the cover media can be text, image, video and audio files. For example, with the text file cover media, methods usually relate to the coding scheme such as line-shifting, word-shifting, feature coding. For image and audio cover medias, methods can be based on least significant bits, discrete cosine transform, fast fourier transform, wavelet transform, etc.

In this work, we present a steganography on the cover media as the video file. The message is considered as an image to be hidden. The study proposed the approach that embeds the secret image pixels in each frame of the video by coefficient positions.

B. Papasratorn et al. (Eds.): IAIT 2013, CCIS 409, pp. 35–46, 2013.

The coefficients of the transform frames with the similar values to that of the secrete image are considered. The lifting based multi-level wavelet transform is used for transforming the domain.

The paper is organized into following sections. Section 2 is the backgrounds and literature review. The steganography model and wavelet transform are described in Section 3. Section 4 discusses the experimental results and the conclusion is given in Section 5.

2   Backgrounds and Literature Reviews

There are many works that have been done in steganography in the past ten years. Some of them are based on the spatial domain and some is based on the frequency domain. Some are interested in the image as cover media and some are interested in the video cover media. We are interested in frequency domain where the video is used as a cover media.

Based on the frequency domain methods, two transformations are commonly used: wavelet and DCT. Some of them works on images and some works on video or audio cover media. Wu and Sun [19] proposed the method for image sharing and checking for the validity of it. The method for reconstruction is developed for the case of an altered stego image Furuta, Noda, Niimi, and Kawaguchi [10] proposed the method based on 3-D set partitioning in hierarchical trees (SPIHT) algorithm for video compression and bit-plane complexity segmentation (BPCS) steganography. Kavitha and Murugan [12] sent maximum hidden information while preserving security against detection by an unauthorized person. A steganographic system is secured and effective when the statistics of the cover message and stego data are identical. The system proposes to increase the strength of the key by using UTF-32 encoding in the swapping algorithm and lossless stegano technique in the AVI file. Liu, Liu and Ni [5] proposed a novel, low complexity chaotic steganography method applicable to MPEG-2 videos. Prabakaran and Bhavani [14] studied the modified secure and high capacity based steganography scheme of hiding a large-size secret image into a small-size cover image. They used arnold transformation to scramble the secret image. Discrete wavelet transform (DWT) is used to perform in both images and used alpha blending operation.

Some of the work considered the DCT transformation while some considered the wavelet transformation. These following work uses the wavelet transform on the cover image while our paper considers embedding images in the video file based on wavelet coefficients. Alkhraisat and Habes [2] proposed a new method for hiding the secret image inside the cover image. Elham, Jamshid and Nima [9] proposed to apply the wavelet transform and the genetic algorithm to embed data in the discrete wavelet transform coefficients in 4x4 blocks on the cover image. Safy, Zayed and Dessouki, [16] proposed the adaptive steganographic technique which uses the bits of the payload to embed in the integer wavelet coefficients of the cover image. Sarreshtedari and Ghaemmaghami [17] proposed the image steganography using the wavelet transform coefficients of the original image to embed the secret data by maintaining integrity of the wavelet coefficients at the high capacity embedding. Reddy and Raja [15] proposed a performance analysis of IWT and DWT on non-LSB with better PSNR value in the case of IWT compared to DWT. Battacharya, Dey and Chaudhuri [4] presented a steganography technique for hiding multiple images in a color image based on DWT and DCT. Yang, Lin and Hu [20] proposed a simple reversible data hiding scheme based on IWT. This model shows that both the host media and secret message can be completely recovered, without distortion. Dinesh and Ramesh [7] proposed a method in DWT transforms that allows to perfect embedding of the hidden message and reconstruction provide an efficient capacity for data hiding without sacrificing the original image quality.

2.1   Discrete Wavelet Transform [8, 18]

The frequency domain transform we applied in this research is Haar-DWT, the simplest DWT. A 2-dimensional Haar-DWT consists of two operations, one is the horizontal operation and the other is the vertical one. Both are separate the image into a lower resolution approximation image or band (LL) as well as horizontal (HL), vertical (LH) and diagonal (HH). The Haar wavelet transform has the benefits of its ease. It is fast and uses small memory space. The calculation can be done in place. It is also, reversible without edge effect. However, it has some limitation on the discontinuity. The result of wavelet transform is a set of wavelet coefficients. The process of a 2-D Haar-DWT are as follows:

$$\psi(x) = \sum (-1) c \, \varphi(2x - k) \tag{1}$$

where $\varphi =$ the host function that is calculated from , $\phi_{jk} = \phi(2^j x - k)$, $c_{M-k} =$ the translation factor.

2.2   Lifting Based Multi-level Wavelet Transform [1, 3]

The lifting scheme is an algorithm used for implementation hardware and software of DWT. It is constituted of steps of predictions and updating described by Fig 1.

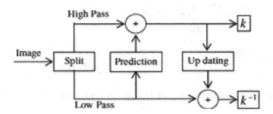

Fig. 1. Lifting scheme forward transform[6]

Fig.1 presents the lifting scheme of the wavelet filter computing on the one-dimension signal. It contains the following steps.

- Split step: The signal is split into even and odd points. The maximum correlation between adjacent pixels can be used for the next step.
- Predict step: The even samples are multiplied by the predicted factor. The results are summed to the odd samples to generate the new coefficients.
- Update step: the new coefficients computed by the predict step are multiplied by the update factors. The results are summed with the even samples to get the coarse coefficients.

The advantage of lifting scheme is the forward and inverse transform was obtained from the same architecture. The inverse goes from right to the left, by inversing the coefficients of normalized and changes the sign positive to negative. k is the constant of normalization and the steps of the predictions and the updating at decomposition in polyphase matrix. The polyphase representation of discrete filter h(n) is defined as:

$$h(z) = h_e(z^2) + z^{-1}h_o(z^2)$$ (2)

where $h_e(z)$ and $h_o(z)$ are respectively obtained from the even and odd zeta transform respectively. If we represent $g_e(z)$ and $h_o(z)$ the low pass and high pass coefficients of the synthesis filter respectively, the polyphase matrix written as:

$$p(z) = \begin{bmatrix} h_e(z) & g_e(z) \\ h_o(z) & g_o(z) \end{bmatrix}$$

The filters h (z) e , h (z) o , g (z) e and g (z) o are Laurent polynomials, as the set of all polynomials exhibits a commutative ring structure, within which polynomial division with remainder is possible, long division between two Laurent polynomials is not a unique operation. Fig.2 is the difference between the two wavelet transforms.

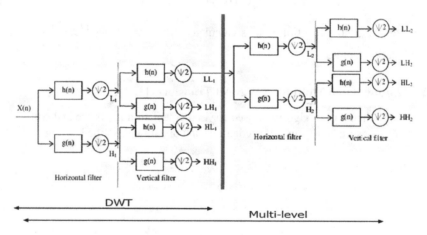

Fig. 2. Difference between discrete wavelet transform and lifting based multi-level wavelet transform [6]

3   Proposed Framework

In this work, we are interested in the hiding image in the video media. The secret data is an RGB image. The proposed embedding model is as shown in Fig 3. The proposed doffing model is as shown in Fig 4.

From Fig. 3, there are following steps. Step 1): Bring secret image and video file to transform using lifting based multi-level wavelet transform; then find and keep the positions with the same coefficient of color between the secret image and the frame of the video. Since we are interested in hiding in the frames containing pixels with the same coefficient as those of the secret image, this step searches for these pixels. Also, we are using the color image which is divided into RGB plane for each plane, we do this search. Step 2): Embed the pixels of the secret image with the same coefficient into those frames. In this work, we attempt to find the positions with the same coefficient values for each wavelet plane. If the number of coefficients that are same for the cover video frames is greater than that of the hidden image, the algorithm works fine. Also, if there are many positions with the same value, we randomly choose one. However, the values of the coefficients are not exactly matched, we find the coefficients with the "closest" values from the cover video frames. The "closest" means the values with the least absolute difference first. When there are two values with the save absolute values, we prefer the darker positions (the smaller value). Among these, we have to check whether the coefficient positions are already used. If not, we can use them. Otherwise, we do not consider them. At last, we cannot find any coefficient positions, e.g. the picture is dark background or white backgrounds. We randomly pick positions.

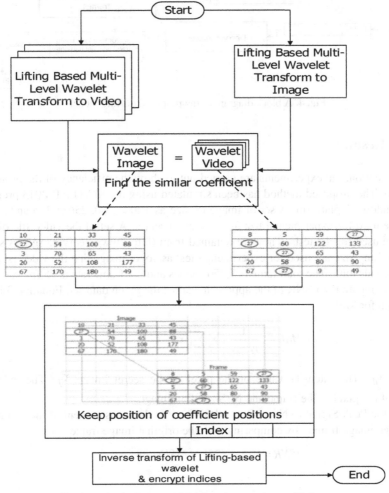

Fig. 3. A block diagram of finding the wavelet coefficients

After embedding, the indices are kept in a file separately from the stego video. We keep the frame number, the row and column positions etc. They are also encrypted. For example, (1,5,5) means we keep the position at frame1, row5 and column5. Then perform the inverse transform back for all the stego video frames.

On the decryption side, Fig. 4 presents the steps which are described as follows: Doff pixel of the each frame of video file using the lifting discrete wavelet transforms. Then, decrypt the index files. The indices are used to locate frames and positions to hide. Extract the values from the coefficients. Save them to as image coefficients. Then perform the inverse lifting wavelet transforms to obtain the secret image.

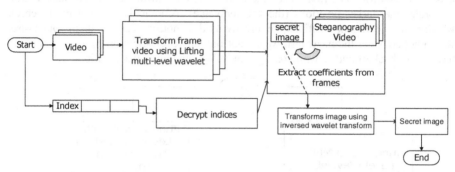

Fig. 4. A block diagram of the proposed doffing model

4   Results

In this section, the experiments are carried out to show the efficiency of the proposed scheme. The proposed method has been simulated using the MATLAB 2013 program on Windows 7 platform. A set of image of size as 100×100, 256×256 and 512×512 are used for experimental test as an original secret. A set of the video file of any size are used for the tests. They are obtained from (http://www.reefvid.org/). A set of video of any size are used for experimental test as cover image that the video is about 307 seconds long. The total fame is 7,750 frames and the frame rate is 25 fps.

We compute the PSNR of the approach against the given data set. Equation 3 is the equation for MSE.

$$MSE = \left[\frac{1}{N * N}\right] \sum_{i=1}^{N} \sum_{J=1}^{N} \left(x_{ij} - \overline{x}_{ij}\right)^2 \tag{3}$$

where: x_{ij} : The intensity value of the pixel in the secret image, $\overline{x}_{ij}$: The intensity value of the pixel in the frame and N: Size of an Image.

For the Peak Signal to Noise Ratio (PSNR), it is the measurement of the quality of the stego image frame   by comparing with the original image frame.

$$PSNR = 10\log_{10} 255^2 / MSE(db) \tag{4}$$

For the video, the average PSNR values of all the video frames are calculated. Table 1 shows the PSNR values of embedded video using lifting based multi-level wavelet transform with the similar coefficients (LMWT-Sim), using multi-level wavelet transform with the random coefficients (LMWT-Random), discrete wavelet transform with the similar coefficients (DWT-Sim) and discrete wavelet transform with random coefficients (DWT-Random). The PSNR of LMWT-Sim is better for all the methods due to the lifting scheme has been developed as a flexible tool suitable for constructing the second generation wavelet. It is composed of three basic operation stages: splitting, predicting, and updating.

The average PSNR values of the video frames are calculated to compare the stego video with the original video. However, for the average PSNR values, we calculate from all frames and then divide with the total number of all frames.

$$\frac{\sum_{i=1}^{n} PSNR_i}{n} \tag{5}$$

where $PSNR_i$ = PSNR of frame i

N = the total number of frames.

Table 1. Comparison of the methods with different images and different video files

Video name	Secret image	LMWT-Sim	LMWT-Random	DWT-Sim	DWT-Random
		PSNR	PSNR	PSNR	PSNR
clip235 (data rate: 2677 kbps, frame rate:25 frames/second)	Lena image (100*100)	54.594	40.374	49.558	35.966
	Lena image (256*256)	53.221	40.229	48.795	34.107
	Lena image (512*512)	53.101	39.495	46.669	31.580
clip396 (data rate: 3103 kbps, frame rate: 25 frames/second)	Lena image (100*100)	56.483	43.783	48.566	36.798
	Lena image (256*256)	54.205	42.173	47.395	34.704
	Lena image (512*512)	54.089	41.059	46.290	32.176
clip535 (data rate: 2453 kbps, frame rate: 25 frames/second)	Lena image (100*100)	58.238	45.382	51.395	35.363
	Lena image (256*256)	56.494	43.208	50.990	34.227
	Lena image (512*512)	55.960	41.897	49.281	32.683

Fig. 5 compares PSNR when the frame drop percentage are varied by 10%, 20% 30% 40% and 50% of all frames of the video file. Dropping frame is random and is done for the stego video. The dropped frames are skipped and the overall PSNR of the secret images are calculated.

Fig. 6 compares the PSNR values of the various method for the varying payload size. For example, when the payload is 10%, we consider the case where the size of the secret image size is 10% of the total size of all the frames. Obviously, the larger payload, the worse PSNR. Still, LMWT-Sim performs better for all the cases. Also, the lower payload size, the better the performance is.

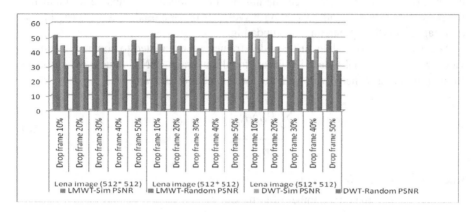

Fig. 5. Comparison of different drop frame rates with different video files with the lena image 512*512

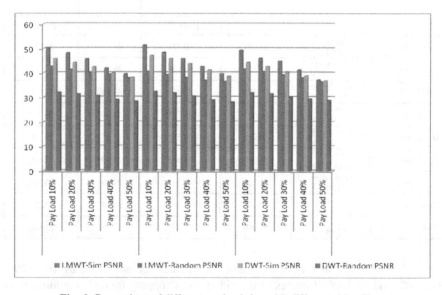

Fig. 6. Comparison of different payload size with different video files

Table 2 shows the coefficients of the original video, secret i e, and the direct combination of them and the combination from our "similar" approach. It shows that the secret image coefficients are hidden completely in the video frame coefficients. Though we can see the region where it is not perfectly hidden due to the number exact coefficient matches, those coefficients are likely hidden in the left side regions of the graph in the figure.

Table 2. Wavelet cofficient histogram of clip 235 of original video and stego video

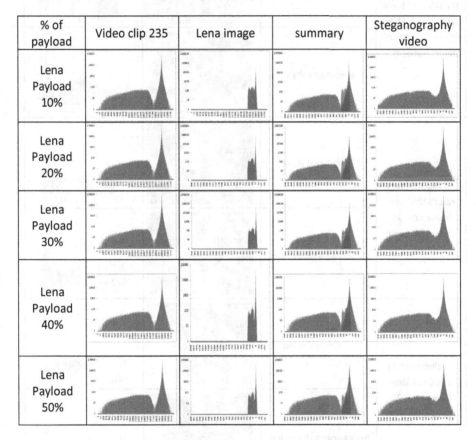

% of payload	Video clip 235	Lena image	summary	Steganography video
Lena Payload 10%				
Lena Payload 20%				
Lena Payload 30%				
Lena Payload 40%				
Lena Payload 50%				

Table 3 is the histogram of the coefficients of the original video and the stego video. We can see the some difference between the original video and the stego video. The size of difference depends on the coefficient of the secret image.

Table 3. Wavelet cofficient histogram of original video and stego video

Video file	Type of video	Sample frame of video file	Histogram of video file
clip235 (data rate: 2677 kbps, frame rate:25 frames/second)	Original video		
	Steganography video		
clip396 (data rate: 3103 kbps, frame rate: 25 frames/second)	Original video		
	Steganography video		
clip535 (data rate: 2453 kbps, frame rate: 25 frames/second)	Original video		
	Steganography video		

5   Conclusion

In this paper, we study the steganography method with lifting multi-level wavelet and the traditional DWT with various coefficient selections: randomly and similar selection. The similar coefficients are selected to hide the image wavelet coefficients.

This approach works very well for all the test cases when measuring the PSNR values of the stego videos and in different scenario such as frame dropping rates and payload sizes. The hiding in coefficients of lifting multi-level wavelet gives better results compared to the random approach of discrete DWT about 40% .

References

1. Acharya, T., Chakrabarti, C.: A Survey Lifting-based Discrete Wavelet Transform Architectures. Journal of VLSI Signal Processing 42, 321–339 (2006)
2. Alkhraisat, M., Habes, M.: 4 least Significant Bits Information Hiding Implementation and Analysis. In: ICGST Int. Conf. on Graphics, Vision and Image Processing (GVIP 2005), Cairo, Egypt (2005)
3. Barua, S., Charletta, J.E., Kotteri, K.A., Bell, A.E.: An efficient architecture for lifting-based two-dimensional discrete wavelet transforms. Intergration, The VLSI Journal 38, 341–352 (2004)
4. Battacharya, Dey, T.N., Chauduri, S.R.B.: A session based multiple image hiding technique using DWT and DCT. J. Comput. Applic. 38, 18–21 (2012)
5. Bin, L., Fenlin, L., Daping, N.: Adaptive compressed video steganography in the VLC-domain Daping. In: Wireless, Mobile and Multimedia Networks, pp. 1–4. IET (2006)
6. Dhaha, D., Medien, Z., Taoufik, S., Mohamed, A., Belgacem, B., Mohsen, M., Rached, T.: Multi-level Discrete Wavelet Transform Architecture Design. In: Proceedings of the World Congress on Engineering, IWCE 2009, London, U.K, July 1-3, pp. 191–195 (2009)
7. Dinesh, Y., Ramesh, A.P.: Efficient capacity image steganography by using wavelets. J. Eng. Res. Applic. 2, 251–259 (2012)
8. Donoho, D.: Nonlinear Wavelet Methods for Recovery of Signals, Densities, and Spectra from Indirect and Noisy Data. In: Daubechies, I. (ed.) Different Perspectives on Wavelets, Proceeding of Symposia in Applied Mathematics, vol. 47, pp. 173–205. Amer. Math. Soc, Providence (1993)
9. Elham, G., Jamshid, S., Nima, F.: High Capacity Image Steganography using Wavelet Transform and Genetic Algorithm. In: Multi Conference of Engineers and Computer Scientists, vol. 1 (2011)
10. Furuta, T., Noda, H., Niimi, M., Kawaguchi, E.: Bit-plane decomposition steganography using wavelet compressed video. In: Proceedings of the 2003 Information, Communications and Signal Processing, and Fourth Pacific Rim Conference on Multimedia, vol. 2, pp. 970–974. IEEE (2003)
11. Williams, J.R., Kevin, A.: Introduction to Wavelets in Engineering. International Journal for Numerical Methods in Engineering 37(14), 2365–2388 (1994)
12. Kavitha, R., Murugan, A.: Lossless Steganography on AVI File Using Swapping Algorithm. In: Conference on Computational Intelligence and Multimedia Applications, vol. 4, pp. 83–88. IEEE (2007)
13. Michel, M., Yves, M., Georges, O., Jean, P.: Wavelet Toolbox for Use with MATLAB. In: Wavelet Toolbox User's Guilde 1996 - 1997. The MathWorks, Inc.
14. Prabakaran, G., Bhavani, R.: A modified secure digital image steganography based on Discrete Wavelet Transform. In: Computing, Electronics and Electrical Technologies (ICCEET), pp. 1096–1100. IEEE (2012)
15. Reddy, H.S.M., Raja, K.B.: Wavelet based non LSB steganography. J. Adv. Network. Applic. 3, 1203–1209 (2011)

16. El Safy, R.O., Zayed, H.H., El Dessouki, A.: An Adaptive Steganographic Technique Based on Integer Wavelet Transform. In: Networking and Media Convergence, pp. 111–117 (2009)
17. Sarreshtedari, S., Ghaemmaghami, S.: High Capacity Image Steganography in Wavelet Domain. In: Consumer Communications and Networking, pp. 1–6 (2010)
18. Vetterli, M., Herley, C.: Wavelets and Filter Banks: Theory and Design. IEEE Transactions on Signal Processing 40, 2207–2232 (1992)
19. Wu, X., Sun, W.: Secret image sharing scheme with authentication and remedy abilities based on cellular automata and discrete wavelet transform. Journal of Systems and Software 86(4), 1068–1088 (2013)
20. Yang, C.Y., Lin, C.H., Hu, W.C.: Reversible data hiding for high-quality images based on integer wavelet transform. J. Inform. Hiding Multimedia Signal Process 3, 142–150 (2012)

Rotor Time Constant Identification Approaches Based on Back-Propagation Neural Network for Indirect Vector Controlled Induction Machine

Moulay Rachid Douiri and Mohamed Cherkaoui

Mohammadia Engineering School, Department of Electrical Engineering,
Ibn Sina Avenue, 765, Agdal-Rabat, Morocco
douirirachid@hotmail.com

Abstract. Nowadays, indirect field oriented control (IFOC) is a promising induction machine control method which leads to excellent motor dynamic performances. It is well known that in this IFOC scheme, the induction machine parameters change widely during the operation of the drive especially the value of rotor time constant which varies with rotor temperature and flux level of the machine. Therefore, the quality of the drive system decreases if no means for compensation or identification is applied. This paper deals with rotor time constant identification for vector controlled induction motor based on measurement of the stator voltages, currents and speed by applying the back-propagation neural networks approach in order to implement a robust control law for industrial application. A convenient formulation is in order to compute physical parameters of the machine. The back-propagation learning process algorithm is briefly presented and tested with different configuration of motor induction. Verification of the validity and feasibility of the technique is obtained from simulation results.

Keywords: artificial neural network, indirect field oriented control, induction motor drives, rotor time constant.

1 Introduction

In the field oriented control scheme, the stator current of an induction motor current is decoupled into torque and flux producing components, respectively, hence allowing independent control of torque and flux, like in a separately excited dc motor. This allows the drive system to produce the desired output torque and speed with much faster and more stable responses, compared with the conventional constant volt per hertz control scheme. The Indirect Field Oriented Control (IFOC) drive uses rotor speed information and the motor electrical parameters to compute the rotor flux position, and is therefore more easily adaptable on existing drives [1],[2]. The major problem associated with IFOC drives using rotor flux orientation, is the time variation of the rotor time constant, leading to an incorrectly calculated slip frequency command. Consequently, the required decoupling between torque and flux is lost, and the dynamic response of the drive is significantly degraded [3],[4],[5]. To maintain

B. Papasratorn et al. (Eds.): IAIT 2013, CCIS 409, pp. 47–57, 2013.

robustness of the drive, on-line identification of the rotor time constant or compensation for the parameter variations is required.

Many techniques has been reported [6],[7],[8] to solve the problem of motor parameter identification while the drive is in indirect field oriented control operation. Intelligent techniques have also been applied to achieve this goal [9],[10],[11].

Ba-Razzouk, A., et all. [12] proposed a rotor time constant estimation method using the back-propagation neural network, formed by log-sigmoidal neurons, and comprises 5 inputs, 6 neurons on the first hidden layer, 6 neurons on the second and one output neuron. It converges to a sum squared error of $9.26.10^{-4}$ after 14500 iterations (with randomly initialized weights and biases in the beginning of the training).

The main objective of this research is to estimate the rotor time constant of an induction motor drive that provides more precise results than obtained by Ba-Razzouk [12], in order to realize an indirect field oriented control insensitive to the variation of this parameter. To achieve this goal, several sub-objectives are to consider in particular, the development of a simulation library of induction motor, the development of artificial neural network (ANN) learning techniques, and finding appropriate architectures.

This paper is organized as follows: in section 2, describes principles of indirect vector control. In section 3, we present the mathematics equations of rotor time constant. In section 3, we develop the steps for training an ANN to rotor time constant. Section 4 presents the simulation results obtained for this approach. Paper ends with a brief conclusion in Section 5.

Nomenclature

d,q	Direct and quadrature components
R_s, R_r	Stator and rotor resistance [Ω]
i_{ds}, i_{qs}	Stator current dq –axis [A]
i_{dr}, i_{qr}	Rotor current dq –axis [A]
v_{ds}, v_{qs}	Stator voltage dq-axis [V]
v_{dr}, v_{qr}	Rotor voltage dq-axis [V]
L_s, L_r, L_m	Stator, rotor and mutual inductance [H]
λ_{ds}, λ_{qs}	dq stator fluxes [Wb]
λ_{dr}, λ_{qr}	dq rotor fluxes [Wb]
T_{em}	Electromagnetic torque [N.m]
ω_r, ω_e, ω_{sl}	Rotor, synchronous and slip frequency [rad/s]
τ_r	Rotor time constant
J	Inertia moment [Kg.m^2]
n_p	Number of poles
$\sigma = 1 - \dfrac{L_m^2}{L_s L_r}$	Leakage coefficient
s	Differential operator (d/dt)

2   Mathematic Model of IFOC Drive

The dynamic model of a three-phase squirrel cage Y-connected induction motor can be described in a fixed stator d-q reference frame [13],[14] as:

$$
\begin{bmatrix} \dot{i}_{qs} \\ \dot{i}_{ds} \\ \dot{\lambda}_{qr} \\ \dot{\lambda}_{dr} \end{bmatrix} =
\begin{bmatrix}
-\left(\dfrac{R_s}{\sigma L_s} + \dfrac{1-\sigma}{\sigma \tau_r} \right) & -\omega_e & \dfrac{L_m}{\sigma L_s L_r \tau_r} & -\dfrac{L_m}{\sigma L_s L_r} n_p \omega_r \\
-\omega_e & -\left(\dfrac{R_s}{\sigma L_s} + \dfrac{1-\sigma}{\sigma \tau_r} \right) & \dfrac{L_m}{\sigma L_s L_r} n_p \omega_r & \dfrac{L_m}{\sigma L_s L_r \tau_r} \\
\dfrac{L_m}{L_r} & 0 & -\dfrac{1}{\tau_r} & -\left(\omega_e - n_p \omega_r \right) \\
0 & \dfrac{L_m}{L_r} & \left(\omega_e - n_p \omega_r \right) & -\dfrac{1}{\tau_r}
\end{bmatrix}
\times
\begin{bmatrix} i_{qs} \\ i_{ds} \\ \lambda_{qr} \\ \lambda_{dr} \end{bmatrix}
+
\begin{bmatrix} \dfrac{v_{qs}}{\sigma L_s} \\ \dfrac{v_{qs}}{\sigma L_s} \\ 0 \\ 0 \end{bmatrix}
\tag{1}
$$

Moreover, the electromagnetic torque equation can be expressed in terms of the stator current and rotor flux linkage as:

$$
T_{em} = \frac{3}{2} n_p \frac{L_m}{L_r} \left(\lambda_{dr} i_{qs} - \lambda_{qr} i_{ds} \right)
\tag{2}
$$

In an ideally decoupled IM, the rotor flux linkage axis is forced to align with the d-axis. It follows that:

$$
\lambda_{qr} = 0, \ \dot{\lambda}_{qr} = 0
\tag{3}
$$

Using (3), the desired rotor flux linkage in terms of i_{ds} can be found from the last row of (1) as:

$$
\lambda_{dr} = \frac{L_m / \tau_r}{s + \left(1 / \tau_r \right)} i_{ds}
\tag{4}
$$

According to the third row of (1), the slip angular velocity ($\omega_{sl} = \omega_e = n_p\omega_r$) can be estimated using λ_{dr} in (4) and i_{qs} as follows:

$$\omega_{sl} = \frac{L_m}{\tau_r \lambda_{dr}} i_{qs} \tag{5}$$

In the steady state, the desired rotor flux linkage shown in (4) can be represented as $\lambda_{dr} = L_m i^*_{ds}$ in which i^*_{ds} is the flux current command. Moreover, the synchronous angular velocity (we) in the indirect field-oriented mechanism is generated by using the measured rotor angular velocity (ω_e) and the following estimated slip angular velocity:

$$\omega^*_{sl} = \frac{i^*_{qs}}{\tau_r i^*_{ds}} \tag{6}$$

where i^*_{qs} is the torque current command. Consequently, the electromagnetic torque can be simplified as:

$$T_{em} = K_t i^*_{qs} \tag{7}$$

with the torque constant K_t defined as:

$$K_t = \left(\frac{3n_p}{2}\right)\left(\frac{L_m^2}{L_r}\right) i^*_{ds} \tag{8}$$

According to the conventional Indirect Field Oriented Control (IFOC) technique the reference slip pulsation ω^*_{sl} is computed by mean of (6). It is clear that variations of τ_r with temperature or saturation cause an misalignment of the stator current vector with respect to the rotor flux vector resulting in incorrect amplitude and phase of the rotor flux vector as well as an incorrect torque.

The influence of the slip frequency on the rotor flux and torque in an IFOC drive has been used to develop a tuning procedure by exploiting the different time constants of torque and flux. This method is in principle simple and effective, unfortunately as in normal operations the system runs under the control of a closed loop speed regulator, the use of the above mentioned method require some operations on the system. Moreover this procedure is strictly dependent on the sensibility of the system operator.

3   Mathematical Determination of the Rotor Time Constant

Consider the stator voltages equations and calculate the term: ($v_{ds}i_{qs}-v_{qs}i_{ds}$),

$$v_{ds}i_{qs} - v_{qs}i_{ds} = \frac{d\lambda_{ds}}{dt}i_{qs} - \frac{d\lambda_{qs}}{dt}i_{ds} \tag{9}$$

Let us know that:

$$\lambda_{ds} = \frac{L_m}{L_r} \lambda_{dr} + \sigma L_s i_{ds} \tag{10}$$

$$\lambda_{qs} = \frac{L_m}{L_r} \lambda_{qr} + \sigma L_s i_{qs} \tag{11}$$

$$\frac{d \lambda_{dr}}{dt} = \frac{R_r}{L_r}\left(L_m i_{ds} - \lambda_{dr}\right) - \omega_r \lambda_{qr} \tag{12}$$

$$\frac{d \lambda_{qr}}{dt} = \frac{R_r}{L_r}\left(L_m i_{qs} - \lambda_{qr}\right) - \omega_r \lambda_{dr} \tag{13}$$

We replace (λ_{ds} and λ_{qs}) by their values given by (7) and (8), we find:

$$v_{ds} i_{qs} - v_{qs} i_{ds} = \left(\frac{L_m}{L_r}\frac{d \lambda_{dr}}{dt} + \sigma L_s \frac{di_{ds}}{dt}\right) i_{qs} - \left(\frac{L_m}{L_r}\frac{d \lambda_{qr}}{dt} + \sigma L_s \frac{di_{qs}}{dt}\right) i_{ds} \tag{14}$$

We replace ($d\lambda_{ds}/dt$ and $d\lambda_{qs}/dt$) by their values given by (9) and (10), we find:

$$
\begin{aligned}
v_{ds} i_{qs} - v_{qs} i_{ds} &= \frac{L_m}{L_r}\left(-\frac{R_r}{L_r}\left(\lambda_{dr} i_{qs} - \lambda_{qr} i_{ds}\right) - \omega_r\left(\lambda_{qr} i_{qs} - \lambda_{dr} i_{ds}\right)\right) \\
&\quad + \sigma L_s \left(\frac{di_{ds}}{dt} i_{qs} - \frac{di_{qs}}{dt} i_{ds}\right)
\end{aligned}
\tag{15}
$$

Hence, we can derive the expression of the rotor time-constant ($\tau_r = L_r/R_r$):

$$\tau_r = \frac{\left(\lambda_{qr} i_{ds} - \lambda_{dr} i_{qs}\right)}{\frac{L_r}{L_m}\left(\left(\lambda_{ds} i_{qs} - \lambda_{qr} i_{ds}\right) - \sigma L_s \left(\frac{di_{ds}}{dt} i_{qs} - \frac{di_{qs}}{dt} i_{ds}\right)\right) + \omega_r\left(\lambda_{qr} i_{qs} + \lambda_{dr} i_{ds}\right)} \tag{16}$$

Due to the mathematical complexity and quantity calculations of rotor time constant estimators, an implantation using ANN seems interesting.

4   Neural Rotor Time Constant Estimator

Among the various neural networks and their associated algorithms, our choice fell on the study of continuous multilayer neural networks [15]. This type of network has excellent characteristics in the estimation and signal processing. In our application, we developed an ANN that can be used in achieving a high performance control of induction motors controlled by indirect method of rotor flux orientation. ANN we used is multi-layer networks, simple (the neurons of a layer are connected only to neurons of the next layer) and each neuron is connected to all neurons of the next layer. The network consists of an input layer, three hidden layer and an output layer. Neurons used in ANN developed are continuous neurons (square, tansig and linear). The methodology used consisted in preparing a databank fairly representative. This bank should take into account the maximum information on the different modes of training, enrolling in range where it is required to operate. Once this databank prepared and normalized, a part representing 20% is chosen to test the network generalization for data never learned. The remaining 80% is used as databank learning will be used to adapt the weights and biases of the ANN. As we mentioned goal is to realize ANN capable of well generalize, the structure of ANN has been developed following the cross-validation procedure proposed by [16]. Once the databank learning and the structure of ANN determined, the learning phase is started using the toolbox neural network MATLAB. During this learning phase, we proceed regularly to verify the network generalization. At the beginning of this phase, the training error and those generalization decrease progressively as the number of iterations increases. However, from a number of iterations, the generalization error starts to grow while the learning continues to decline. This is due to the fact that ANN begins to learn by heart the training data (memorization).

As the goal is to develop ANN that generalizes, it is necessary that the learning phase to be stopped as soon as the generalization error starts to grow. If both errors are far from the desired error, we add some neurons and restart the learning phase until obtaining a good compromise between the desired errors, learning and generalization.

Once the ANN has converged to an acceptable error, the optimal weights and biases are saved.

Development of the Neural Network

A neural network has been trained for estimating the rotor time constant variation in line using speed measurements, voltage and stator current (v_{ds}, v_{qs}, i_{ds}, i_{qs}, ω_r).

Signals networks learning were prepared from the machine phase model in which we programmed the rotor resistance variations. In addition, survey data from the machine experimental magnetization characteristic were used to develop a model that takes into account the saturation. For each rotor resistance variation, the rotor time constant is calculated and stored. A databank has been constructed from the input signals (v_{ds}, v_{qs}, i_{ds}, i_{qs}, ω_r), and network output τ_r. In preparing this databank, different operating conditions (torque and flux variables) were simulated. For the couple, the operations in the two rotation directions and even stoppage were simulated. It should be noted that learning could also be done with real signals captured in the laboratory, if we can by one means or another to vary the rotor time constant value. This is simpler in the case of a wound rotor machine, which can easily apply variations in rotor resistance. Each time constant value corresponds to a very precise combination of input signals. The artificial neural network role is therefore able to detect in the modifications imposed on the input signals, due to the rotor resistance variation, the time constant value at machine level. Once this databank prepared, it was subdivided at random into two subsets, one for training whose size represents 80% of this data-bank and another representing approximately 20% was reserved for testing the network generalization for data never learned. The databank contains prepared 5000 combinations of input signals - rotor time-constant, which represents a reasonable size for bank learning ANN.

$$I_s^2 = i_{ds}^2 + i_{qs}^2 \qquad (17)$$

$$i_{qs} = \sqrt{I_s^2 - \left(\frac{\lambda_r}{L_m}\right)} \qquad (18)$$

$$\lambda_r = \frac{L_m I_s}{\left(1 + s\tau_r^*\right)\sqrt{\left(\frac{1}{1+s\tau_r^*}\right)^2 + \tau_r^2 \left(\frac{L_m i_{qs}^*}{\tau_r^* \lambda_r^*}\right)^2}} \qquad (19)$$

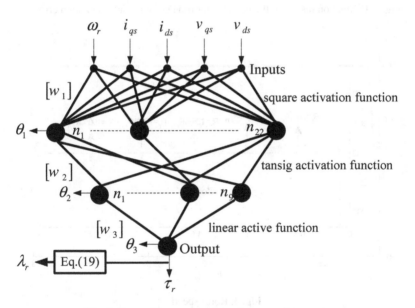

Fig. 1. Rotor time constant based on neural networks

A three-layer network with a total of 37 hard limit neurons is employed to implement the rotor time constant estimator as shown in Fig.1. The first hidden layer has 22 neurons (square activation function neuron with the w_1 and bias θ_1), 8 neurons in the second hidden layer (tansig activation function neuron with the weight w_2 and bias θ_2), and the output layer has one neuron (linear active function neuron with the weight w_3 and bias θ_3). The network is trained by a supervised method. After 63920 training epochs, the sum squared error arrives at $7.44.10^{-6}$.

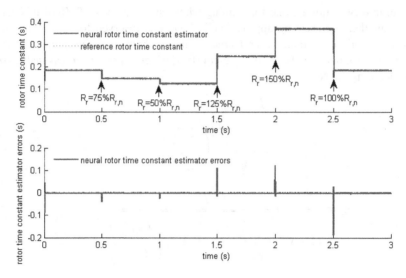

Fig. 2. Estimation results of the neural rotor time constant and estimation errors

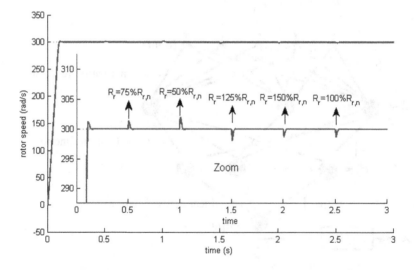

Fig. 3. Rotor speed

Fig.2 shows the results of neural rotor time constant estimating. This result is presented for rotor flux oriented drive operating at nominal set-points flux and torque, in which we have programmed a rotor resistance which varies between 100%, 75%, 50%, 125%, 150% and 100% at $t = 0.5s$, $t = 1s$, $t = 1.5s$, $t = 2s$ and $t = 2.5s$ respectively. The neural network was also used to adjust a rotor flux oriented drive with respect to the rotor resistance variation. The rotor time constant estimated by this ANN is used to correct the set-point slip at vector controller level.

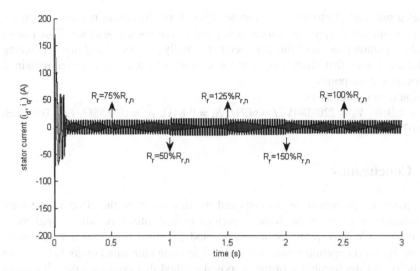

Fig. 4. Stator current (i_d, i_q)

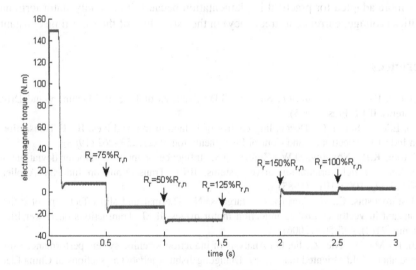

Fig. 5. Electromagnetic torque

You can see in this figure the transient behavior of rotor time constant estimator based ANN. We can also see that it responds precisely and variation index instantly applied to the rotor time constant. Indexical variations were used here in order to verify the dynamic performance estimation scheme. However, in practice the rotor time constant varies exponentially with the heating of the machine.

The rotor speed response shows that the drive can follow the low command speed very quickly and rapid rejection of disturbances, with a low dropout speed (Fig. 3).

The current responses are sinusoidal and balanced, and its distortion is small (Fig. 4).

The current and electromagnetic torque (Figs. 4 and 5) curves remain at their respective set-points despite the variation applied to the rotor resistance. This proves that the adaptation process of this parameter is actually performed and that decoupling is maintained, seen that electromagnetic torque and current in the machine remain at their respective set-points.

Induction motor parameters:

$P_n = 2.2\text{kW}$, $V_n = 220/380\text{V}$, $f = 60\text{Hz}$, $R_s = 0.84\Omega$, $R_r = 0.3858\Omega$, $L_s = 0.0706\text{H}$, $L_r = 0.0706\text{H}$, $L_m = 0.0672\text{H}$, $J = 0.008\text{kg·m}^2$, $n_p = 2$.

5   Conclusions

In this paper we presented the analysis and the discussion of the effect of the rotor time constant variations on the dynamic performance of rotor flux indirect field orientation drives. We have proposed a new method for rotor time constant estimation based on back-propagation neural networks. The computer simulations have shown the validity and the feasibility of the proposed method that possesses the advantages of neural network implementation: the high speed of processing. In addition this method is more adapted for practical implementation because it uses only stator terminal quantities (voltage, current and frequency) in the estimation of the rotor time constant.

References

1. Krause, P.C., Wasynezuk, O., Sudhoff, S.D.: Analysis of Electric Machinery and Drive Systems. IEEE Press (1995)
2. Ho, E.Y.Y., Sen, P.C.: Decoupling control of induction motor drives. IEEE Transactions on Industrial Electronics and Control Instrumentation 35(2), 253–262 (1988)
3. Nordin, K.B., Novotny, D.W., Zinger, D.S.: Influence of motor parameter deviations in feedforward field orientation drive systems. IEEE Transactions on Industry Applications 21(4), 1009–1015 (1985)
4. Mastorocostas, C., Kioskeridis, I., Margaris, N.: Thermal and slip effects on rotor time constant in vector controlled induction motor drives. IEEE Transactions on Power Electronics 21(2), 495-504 (2006)
5. Lu, H., Ma, W., Nie, Z., Jie, G.: Analysis of induction machine system performance influence about field-Oriented inaccuracy. Diangong Jishu Xuebao/Transactions of China Electrotechnical Society 20(8), 84–88 (2005)
6. Wang, K., Chiasson, J., Bodson, M., Tolbert, L.M.: An online rotor time constant estimator for the induction machine. IEEE Transactions on Control Systems Technology 15(2), 339–348 (2007)
7. Gao, W.: A simple model-based online rotor time constant estimator for an induction machine. IEEE Transactions on Energy Conversion 19(4), 793–794 (2004)
8. Lin, F.-J., Su, H.-M.: A high-performance induction motor drive with on-line rotor time-constant estimation. IEEE Transactions on Energy Conversion 12(4), 297–303 (1997)
9. Zidani, F., Naït Saïd, M.S., Abdessemed, R., Benbouzid, M.E.H.: A fuzzy method for rotor time constant estimation for high-performance induction motor vector control. Electric Power Components and Systems 31(10), 1007–1019 (2003)

10. Boussak, M., Capolino, G.A.: Recursive least squares rotor time constant identification for vector controlled induction machine. Electric Machines and Power Systems 20(2), 137–147 (1992)
11. Mayaleh, S., Bayindir, N.: Suha: On-line estimation of rotor-time constant of an induction motor using Recurrent Neural Networks. In: IEEE Workshop on Computers in Power Electronics, pp. 219–223 (1998)
12. Ba-razzouk, A., Cheriti, A., Olivier, G.: Neural networks based field oriented control scheme for induction motors. In: Conference Record - IAS Annual Meeting (IEEE Industry Applications Society), vol. 2, pp. 804–811 (1997)
13. Krishnan, R.: Electric Motor Drives: Modeling, Analysis, and Control. Prentice-Hall, New Jersey (2001)
14. Kerkman, R.J., Rowan, T.M., Leggate, D.: Indirect field-oriented control of an induction motor in the field-weakening region. IEEE Transactions on Industry Applications 28(4), 850–857 (1992)
15. Ban, J.-C., Chang, C.-H.: The learning problem of multi-layer neural networks. Neural Networks 46, 116–123 (2013)
16. Basheer, I.A., Hajmeer, M.: Artificial neural networks: fundamentals, computing, design, and application. Journal of Microbiological Methods 43(1), 3–31 (2000)

Improving Multi-Floor Facility Layout Problems Using Systematic Layout Planning and Simulation

Seyedeh Sabereh Hosseini[*], Seyed Ali Mirzapour, and Kuan Yew Wong

Department of Manufacturing and Industrial Engineering,
Universiti Teknologi Malaysia, 81310 UTM Skudai, Malaysia
{sabere.hosseini,mirzapour.ie}@gmail.com, wongky@fkm.utm.my

Abstract. To find the effects of applying the systematic layout planning (SLP) method on the multi-floor facility layout (MFFL) of a card and packet production company, simulation was used as an evaluation tool. A detailed study of the facility layout such as its operational processes, flow of materials and activity relationships has been done. Long transfer distance, cross-traffic and cost have been identified as the major problems of the current MFFL. Three alternative layouts were suggested by SLP and each layout was evaluated using simulation. Comparison between the alternative layouts and current layout was also made. The simulation results illustrate that the first alternative layout is the best solution to improve the company's layout problems.

Keywords: Multi-floor facility layout problem, Cross-traffic and long distance, Systematic layout planning, Simulation.

1 Introduction

Facility layout problem (FLP) is classified into single floor problem and multi-floor problem. Multi-floor facilities are constructed over a period of years to utilize the area efficiently. Due to travelling time, distance and vertical transporting of materials, multi-floor problems are more complicated than single floor ones. Vertical tranportation is applied in the area which has the limitations of available horizontal space [1]. In recent years, there has been an increasing amount of literature on multi-floor facility layout (MFFL) problems. Lee et al. [2] published a paper in which they applied an improved genetic algorithm to derive solutions for MFFLs having inner structure walls and passages. Krishnan and Jaafari [3] proposed a mimetic algorithm for unequal departmental areas to minimize material handling cost and to maximize closeness rating in MFFL problems. Khaksar-Haghani et al. [4] used an integer linear programming model for designing MFFLs of cellular manufacturing systems to minimize the total costs of intra-cell, inter-cell and inter-floor material handling.

Nowadays, factories have to enhance their potential and effectiveness in production to compete against their market rivals. Thus, production processes must be equipped with the ability to decrease cost and increase effectiveness. In FLPs, minimization of

---

[*] Corresponding author.

B. Papasratorn et al. (Eds.): IAIT 2013, CCIS 409, pp. 58–69, 2013.

total cost or total time of material handling is generally used as the objective function, which depends on distance between facilities [5]. Layout improvement procedures can be categorized into two types: construction type and improvement type. Construction methods try to construct a layout basically "from scratch". Improvement types, on the other hand, aim to develop a layout which would be better than its previous form. Systematic layout planning (SLP) can be used as an improvement technique to find a sensible layout based on material flow analysis and closeness rating [6]. It has been proposed by the American plant design expert, Richard Muther in 1961 [7, 8, 9]. Wiyaratn and Watanapa [7] used the SLP procedure to improve the plant layout of iron manufacturing and decreased the distance of material flow. Zhu and Wang [9] improved the overall layout of log yards using SLP, in which the best layout demonstrated a good process flow and practical significance. In this study, the SLP procedure is applied on a two-floor company to generate a number of layout alternatives. In order to evaluate certain improvement alternatives prior to actual implementation, tools such as computer simulation can be applied [10]. There are many simulation software used for modeling a given process. Adequate modeling and experimentation are important, particularly when financial investment is involved [11]. This paper tries to model and simulate the company's layout by using the ARENA 13.9 software. After running a simulation model in ARENA, performance measures such as the average transfer time, output and completion time can be seen in the reports generated by the software [12]. Therefore, this study attempts to provide an innovative approach by combining SLP and simulation to improve a MFFL problem and assess the proposed alternatives, respectively.

2   Systematic Layout Planning

The SLP method can be used as a proven tool in providing layout design guidelines which are applied to create layout alternatives. Its procedure has 11 steps which are depicted in Fig. 1.

2.1   Original Facility Layout

The case study is a company of card and packet production which is located in Iran. This company produces three different types of cards and packets. The production processes are done on two floors, ground floor and first floor. The scope of this study is focused on the production operation of the company in which its total production is according to customer orders. This company has designed its plant based on a process layout. It has 20 departments and each has a different task. All these departments are labeled in Table 1.

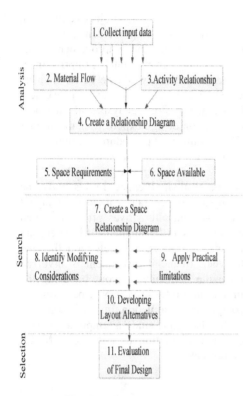

Fig. 1. SLP procedure [13]

Table 1. Label of departments

Label	Department	Label	Department
A	Raw paper storage 1	M	Packaging
C	Press room	N	Trash storage
D	Cutting 1	O	Cutting 2
E	Product 1 imprinting	Q	Final Product storage (card and packet)
F	Product 2 imprinting	R	Product 1 boxing
G	Product 2 Boxing	S	Raw paper storage 2
H	Product 3 Imprinting	T	Product storage (packets)
I	Gold embossing Process	U	Maintenance room
J	Product 3 Boxing	V	Packet assembly
L	Card and Packet inspecting	X	Entrance

Fig. 2 demonstrates the operation process chart showing the chronological sequence of production. From-to-chart analysis for distance and material flow was done to show the relationships between departments for each process. Particularly, the rectilinear distance between departments was computed and the amount of movements on each route was counted. These data were compiled to obtain the total travelling distances between departments, which were then converted into closeness ratings. Table 2 presents the total travelling distance and closeness rating between departments. A further analysis of the company's layout reveals certain issues. The long distance between some departments is one of the problems that the company has. Another problem that can be seen in Fig. 3 is the cross-traffic between departments on the first floor. These problems have resulted in a higher production cost and poorer movement of materials.

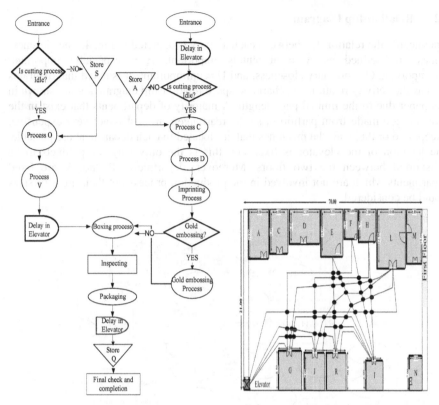

Fig. 2. Process flow chart   **Fig. 3.** Cross-traffic of the existing layout

Table 2. Total travelling distance and closeness rating

Departments	Distance (m)	Closeness Rating	Departments	Distance (m)	Closeness Rating
A – C	272	I	H - J	445.25	E
A – X	618	E	H - I	455	E
C – D	344	I	I - U	383	E
C – U	297	I	I - R	434	E
C – X	85.75	I	I - N	96	I
D – E	514.5	E	I - J	621	E
D – F	745.5	E	J - U	299	I
D – H	1008	A	J - T	954.25	A
D – N	552.5	E	J - N	152	I
D – U	340	I	J - L	2835	A
E – U	375	E	L - R	1650	A
E – R	162.5	I	L - N	117	I
E – N	129	I	L - M	665	E
E – I	812	E	M - U	499	E
F – U	411	E	M - Q	8417.5	A
F – N	114	I	O - V	464	I
F – G	474.5	E	O - U	88	E
G – U	265	I	O - S	147.2	I
G – T	860.75	A	R - U	329	I
G – N	188	I	R - T	1036.8	A
G – L	3430	A	S - X	112.2	I
G – I	864	A	T - V	688	E
H – U	436	E	U - V	138	I
N – R	122	I			
H – N	93.75	I	**Total**	**35184.95**	

2.2   Relationship Diagram

Graphically, the relationship between each activity is depicted in Fig. 4. The closeness values are defined as A = absolutely important, E = especially important, I = important, O = ordinary closeness, and U = unimportant. It is noted that diagrams such as the activity relationship chart and space relationship diagram are not shown in this paper due to the limited page length. A majority of departments that exist in the company are made from partitions, so the rearrangement cost is not very expensive. Except two or three, all the machines that are located in each department are portable. The location of the elevator is fixed and this is the only way for products to be transported between the two floors. Moreover, departments P and W are fixed departments which are not involved in the production process but their areas or sizes would be considered.

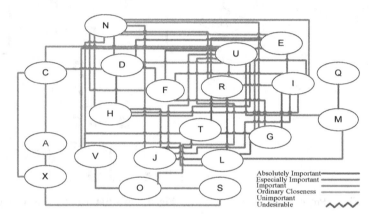

Fig. 4. Relationship diagram

2.3   Developing Layout Alternatives

The closeness values between activities were rearranged from the most important one to the least important one. Based on this priority and the SLP method, the alternative facility layouts were developed. The current and three alternative layouts are displayed in Fig. 5, 6, 7 and 8 respectively.

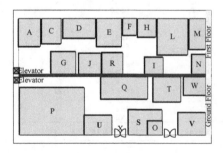

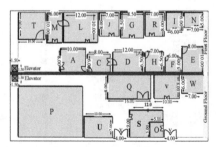

Fig. 5. Current Layout   **Fig. 6.** Layout Design I

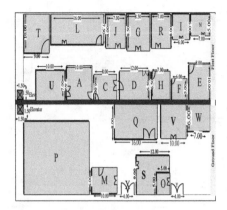

Fig. 7. Layout Design II

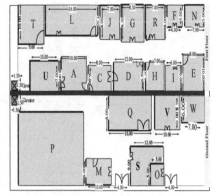

Fig. 8. Layout Design III

3   Simulation Model Development

Subsequently, the simulation model was designed and developed according to the input data collected. ARENA uses the Input Analyzer to fit a probability distribution to the existing data. The variation in the process time was very low, therefore the uniform distribution was selected for all processes except for department L in which the triangular distribution has been used. The model was constructed in two separate views that complement each other. It consists of different modules such as create, process, signal, etc. The logic view of this model as illustrated in Fig. 9 shows that two types of entities (cards and packets) are processed to generate products 1, 2 and 3. The model has seven create modules where the first three are related to packet production while the second three are for card production. The last create module is associated with the maintenance room processes. The travelling time of the entities is taken into account via the route and station modules.

The second view of the simulation model as shown in Fig. 10 is the animation view. Different resources are animated to give a better understanding of how different elements are involved in the processes.

3.1   Assumptions

The following assumptions have been used in simulating the layout:

1. Operators are always available during the shift (1 shift = 8 hours).
2. The simulation run length is considered as 1 month or 22 days.
3. There is no reject and rework.
4. There is no significant equipment or station failure.
5. Materials are always available at each assembly station.

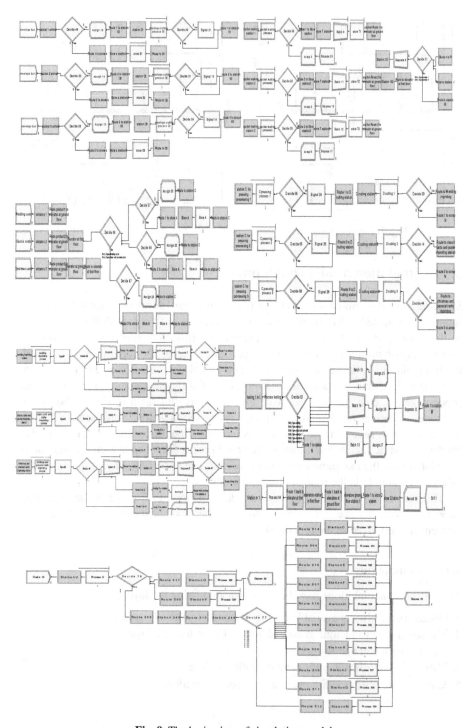

Fig. 9. The logic view of simulation model

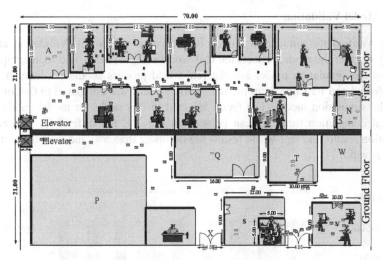

Fig. 10. The animation view of simulation model

3.2   Model Verification

Verification is a process in which the simulation model is ensured to work as expected without any logical error [14]. Debugging was done by running the simulation model. In this case, the model does not have any logical error, since the software did not show any error message during its execution. To check whether the model behaves as expected, the reports produced by the simulation software should be checked. This process is called "sanity check". In this process, a factor was selected and its value reported by the simulation software was compared with that obtained by manual calculation. In order to verify the simulation model, the average transfer time for each of the products was considered.

The average transfer time of product 1 in the current situation is equal to 20.82 minutes. The result generated by simulation is 21.56 minutes (see Table 3). This indicates that the deviation between these two values is only 3.55%. The average transfer time of product 2 is 20.46 and the simulation result is 20.96, so the deviation is equal to 2.44%. For the last comparison, the average transfer time of product 3 is 19.48 whereas the simulation result is 20.24, so the deviation is 3.90%. This analysis explains that the model is acceptable.

Table 3. The simulation results for average transfer time

Transfer Time	Average	Half Width	Minimum	Maximum
Product 1	21.56	(Correlated)	10.0700	21.9000
Product 2	20.96	(Correlated)	10.0400	21.3100
Product 3	20.24	(Correlated)	10.0000	20.7200

3.3   Model Validation

Having verified the simulation model, it is time to validate it. Validation aims at finding whether the model reflects the real-world system [14]. To do so, a comparison between the simulation model and the real-world process should be done. A factor was selected and its value from the real-world system was compared to that obtained from the simulation model. The factor selected in this study for model validation is the total completion time. As can be seen in Fig. 11, the differences between the simulation results and real-world results are not more than 5%, and this shows that the model is valid.

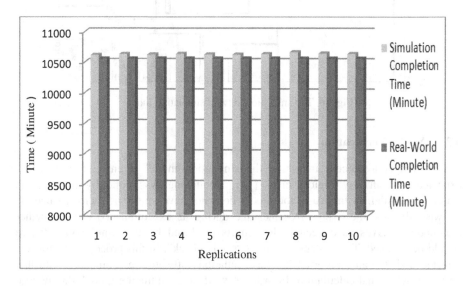

Fig. 11. Comparison between simulated and actual values

3.4   Model Experimentation

For this simulation, the run length was 1 month with 22 days and 8 hours per day which is equal to 10560 minutes. Graphically, the warm-up period was shown to be approximately one day, in order to allow the model to get into the steady state of a normal situation and avoid the start-up variation of the system. To calculate the number of replications, 10 initial simulation runs were considered. Based on the formula used by Nikakhtar et al. [12], the simulation was replicated for 10 times in order to make the experimentation more reliable.

3.5   Evaluation

As demonstrated in Table 4, layout design 1 gives the highest improvement as compared to other alternatives. The total travelling distance has been decreased from 35184.95m to 26244.20m or about 25.41% improvement. The number of cross-traffics in layout design 1 is reduced to 24 which represents 36.84% improvement in comparison to the current layout. The estimation of cost reduction begins with the calculation of the travelling cost per one meter unit. The average payment per one worker is equal to 11 dollars per shift and the total working time per shift is 480 minutes (8 hours × 60 minutes per hour), so the cost of one worker per minute is 0.023 dollars per minute. The travelling time per distance of a worker is obtained by estimation. It is estimated that a worker will move at about 20 m/minute from one point to another. As a result, the travelling cost per meter is obtained by multiplying the cost of one worker per minute with the inverse of the worker's moving speed.

$$\text{Travelling cost per meter} = \left(\frac{\$\, 0.023}{\text{min}} \right) \times \left(\frac{1\ \text{min}}{20\ \text{m}} \right) = \$0.00115/\text{m}$$

The estimated cost for each layout alternative is obtained by multiplying the total distance travelled for each layout with the cost coefficient gained from the calculation above. As can be seen in Table 4, layout design 1 saves more money than other layouts; the cost has declined from $40.46 to $30.18. The improvement in total travelling cost is about 25.41%, which indicates that the company can save up to $10.28 per day.

Table 4. The results that have been obtained manually

	Total travelling distance (m)	Number of cross-traffics	Total travelling cost ($)
Current Layout	35184.95	38	40.46
Layout Design 1	26244.20	24	30.18
Layout Design 2	29084.15	30	33.45
Layout Design 3	29978.15	27	34.47

Table 5 shows the results that have been obtained by simulation. By comparing each performance measure of the alternative layouts with the original layout, it can be found that the improvement in average transfer time for products 1, 2 and 3 of layout design 1 is about 21.33%, 25.67% and 17.34% respectively. It is apparent from this table that there is also an improvement in terms of output and completion time of layout design 1 as compared to other alternatives.

In summary, the best alternative of the case study is layout design 1 which has the highest improvement in total travelling distance and cost, cross-traffic, transfer time, output and completion time. Hence, the benefits of implementing this layout design are cost and time savings for both finished products and in-process products.

Table 5. The results that have been obtained by simulation

		Average transfer time (min)	Average output	Average completion time (min)
Current Layout	Product 1	21.56	4615	10643
	Product 2	20.96		
	Product 3	20.24		
Layout Design 1	Product 1	16.96	5310	10275
	Product 2	15.58		
	Product 3	16.73		
Layout Design 2	Product 1	19.44	4950	10472
	Product 2	18.11		
	Product 3	19.17		
Layout Design 3	Product 1	19.96	4905	10561
	Product 2	18.25		
	Product 3	19.20		

4   Conclusions

In this paper, the SLP procedure has been applied to analyze and rearrange the production layout of a card and packet production company. High total travelling distance, cross-traffic and cost have been identified as the major layout problems of this company. SLP was used as an analysis and synthesis tool to develop different layout alternatives. Three corresponding alternatives with different characteristics and arrangements were generated. These alternatives were evaluated quantitatively to determine the best solution. For this reason, simulation was used as it is a cost-effective and efficient way to assess their effectiveness after the application of the SLP method. The simulation models of the original system and improved layouts were analyzed and compared. Finally, the layout alternative with the best results in terms of distance, time, cost, cross-traffic and output was identified.

References

1. Bozer, Y.A., Meller, R.D., Erlebacher, S.J.: An improvement-type layout algorithm for single and multi-floor facilities. Management Science 40(7), 918–932 (1994)
2. Lee, K., Roh, M., Jeong, H.: An improved genetic algorithm for multi-floor facility layout problems having inner structure walls and passages. Computers & Operations Research 32(4), 879–899 (2005)
3. Krishnan, K.K., Jaafari, A.A.: A mixed integer programming formulation for multi floor layout. African Journal of Business Management 3(10), 616–620 (2009)
4. Khaksar-Haghani, F., Kia, R., Mahdavi, I., Javadian, N., Kazemi, M.: Multi-floor layout design of cellular manufacturing systems. International Journal of Management Science and Engineering Management 6(5), 356–365 (2011)

5. Kohara, D., Yamamoto, H.: Efficient Algorithms Based on Branch and Bound Methods for Multi Floor Facility Layout Problems. In: Proceedings of the 9th Asia Pacific Industrial Engineering & Management Systems Conference, Bali, Indonesia, pp. 387–395 (2008)

6. Ma, C.P., Yan, Z.G.: Analysis and Optimization of Assembly Workshop System Based on SLP. Logistics Engineering and Management 31, 46–49 (2009)

7. Wiyaratn, W., Watanapa, A.: Improvement Plant Layout Using Systematic Layout Planning (SLP) for Increased Productivity. World Academy of Science, Engineering and Technology 72(36), 269–273 (2010)

8. Wiyaratn, W., Watanapa, A., Kajondecha, P.: Improvement Plant Layout Based on Systematic Layout Planning. IACSIT International Journal of Engineering and Technology 5(1), 76–79 (2013)

9. Zhu, Y., Wang, F.: Study on the General Plane of Log Yards Based on Systematic Layout Planning. In: Proceedings of the International Conference on Information Management, Innovation Management and Industrial Engineering, vol. 3, pp. 92–95 (2009)

10. Sutee, U., Yarlagadda, P.K.: Simulation-Based Comparison of Pull-Push Systems in Motorcycle Assembly Line. Applied Mechanics and Materials 241, 1507–1513 (2013)

11. Mirzapourrezaei, S.A., Lalmazloumian, M., Dargi, A., Wong, K.Y.: Simulation of a Manufacturing Assembly Line Based on WITNESS. In: Proceedings of the Third International Conference on Computational Intelligence, Communication Systems and Networks (CICSyN), Bali, Indonesia, pp. 132–137 (2011)

12. Nikakhtar, A., Wong, K.Y., Zarei, M.H., Memari, A.: Comparison of two simulation software systems for modeling a construction process. In: Proceedings of the Third International Conference on Computational Intelligence, Modelling and Simulation (CIMSim), Langkawi, Malaysia, pp. 200–205 (2011)

13. Tompkins, J.A., White, J.A., Bozer, Y.A., Tanchoco, J.M.A.: Facilities Planning, 4th edn. John Wiley, Hoboken (2010)

14. Al-Sudairi, A.A.: Evaluating the effect of construction process characteristics to the applicability of lean principles. Construction Innovation: Information, Process, Management 7(1), 99–121 (2007)

Icon Placement Regularization for Jammed Profiles: Applications to Web-Registered Personnel Mining

Hiroyuki Kamiya, Ryota Yokote, and Yasuo Matsuyama

Waseda University, Department of Computer Science and Engineering,
Tokyo, 169-8555, Japan
{kamiya,rrryokote,yasuo}@wiz.cs.waseda.ac.jp
http://www.wiz.cs.waseda.ac.jp/

Abstract. A new icon spotting method for designing a user-friendly GUI is described. Here, each icon can represent continuous and discrete vector data which are possibly high-dimensional. An important issue is icon-margin adjustment or uniforming while the relative positioning is maintained. For generating such GUI, multidimensional scaling, kernel principal component analysis (KPCA) and regularization were combined. This method was applied to a set of city locations and a big data set of web-registered job hunter profiles. The former is used to check to see location errors. There were only little mis-allocations. The latter is a set of high dimensional and sparsely discrete-valued big data in the real world. Through these experiments, it was recognized that the presented method, which combines multidimensional scaling, KPCA and the regularization, is applicable to a wide class of jammed big data for generating a user-friendly GUI.

Keywords: Icon spotting, uniforming, GUI, data mining, regularization.

1 Introduction

In developing a new ICT service such as social networking, user data mining from a service provider has raised a class of crucial topics. Web sites, Facebook [1] and Twitter [2] give typical resources as targets for user data analysis. Nevertheless, in most companies and universities, a large amount of data is sleeping even on open resources. Such data could be utilized for new creative services once they were analyzed effectively. In such a situation, designing an effective graphical user interface (GUI) becomes necessary since the final judgment is made by human stakeholders. There are many faces on the *effectiveness*. In this paper, we present a new design method for user-friendly GUI which alleviates jammed allocation of icons. For instance, on big data from a matching site of job hunters and companies, the concentration of popularity show extremely jammed icon allocations. In such cases, clicking a target icon is impossible without blowing up the GUI to the largest size. However, such a view does not give GUI users to

B. Papasratorn et al. (Eds.): IAIT 2013, CCIS 409, pp. 70–79, 2013.

grasp a landscape view. In this paper, we present a user-friendly placement of profile icons to alleviate such inevitable icon jamming.

There are three main steps in this paper's method.

(1) If each source data is symbolic or discrete-valued, it is necessary to change it to a real-valued vector.
(2) Joint dimension reduction and multidimensional scaling (MDS) [3] is applied to the real-valued vector set. In this paper, kernel principal component analysis (KPCA) [4] [5] is used for the dimension reduction.
(3) Regularization of jammed icon positioning is the last and the most important step for generating the user-friendly GUI. Even if the kernel is chosen appropriately with its best ability, further automatic adjustment will be necessary for a highly condensed icon set. Thus, the total system is a class of self-organizing map generator for a composite data set [6] [7]. However, data to be organized themselves are given in a batch, not one-by-one.

As experimental examples, two types of data sets are used.

(a) One is a set of capital cities specified by positions. This set is used only to show there is little mis-allocations of icons by our method.
(b) The other is a big data set of Web-registered job hunter profiles. This is a collection of real-world and high-dimensional sparse discrete data. The site of Company Navigation (Kaisya-navi) [8] was used.

The rest of text is organized as follows. In Section 2, a method to convert discrete vector relationship to real valued ones is described. In section 3, a joint method of KPCA and MDS is described. The form of the kernel is explained there. Section 4 describes a remapping method which uses a penalty function for the icon positioning regularization. Section 5 gives experimental results. One is on the city mapping for evaluating mis-allocations. The second experiment is on the main target of the company navigation. The last section gives concluding remarks.

2   Conversion of Questionnaire Data to Real-Valued Set

Questionnaire data or *enquête* can lead to a big set of data. Since a complicated answer style is avoided by users, almost on-off selections are applied. On the other hand, a correct opinion extraction is necessary. Therefore, an enough number of queries is prepared by site designers. This generates a big data of discrete-valued high dimensional answers. In the case of the Company Navigation (Kaisya-navi) [8], a composite of Boolean values, discrete values and continuous values are allowed. Users may set a null when an item is a nuisance to specify. Thus, the Company Navigation holds more than 100,000 user profiles.

For the purpose of creating a user map, user profiles are reformatted by vector quantization [9] to generate a user profile matrix.

$$X = [x_1 \cdots x_n]^T \tag{1}$$

Here, n denotes the number of the users. Each column

$$\boldsymbol{x}_i = [x_{i1}, \cdots, x_{id}]^T \tag{2}$$

is a d-dimensional vector for ith user's profile. Each component x_{ij} has a value of

$$x_{ij} \in \{-1, 0, 1\}. \tag{3}$$

Thus, each person's answer set is changed to numerals. Note that user profile is registered by a user's input via a keyboard or a smartphone. For usability of the service, most elements are null by default. Thus, most elements of x_{ij} are 0, although the distribution of $\{-1, 0, 1\}$ is not uniform. Therefore, we normalize each column vector $\boldsymbol{X}$ so that it has a zero mean and a unit variance for the computational stability.

After the normalization, we compute the distortion or dissimilarity between two users by the negative inner product.

$$d(\boldsymbol{x}_i, \boldsymbol{x}_j) = -\boldsymbol{x}_i^T \boldsymbol{x}_j \tag{4}$$

Note that $\boldsymbol{x}_i$ is not a metric, however, a nonlinear transformation using a Gaussian kernel is applicable. This will appear in Section 3.

3   Data Mapping

3.1   Mapping by PCA

Multidimensional scaling (MDS) [3] is a method to locate data points to a low dimensional space using a distortion or a dis-similarity measure. MDS can be utilized for data mapping for visualization [10]. Principal Component Analysis (PCA) is a linear dimensionality reduction method, and is a class of MDS with an Euclidian distance. PCA is conducted by an eigenvalue decomposition of a covariance matrix.

$$\frac{1}{n} \boldsymbol{X}^T \boldsymbol{X} = \boldsymbol{E} \boldsymbol{D} \boldsymbol{E}^T \tag{5}$$

Here, $\boldsymbol{E} = [\boldsymbol{e}_1 \cdots \boldsymbol{e}_n]$ is an orthogonal matrix whose column vector is an eigenvector. $\boldsymbol{D} = \mathrm{diag}(d_1, \cdots, d_n)$ is a diagonal matrix whose diagonal element is an eigenvalue sorted in a decreasing order. Each column vector of $\boldsymbol{X}$ given by (3) is pre-centered to satisfy zero mean.

The dimensionality reduction is achieved by multiplying selected m eigenvectors to $\boldsymbol{X}$. Thus, first m principal components are given by

$$\boldsymbol{Y} = \boldsymbol{X} [\boldsymbol{e}_1 \cdots \boldsymbol{e}_m]. \tag{6}$$

3.2   Mapping Using KPCA

By the PCA, the distortion matrix was changed to a numerical expression without containing explicit distortion numerals. A dimension reduction was also achieved. However, this result by the linear PCA still inherits undesirable property of three-valued user profiles of (3). Therefore a kernel PCA (KPCA) [4] [5] is applied to the user profiles.

Given a kernel matrix $\boldsymbol{K} = \{k_{ij}\}_{i,j=1\cdots n}$, we apply centering and eigenvalue decomposition to this matrix:

$$\left(\boldsymbol{I} - \frac{1}{n}\boldsymbol{1}_{n\times n}\right) \boldsymbol{K} \left(\boldsymbol{I} - \frac{1}{n}\boldsymbol{1}_{n\times n}\right) = \boldsymbol{U}\boldsymbol{\Lambda}\boldsymbol{U}^T \tag{7}$$

Here, $\boldsymbol{I}$ is an identity matrix, $\boldsymbol{1}_{n\times n}$ refers to a matrix whose elements are 1. $\boldsymbol{U} = [\boldsymbol{u}_1 \cdots \boldsymbol{u}_n]$ is an orthogonal matrix, and $\boldsymbol{\Lambda} = \mathrm{diag}(\lambda_1, \cdots, \lambda_n)$ is a diagonal matrix. Using an eigenvector and an eigenvalue, first m nonlinear principal components are calculated by

$$\boldsymbol{Y} = [\boldsymbol{u}_1 \cdots \boldsymbol{u}_m]\,\mathrm{diag}\left(\sqrt{\lambda_k n}\right). \tag{8}$$

In the case of the Gaussian kernel, the kernel value can be calculated by using a distortion of (4).

$$k_{ij} = \exp(-d(\boldsymbol{x}_i, \boldsymbol{x}_j)^2/\sigma^2) \tag{9}$$

As explained above, we use a two-step method. The first step is a usual PCA. The second step is a KPCA with partial local profiles. This is because a monolithic KPCA suffers from high computational complexity for the size of big data. This transformation provides an efficient feature extraction for the data mapping. Given a specific user, say $i = i_0$, similar yet other user profiles are selected by reflecting the distortion to this person. More experimental details will be given in later sections.

4   Automatic Margin Adjustment for Icon Spotting

Most methods of mapping and dimensionality reduction focus only on the reduction of mapping errors that reflects the distance preservation [11]. Mapping accuracy surely contributes to an accurate data analysis. Whereas, an exact mapping may not be the most desirable one as a GUI [10]. Readers of this paper can easily recall the cases of a weather map and a railroad map. They are designed to obtain little map-location error with high usability. However, the visibility is a much more important factor for a GUI. By considering this necessity, a user map generated by PCA and KPCA will be more tuned in this section by using the regularization in terms of a cost function minimization.

The proposed method is a class of uniforming. Histogram equalization which is frequently used in image processing is a similar method, however, that method is usable only for one-dimensional values. Contrary to this, our method gives more uniformly scattered data points on a multi-dimensional map. Details of this method is explained as follows.

Given a set of accurate positions $\boldsymbol{s}_1, \cdots, \boldsymbol{s}_n$ and a set of modified positions $\boldsymbol{z}_1, \cdots, \boldsymbol{z}_n$, we measure a mapping error by

$$\|\boldsymbol{s}_i - \boldsymbol{z}_i\|^2 \tag{10}$$

in terms of a squared L2-norm. In addition to this, the local uniformity between data points i and j is measured by

$$\exp\left(-\frac{\|z_i - z_j\|^2}{\sigma^2}\right). \tag{11}$$

Here, σ is a design parameter which adjusts the degree of scattering. This exponential function is maximized when z_i is equal to z_j. In other words, if data points i and j are set to overlap on a map, the local uniformity has the maximal penalty.

Using the above criterion, the contrast function to be minimized for i is given below.

$$E(z_i) = \|s_i - z_i\|^2 + \sum_{j=1}^{n} A\exp\left(-\frac{\|z_i - z_j\|^2}{\sigma^2}\right) \tag{12}$$

The first term corresponds to a mapping error of z_i, and the second term is a penalty to local congestion around z_i. The square function penalty becomes rapidly increased if the data point z_i is far from the original point s_i. This implies that s_i regularizes z_i with the squared L2-norm. On the other hand, the exponential function becomes to zero if z_j is far enough from z_i. Thus, the function (12) reflects a joint property of allocation errors and position jamming.

An update rule with respect to z_i is obtained by a differentiation of the cost function $E(z_i)$.

$$\frac{\partial}{\partial z_i}E(z_i) = (s_i - z_i) - \sum_{j=1}^{n} \frac{A}{\sigma^2}(z_i - z_j)\exp\left(-\frac{\|z_i - z_j\|^2}{\sigma^2}\right) \tag{13}$$

Here, the scalar multiplier $1/2$ is omitted. An iteration for the minimization is summarized below. First, $s_1, \cdots, s_n$ are set to $z_1, \cdots, z_n$ as initial values.

$$z_i \leftarrow s_i \tag{14}$$

Second, using gradient descent optimization, $z_1, \cdots, z_n$ are fine-tuned to be scattered uniformly.

$$z_i \leftarrow z_i - \mu\frac{\partial}{\partial z_i}E(z_i) \tag{15}$$

Here, μ is a learning constant. The update of (15) is iterated. Position data $s_1, \cdots, s_n$ to be reallocated are assumed to be given in advance at the start of each iteration so that they work as teacher signals. That is, $s_1, \cdots, s_n$ are set to

$$s_i = y_i, \tag{16}$$

where $Y = [y_1 \cdots y_n]^T$ is given by Eq. (6) or (8).

Note that the update of Eq. (15) can be used as a stochastic gradient descent way, if lower complexity and less memory consumption are required. This is possible at the cost of the total learning speed.

5 Preliminary Experiment to Check Mis-allocations: City Mapping

In order to check the mis-allocation possibility, we conducted an experiment to check to see how the proposed regularization method works. For this purpose, we used a set of prefecture capitals whose locations are given by exact positions of longitudes and latitudes. There is no need of the PCA/KPCA for this data set.

Figure 1 shows the map of 47 prefectures in Japan, which means the positions of the prefecture capital city. This result were given by the ability of Google Maps [12]. The horizontal and vertical axes indicate the longitude and latitude respectively. In spite of the accurate positions, it is difficult to understand cities on this map nor clicking city names as icons because of the excessive overlapping. For instance, Tokyo is perfectly hidden by nearby prefectural capitals since the distribution of this area is locally dense too much.

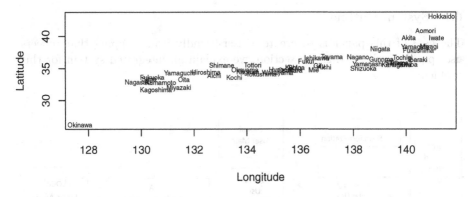

Fig. 1. The accurate map of Japanese cities: This map shows exact mapping of city locations. Whereas, the total view is too busy because it is too correct. Users cannot easily pick up a certain city by a cursor.

Next, we apply the method of the position regularization given in Section 4. For the purpose of improving the visibility of Fig. 1, we applied the proposed remapping to the map of Fig. 1. The parameters were set to $A = 10$, $\sigma = 1$, $\mu = 0.1$ respectively. The number of iterations was 100. Figure 2 shows the result of this experiment for city remapping..

Comparing Fig. 1 with 2, prefecture locations in Fig. 2 have positional displacements on the longitude and latitude. The city overlapping is reduced well. The visibility is much more improved. This is because the distribution became more uniform by the regularization. An important observation is that ordering of cities in the sense of the longitude and the latitude is perfectly preserved without any human handcrafting.

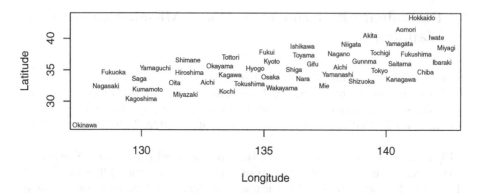

Fig. 2. A tuned map of Japanese cities: The view of the city collection is regularized. Relative positions of cities are maintained by the presented method of this paper.

6   Web-Data Mapping: An Application to Big Data

6.1   System Outline

The goal of this paper is to create a user-friendly icon mapping that reflects user profiles well. In this sub-section, we explain an integrated system for this problem.

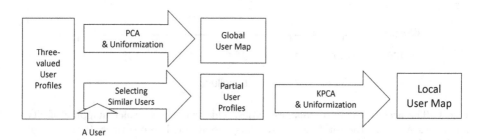

Fig. 3. The system flow for creating user maps

Figure 3 illustrates a flow of the total system. First, user profiles X as the format of (1) and (3) were given. Then, a low dimensional map Y was computed by PCA (6) or KPCA (8) from X. Finally, using Eq. (14), (15) and (16), the map Y was reorganized to generate $Z = [z_1 \cdots z_n]^T$.

PCA can be applied to all user profiles X. However, KPCA cannot be used for raw X because of its complexity. Thus, we used a KPCA on identifiable users. Referring to the user $i = i_0$, other similar users $j' = j'_1, \cdots, j'_l$ are selected with respect to their similarities. The similarities are calculated by Eq. (4). We apply KPCA to these selected user profiles. Here, l denotes the number of similar users. The size of l is much less than n and is small enough to be able to calculate

KPCA. Here, n is the number of all users. The typical example is that n and l are $n = 100,000$ and $l = 100$.

As the result, we obtain global and local user maps. A global user map is given by PCA. A local user map is given by user selection and KPCA, They contain global and local properties about user profiles, respectively.

6.2   Mapping of Web-Registered Job Hunters

For a check of practical usability, a data set form the registered Company Navigation (Kaisya-navi) [8] is extracted. Note that this database is continually accumulating.

In order to check the usability of this paper's method, datasets of active users were selected. Its size is $n = 2000$. The dimensionality of feature vector is $d = 150$. The user profile depends on the service type. It satisfies the condition of (3).

The design parameters for this experiment are as follows. The dimensionality reduction was to $m = 2$. Thus, PCA and KPCA gave a map on a 2-dimensional plane. The number of similar users was set to $l = 10$. Under these conditions, the global and local maps were generated. Note that the number of users was set smaller in this paper than the actual system for the purpose of graphical illustrations.

Figure 4 shows the global map of all job hunters given by the proposed system. The horizontal and vertical axis indicate the first and second principal components. This is a result by this paper's method. A point on the map represents one user. If a user was similar to another one, these points were set nearby on the map. Thus, a user group that contains common profiles was mapped as a jammed cluster. This is inevitable since popular occupational categories receive registrations from many Web users. On the other hand, in the next illustration, a favorable property which is not grasped by a single view can be identified.

Figure 5 shows a regularized global map where users of $i = i_0$ were picked up randomly. Here, the chosen users were students of ICT major (information and communication technology major). In this figure, the filled red circle indicates the user per se. The arrow identifies the position of this person. The other points were scaled with respect to the similarities to him or her. Here, a big circle indicates high similarity. There is a cluster including many big circles at the upper left in this figure. This means that students majoring ICT were collected at the upper left in the map. On the other hand, there is another cluster in the right hand side, although each similarity is small.

Fig. 4 and 5 are global maps where the congestion essentially occurs because of the data size. An important issue is that this icon jamming remains to reside, or not, when a local area was illustrated by an enlarged drawing. This is the last step to be checked for the authorization of the presented icon placement regularization.

Figure 6 illustrates a local map personalized to an aforementioned specific user. The circle indicates the chosen user. Each icon by a text explanation means

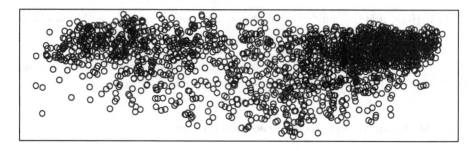

Fig. 4. The global user map of all job hunters: This is a big collection of job hunter profiles. Overlapping around the upper right corner is inevitable because this region corresponds to contemporary popular companies. Although, once personalized, a user friendly interface appears (compare with Fig. 5 and Fig. 6).

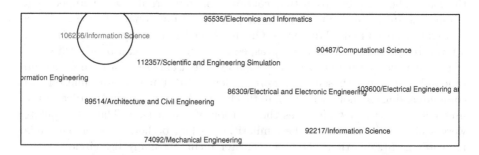

Fig. 5. A personalized global user map

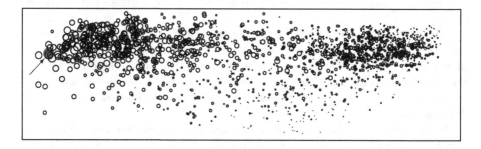

Fig. 6. An enlarged local user map

a user ID and his/her major, respectively. Even for such a space-consuming icons, users can click them without confusion.

By the experiments of Fig. 4-6, one can regard the presented icon allocation system as self-organization can work as a user-friendly GUI.

7   Concluding Remarks

In this paper, a new GUI design method for user profile's data mining was presented. The proposed system utilizes PCA, KPCA and the regularization that improve visibility and clicking easiness. The experimental result using the real user profiles which were registered by job hunters were presented. The result showed that the designed system is a ready-to-use one. Since the method contains a normalization phase for mixture data of discrete and real numbers, applications to a variety of data sets drawn from Web sites are possible. Important applications include a student mapping for MOOCs (Massively Open Online Courses) which is going to be a revolutionary education system.

References

1. Facebook, https://www.facebook.com
2. Twitter, https://twitter.com
3. Cox, T.F., Cox, M.A.A.: Multidimensional Scaling, 2nd edn. Chapman & Halls/CRC, Boca Raton (2001)
4. Schölkopf, B., Smola, A., Müller, K.R.: Nonlinear Component Analysis as a Kernel Eigenvalue Problem. Neural Computation 10(5), 1299–1319 (1998)
5. Shawe-Taylor, J., Cristianini, N.: Kernel Methods for Pattern Analysis. Cambridge University Press, Cambridge (2004)
6. Kohonen, T.: Self-Organizing Maps. Springer, Berlin (1995)
7. Matsuyama, Y.: Harmonic Competition: A Self-Organizing Multiple Criteria Optimization. IEEE Trans. Neural Networks 7, 652–668 (1996)
8. Company Navigation, or Kaisya-navi, http://sk.kaisyanavi.jp
9. Gersho, A., Gray, R.M.: Vector Quantization and Signal Compression. Kluwer Academic Publishers, Boston (1992)
10. Maejima, M., Yokote, R., Matsuyama, Y.: Composite Data Mapping for Spherical GUI Design: Clustering of Must-Watch and No-Need TV Programs. In: Huang, T., Zeng, Z., Li, C., Leung, C.S. (eds.) ICONIP 2012, Part V. LNCS, vol. 7667, pp. 267–274. Springer, Heidelberg (2012)
11. Niu, D., Dy, J.G., Jordan, M.I.: Dimensionality Reduction for Spectral Clustering. In: Proc. Int. Conf. on Artificial Intelligence and Statistics, Fort Lauderdale, FL, pp. 552–560 (2010)
12. Google Maps, https://maps.google.com
13. Coursera, https://www.coursera.org/
14. edX, https://www.edx.org/

A Paradigm Approach to Generate Trust Index Using 3C3G Framework for B2C E-Commerce Websites

Baljeet Kaur and Sushila Madan

Department of Computer Science, Banasthali Vidyapith, India
baljeet.ka@gmail.com, sushila_lsr@yahoo.com

Abstract. The growth in the number of Internet users across the globe has triggered the advancement in the field of E-Commerce. E-Commerce sales have been skyrocketing across the world. For the successful implementation of a B2C E-business, it is necessary to understand the trust issues associated with the online environment which holds the customer back from shopping online. This paper proposes a framework for assessing the level of trust in any B2C E-Commerce website. The study aims to identify the trust factors pertaining to B2C E-Commerce websites from the perspective of the Indian customer and calculate the trust index of the website based on these factors. This was done by first distinguishing the trust factors, taking experts' judgments on them and then studying the customers' responses regarding B2C E-Commerce websites with respect to the trust parameters and examining their significance. Additionally, it worked on the development of a fuzzy system using Mamdani fuzzy inference system for the calculation of the trust index depicting customers' confidence level in any B2C E-Commerce website.

Keywords: Ecommerce Trust, Trust, Trust Factors, Online Trust, Trust Index, Customer's Trust, Fuzzy System.

1   Introduction

In 1971, with the development of ARPANET, the foundations of E-Commerce had been laid. Essentially, E-Commerce germinated in 1979 with Michael Aldrich demonstrating the very first online shopping system. It came to India in 1996 when Indiamart established B2B marketplace. E-Commerce since then has become a significant tool for businesses to sell to customers along with engaging them. There is continuous growth in E-Commerce and the number of people purchasing products online is increasing day by day. Convenience, greater supply, lower prices and ability to compare prices from different vendors easily are four main reasons cited by people for shopping online[6]. Various reports on Indian E-Commerce markets suggest that the market size of online retail industry in India is likely to touch Rs 70 billion by 2015. With such numbers being forecasted, online merchants have a primary concern of attracting more and more customers and making them trust in the formers' businesses. To purchase from an e-vendor especially in an environment of uncertainty, anonymity, lack of control and potential opportunism is not that easy for the customers. The customers feel hesitant while transacting with the companies they

B. Papasratorn et al. (Eds.): IAIT 2013, CCIS 409, pp. 80–92, 2013.

don't know about primarily because of missing physical cues. Trust issue is a major concern for many customers and a strong reason for not shopping online.

2 Existing Trust Frameworks for B2C Websites - A Comparison

Trust being a crucial element of E-Commerce and a significant contributor to its growth, it has attracted the attention of various researchers. Many of them have proposed different frameworks to understand the issues involved with the customers' trust and various factors impacting the same.

Matthew Lee and Efraim Turban's CTIS Model. Matthew K.O. Lee and Efraim Turban[8] studied various antecedent influences on customer trust in Internet shopping. There study focussed on four such antecedents: trustworthiness of the Internet merchant, trustworthiness of the Internet as a shopping medium, infrastructural (contextual) factors (e.g. security, third-party certification), and other factors (e.g. company size, demographic variables). As per the study, the trustworthiness of the Internet merchant is dependent on the merchant's ability, integrity and benevolence. Customer trust in the other antecedent i.e. Internet as a shopping medium is influenced by perceived technical competence, perceived performance level and the degree to which a customer understands the workings of the Internet shopping medium (also referred as "medium understanding"). Contextual factors focus on security, privacy, third- party certifications, escrow and insurance services while the other factors include size of an Internet shop and demographic variables of the buyers, such as sex, age, and Internet usage experience. According to their CTIS model, the mentioned factors along with individual propensity to trust influence customer trust in Internet shopping. However, their study could not find empirical support for the effect of third-party certification and also, the sample used in their study were mainly prospective Internet shoppers and not the actual Internet shoppers.

Online B2C Perceived Trust Model. Brian J. Corbitt, Theerasak Thanasankit, Han Yi's [5] online B2C perceived trust model is based on the relationship of key factors related to trust in the B2C context. They identify perceived market orientation, perceived site quality, perceived technical trustworthiness, perceived risk and user's web experience as key factors impacting trust. Their research suggest that people are more likely to purchase from the web if they perceive a higher degree of trust in E-Commerce and have more experience in using the web. They also claim that the people with a higher level of trust in E-Commerce are more likely to participate in E-Commerce. The authors revealed positive 'word of mouth', money back warranty and partnerships with well-known business partners as effective mechanisms to reduce risk. Though their study has contributed significantly to the literature of trust, but a more complete set of trust antecedents and consequences could be identified and the relationships they have discussed could be explored further.

Integrated Model of Online Trust Formation. The Integrated model of online trust formation by Xianfeng Zhang and Qin Zhang[12] is based on three online trust forming approaches i.e. the cycle approach (this emphasizes on how trust relationship is kept), the stage- development approach (focuses on trust in different stages) and the factor approach (pays attention on different factors). The model is linked by three vital ties and incorporates the trustor factors (demographic factors, knowledge on the Internet, past experience, personality based factors, time pressure, disability etc.), trustee factors (perceived size, perceived reputation, perceived brand recognition, perceived commodity quality, perceived service level, perceived trustworthiness, perceived system reliability, perceived interface design level, perceived information quality show etc.), system trust factors (situational normality, structural assurance and facilitating conditions), former online interactions and external environmental factors. The model proposed by them also reflects the dynamic development claiming that initial trust may turn into robust trust after long-term interactions. Though the authors have listed a significant number of trust factors, however, the authors briefly touched upon them and failed to discuss how each of them affects customers' trust in online shopping.

Trust Management Model. Alireza Pourshahid, Thomas Tran[1] propose a trust management system that they expected would be of some help to the prospective buyers to make good trust decisions. Their model is based on the user's requirements notation. It is a conceptual model which evaluates trustworthiness of different parties and suggests the best trustee to the trustor based on the trustor's goals. Their model is different from the other reputation or trust management systems in terms of choice of the trustee for a trustor as this choice is not based on any predefined or limited attributes. Instead, it is a dynamic choice based on the trustor's preferences. Their model attempts to demonstrate that most of the trustee's behaviour is toward reducing risks for the trustor. The model does not talk about the technical details (technology risks) associated with formation of trust.

A Unified Model of Trust in E-Commerce. Prashant Palvia's unified model of E-Commerce relational exchange[11] focused both on the antecedents and consequents of intention to use a vendor's website in developing long- term relationship with customers. The research model proposed by them incorporated key concepts from Technology Acceptance Model, trust and relational exchange. The model integrated the three of these via Theory of Reasoned Action (TRA)[9]. Their research found that shared beliefs in the integrity, competence, and benevolence of the e-vendor positively affected customers' trust of an e-vendor. The researchers also claim that the usage attitude toward an e-vendor's site was not only influenced by perceived ease of use and perceived usefulness but also by the perceived trustworthiness of the web vendor. Their study focussed on satisfaction, value, loyalty and word of mouth as the consequents of intention to use. According to them, developing and nurturing customers' trust is a vital requirement in order to create long term relationships. However, their study was done on students which could be future online buyers but were not the actual online buyers at that time.

Trust Factor Evaluation - Expert System Approach. Mehrbakhsh Nilashi, Karamollah Bagherifard, Othman Ibrahim, Nasim Janahmadi, Mousa Barisami[10] proposed an application of expert system on trust in electronic commerce. They studied the impact of design of websites, security of websites and familiarity of websites on customers' trust in online transactions. Their model used adaptive network fuzzy inference system to analyse the results. The researchers tried to evaluate and quantify trust in B2C E-Commerce websites. The study failed to incorporate the customers' personality traits like propensity to trust, knowledge of Internet etc. for evaluating the trust in B2C websites.

Aris, Mustaffa Et Al's Framework of Trust. Aszifa Aris, Norlia Mustaffa, Nasriah Zakaria, Nurul Syafika Nadiah, Mohd Zabarudin's[2] framework of trust is based on the three main antecedents of initial trust: the website quality, assurance and reputation. They consider website design cues, website appeal, interactivity, usefulness, ease of use and customization/ personalization as the sub-factors in the website quality; web assurance, internal e-assurance, perceived security, perceived privacy, security control and structural assurance as sub-factors in assurance and company reputation, reputation advertising and branding as sub-factors in reputation. They further categorize website quality and assurance into cognitive-based trust and emotional-based trust constructs. However, their study did not give due significance to the reputation factors claiming it cannot be controlled but that is not the case. Organization's reputation can be very well controlled by the organization itself by taking due measures.

3   3C3G Framework of Trust for B2C E-Commerce Websites

Previous frameworks of trust for B2C websites had several shortcomings as discussed in the previous section. Based on those shortcomings of the previous frameworks, a research model named 3C3G Framework of Trust for B2C Websites is proposed in this section. The framework proposes to generate the trust index of the commercial B2C websites by evaluating the websites on the three classes of trust factors. The model follows six steps as shown in Figure 1. The steps of the framework are explained in detail in the following sub-sections.

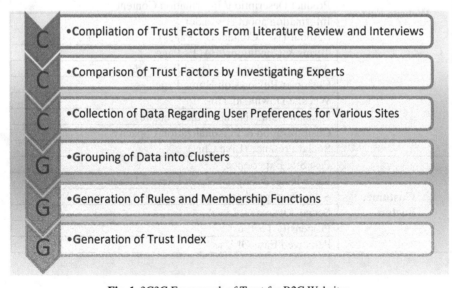

Fig. 1. 3C3G Framework of Trust for B2C Websites

3.1   Compilation of Trust Factors from Literature Review and Interviews

This is the very first step of this study and it involved gathering of data from Indian customers who have been involved in the E-Commerce operations. There were two sources of data i.e. primary and secondary. Primary data has been gathered from Indian customers for the purpose of the present study. Both types of prospective customers/ customers of commercial websites are considered, ones who shop online and the others who don't go for online shopping because of various reasons. The methodology followed was of conducting personal interviews for the collection of data related to the objectives of this research. About 237 people were interviewed

Table 1. Trust Factor Categories[3]

Organizational Factors	Brand Recognition
	Money Back Guarantee/ Return & Exchange Policy
	Order Fulfilment (Order Tracking, Logistics)
	Offline Presence
	Competence (Good Discounts, Free Shipping)
	Perceived Size of Organization
Website Factors	Website Look & Feel
	Navigation
	Payment Related Issues (Cash On Delivery, Secure Payment Gateways, Second Level Authentication, Multiple Payment Options)
	Privacy Policy
	Third Party Trust Seals
	Security Protocols(https), SSL Certificates, Padlock Sign
	Product Description/ Information Content
	Information about E-Vendor ('About Us', 'Contact Us' Pages)
	Terms & Conditions/ FAQ's Page
	Absence of "Pop Up"/ Third Party Ads
	Customer Reviews on Home Page
	Website Download Time
	Domain Name (Name of the Website)
	Customization & Personalization Capacity
	Social Presence (Live Chat)
Customer Factors	Past Site Experience
	Knowledge & Experience in Internet Usage
	SocioDemographics
	Social Awareness Level
	Propensity To Trust
	Perceived Ease Of Use

and were asked about various trust factors which exist in Indian E-Commerce market. Secondary data was gathered from extensive literature review on trust factors that exist in online market space. Various factors which have an impact on the E-Commerce trust, in any form, were collected and categorized[3]. Table 1 lists all the factors were collected along with their categories.

3.2   Comparison of Trust Factors by Investigating Experts

In the second round of study, a web based survey was used to investigate 74 experts from Indian E-Commerce market. Experts' judgments were gathered based on the linguistic scale to establish pair-wise comparisons matrix for sub-factors through pair-wise comparisons questionnaire and grouping factors in three major groups to determine the trust model for B2C E-Commerce websites for Indian E-Commerce market space. Various decision matrices were used[4]. Experts were asked to fill in the decision matrices with values ranging from Equal Importance (1) to Extreme Importance (9). The panel of experts chosen for this study included subject matter experts, both from the customers' side and also from the e-vendors' side. Special attention was focused on choosing experts who understand Indian B2C E-Commerce set up really well.

The data gathered from this survey was analyzed using Analytic Hierarchy Process. The Analytic Hierarchy Process, often called AHP, is a mathematical technique designed to solve complex problems involving multi criteria. AHP has been used because of its ease of applicability along with hierarchical modelling of the problem, the possibility to adopt verbal judgments and the verification of the consistency. A hierarchy of trust factors was created as shown in Figure 2. Expert choice software (AHP based software) was used to calculate priorities, inconsistencies and synthesize the results.

The results of the synthesis gave relative weights to all the sub-factors in the three categories. Figure 3 shows the relative weights of the sub-factors in the category of organizational trust factors. As can be seen in Figure 3, Brand Recognition is the most important trust factor amongst the organizational trust factors. It is weighted 0.272 and hence it is of the top most priority. Order Fulfilment, Money Back Guarantee/ Return & Exchange Policy and Competence occupy second, third and fourth position and are weighted 0.175, 0.164 and 0.145 respectively. Last two positions are occupied by Perceived Size of Organization and the Offline Presence which are weighted at 0.13 and 0.114 respectively. Inconsistency rate of this set of pair-wise comparisons is 0.04 and it is acceptable as the value is less than 0.10.

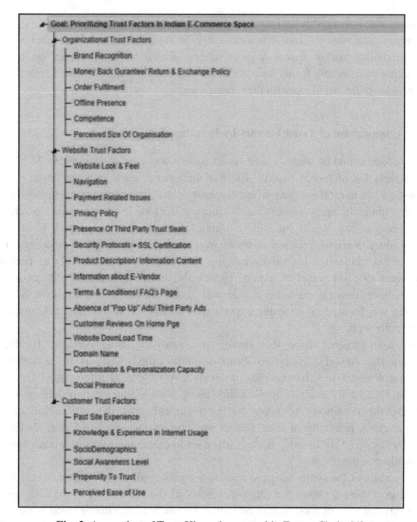

Fig. 2. A snapshot of Trust Hierarchy created in Expert Choice[4]

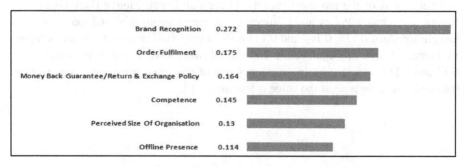

Fig. 3. Priority of sub-factors in Organizational Trust Factors

Next Figure 4 shows the relative weights of the sub-factors in the category of website trust factors. According to the results of the synthesis, Payment related matters like availability of secure gateway, cash on delivery option, second level authentication and choice of various payment options possess highest weight-age at 0.21. Subsequent priorities are of Information about e-vendor (weighted 0.123), Security Protocols(weighted 0.085), Presence of Third Party Trust Seals(weighted 0.071), Privacy Policy(weighted 0.068), Customer Reviews on Home Page(weighted 0.065), Absence of Pop up ads or Third Party ads(weighted 0.055), Navigation(weighted 0.051), Product Description and Information Content(weighted 0.047), Website Look and Feel(weighted 0.038), Domain Name(weighted 0.037), Website Download Time(weighted 0.037), Social Presence(weighted 0.033), Customization and Personalization Capacity(weighted 0.032) and presence of Terms and Conditions or FAQ's page(weighted 0.021) occupying the last position. Inconsistency rate of this set of pair-wise comparisons is 0.06 and it is acceptable as the value is less than 0.10.

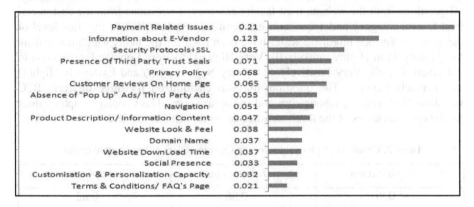

Fig. 4. Priority of sub-factors in Website Trust Factors

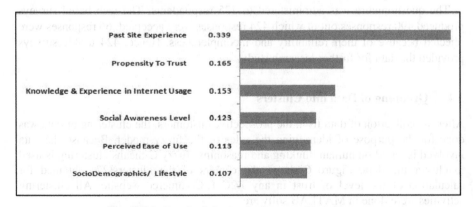

Fig. 5. Priority of sub-factors in Customer Trust Factors

As shown in Figure 5, Past Site Experience is of most importance in the customer trust factors. It is weighted at 0.339; hence it is at the top priority followed by Propensity to Trust (weighted at 0.165), Knowledge and Experience in Internet Usage (weighted at 0.153), Social Awareness Level (weighted at 0.123), and Perceived Ease of Use (weighted at 0.113). Sociodemographics is of least importance in this category weighted at 0.107. Inconsistency rate of this set of pair-wise comparisons is 0.03 and it is acceptable as the value is less than 0.10.

3.3   Collection of Data Regarding User Preferences for Various Sites

In this round of study, the data for the purpose of studying the customers' responses regarding B2C E-Commerce websites was collected by through questionnaires. The study was conducted on the trust factors gathered from the previous steps which have significant contribution to the trust formation in B2C E-Commerce websites. The questionnaire consisted of 4 questions from the organizational trust factors category, 10 questions from the website trust factors category, 4 questions from the customers' trust factors category and 1 question has been observed relative to the trust level of the website. Various linguistic scales have been used for the items which range from Very Easily(4) to Highly unlikely(0); Very High (4) to Very Low(0); Excellent(4) to Extremely Bad(0); Very Positively(4) to Very Negatively(0) and Extremely High(4) to Extremely Low(0). The questionnaire was customized for three different B2C websites- flipkart.com, jabong.com and indiaplaza.com. The Cronbach alpha values for the questionnaires of the three websites are as reported in Table 2:

Table 2. Cronbach Alpha values for the Questionnaires of the Three Websites

Flipkart.com	Jabong.com	Indiaplaza.com
0.86	0.86	0.82

The questionnaire was administered to 725 respondents. The web based surveys produced 490 responses out of which 424 responses were accepted. 66 responses were rejected because of their reliability and incompleteness. Hence, 424 usable surveys provided the data for further research study.

3.4   Grouping of Data into Clusters

After the collection of data from the prospective customers, the clustering of data was done for the purpose of identifying the rules of the fuzzy model. Because the data involved is based on human thinking and reasoning, fuzzy C-means clustering is used to cluster the data. Figure 6 shows the centers of the clusters(27) obtained for calculation of the level of trust in any B2C E-Commerce website. All clustering activities were done in MATLAB software.

```
1-   6.0155067894243268e+000   2.9046512830831526e+001   7.4385295268743903e+000   2.9278193928146323e+000
2-   6.9610472918595212e+000   5.7142813409917148e+000   6.7575336185807222e+000   1.1392363535981014e+000
3-   8.5974775111085804e+000   2.8231083426934063e+001   1.1654332978151759e+001   3.2619032747207411e+000
4-   1.4506271052196700e+001   3.5116416695801036e+001   7.8860834681973326e+000   3.0140249901505571e+000
5-   1.6994725163469315e+000   1.8378626314079341e+000   1.4515428784309039e+001   2.2138088402211560e-002
6-   1.8430296989695545e+001   1.6319597003394428e+001   7.2322507187381815e+000   2.2801474964324529e+000
7-   9.7087503958497390e+000   3.4054241371636202e+001   2.1939597009852028e+000   1.9639061981613919e+000
8-   1.1284976367204279e+001   5.9539859557158392e+000   1.1450951357726664e+001   2.2432503110582984e+000
9-   1.3488431226048794e+001   3.6759634108955019e+001   1.4798857593190230e+001   3.8246312815028804e+000
10-  1.2859753408031449e+001   3.9090491936645321e+000   1.1486768479179339e+000   1.2930216299397743e+000
11-  1.1029971555968772e+001   3.3153637894706769e+001   2.0915598062753966e+000   2.0846897709988430e+000
12-  2.4967388996075894e+000   3.7087412082760316e+001   6.7174828150895272e+000   2.3937558525388192e+000
13-  1.0808321480746039e+001   2.4702479088881404e+001   2.6607354848171658e+000   2.4034957528609162e+000
14-  3.3934338496623271e+001   3.2054124115445971e+001   1.8341864715871570e+000   1.2033136496957355e+000
15-  1.2070492657728447e+001   1.7849477403376589e+000   8.3020958750665161e+000   1.7367274843457290e+000
16-  2.8115534127130295e+000   2.9063743203865783e+001   1.3863836089347383e+000   2.1029207630402351e+000
17-  6.8556127369691895e+000   3.2126815996970876e+001   2.8599078060860013e+000   9.1588817286877982e-003
18-  6.9446341881861673e+000   2.3135365956804225e+001   1.1319113978178117e+001   2.4164812516076237e+000
19-  1.6305698522275573e+000   1.9103530984247914e+001   1.2618012266464133e+000   2.2373662853160425e+000
20-  4.3026703265171822e+000   8.3603472497601857e+000   7.7625904013266043e+000   2.7318114019878141e-002
21-  3.6011889647080593e+000   1.7144511132168415e+001   4.3962191331528355e+000   7.8230658123168229e-003
22-  1.2470536930080363e+001   1.6493006739967321e+001   6.5559691957579205e+000   1.8119103504168907e+000
23-  7.8041166803261752e+000   6.6135338311845970e+000   1.4679897789045731e+001   1.4243171598540886e+000
24-  7.1501238128734719e+000   2.4231067101017329e+001   2.9163011661234615e+000   2.0974867345918366e+000
25-  2.6592346162164788e+000   4.3277652324243441e+000   3.7405335202010950e+000   3.1974759083685651e-002
26-  6.8915113148348479e+000   2.1459024274276864e+001   8.5582159974424763e+000   1.3169596008623074e+000
27-  1.2540103280032660e+001   1.9964521258630590e+001   1.2923170500289711e+001   2.8571157967421583e+000
```

Fig. 6. Cluster Centers

3.5 Generation of Rules and Membership Functions

After clustering the data, an attempt is made to quantify the trust measure from the three categories of the trust factors - organizational trust factors, website trust factors and customer trust factors based on the Mamdani fuzzy inference system. Mamdani method is the most commonly used fuzzy inference technique based on the fuzzy rules proposed by Ebrahim Mamdani in 1975. Mamdani method is widely accepted for capturing expert knowledge. It allows us to describe the expertise in more intuitive, more human-like manner.

The fuzzy rules for this research study are generated by ordering, analyzing and clustering the respondents answers in the questionnaires. 27 rules are formed that describe the level of trust based on the degree of trust from the three categories of factors. The degree of the level of trust represented by the trust index has been graded from very low to very high. The example of rules generated for the present research study is as follows:

> If Organizational_Trust_Factors_Level is High
> and Website_Trust_Factors_Level is High
> and Customer_Trust_Factors_Level is High
> Then Trust_Index is Very High

> If Organizational_Trust_Factors_Level is High
> and Website_Trust_Factors_Level is High
> and Customer_Trust_Factors_Level is Moderate
> Then Trust_Index is High

Besides discovering the rules for quantifying trust, required membership functions for the three inputs - organizational trust factors, website trust factors and customer trust factors; and one output-trust index were also created. Figure 7 shows the fuzzy system to obtain the level of trust from the three categories of factors.

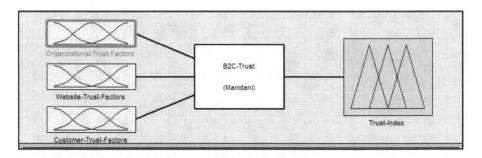

Fig. 7. Fuzzy System to obtain Trust

Gaussian membership function was used for the input variables in the fuzzy system. A Gaussian membership function is specified by two parameters {m, σ} as follows:

$$gaussian(x: m, \sigma) = exp(- \frac{(x-m)^2}{\sigma^2})$$

where m and σ denote the center and width of the function, respectively[7]. Figure 8 shows the membership functions for the fuzzy system.

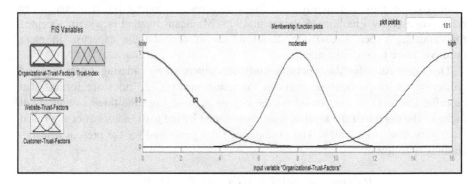

Fig. 8. Membership Functions for the Fuzzy System

3.6   Generation of Trust Index

After developing the fuzzy system using Mamdani fuzzy inference system, the fuzzy model of trust was implemented using Simulink. The equations used in the system were implemented in Simulink with standard blocks. The Simulink implementation of the fuzzy system can be seen in Figure 9. The Simulink model for the fuzzy trust system is developed using one fuzzy logic controller, a process, one multiplexer, one difference element, three constant bocks and a display window.

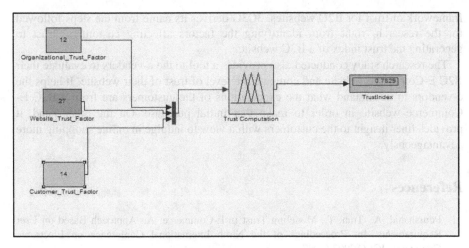

Fig. 9. Generation of Trust Index

The framework suggests the range for the trust as shown in Table 3.According to Table 3, any value of trust index less than 0.3 constitutes low trust range. It suggests very less chances of the customer buying from the website and indicates that the e-vendor should try very hard to improve upon its brand and website to induce customers' trust. While, any value of trust index greater than 0.3 but less than 0.6 constitutes moderate trust and indicates that e-vendor has still more scope for improvement in his e-business.

Table 3. Range of Trust

Trust Index	Linguistic Value
0-0.3	Low Trust
0.31-0.6	Moderate Trust
0.61-0.97	High Trust

Values of trust index between 0.61 and 0.97 indicate high trust range and connote bright chances of customers buying from that particular B2C website.

4   Conclusion

The study was carried out with the objective to understand trust issues prevalent in B2C E-Commerce operations in India with respect to the customer's perspective. It tried to fill the gaps highlighted in the literature review by examining the different dimensions of customers' trust in B2C E-Commerce and proposed the 3C3G framework of trust for B2C websites. 3C3G derives its name from the steps followed for the research, right from identifying the factors affecting customers' trust to generating the trust index of a B2C website.

The research study conducted also provides a tool to the e-vendors to evaluate their B2C E-Commerce website and compute the level of trust of their website. It helps the e-vendors to understand what the expectations of the customers are from a B2C E-Commerce website in order to make that initial purchase. On the other hand, it provides finer insight to the customers with a view to indulge in online shopping more advantageously.

References

1. Pourshahid, A., Tran, T.: Modeling Trust in E-Commerce: An Approach Based on User Requirements. In: Proceedings of the Ninth International Conference on Electronic Commerce, ICEC 2007 (2007)
2. Aris, A., Mustaffa, N., Zakaria, N., Nadiah, N.S., Zabarudin, M.: A Review on Initial Trust Antecedents in E-Commerce. Journal of Research and Innovatio. Information Systems, http://seminar.spaceutm.edu.my/jisri/download/Full%20Paper/ G_TrustAntecedentsEC_CReady.pdf
3. Kaur, B., Madan, S.: Identifying Customers' Preference for Trust Factors in Adoption of B2C E-Commerce in India. International Journal of Computer Science and Technology 4(2), Ver 4 (April-June 2013)
4. Kaur, B., Madan, S.: An Analytical Study of the Trust Concerns of Online Buyers in India. Journal of Computing 5(6) (June 2013)
5. Corbitt, B.J., Thanasankit, T., Yi, H.: Trust and E-Commerce: A study of consumer perceptions. Electronic Commerce Research and Applications 2, 203–215 (2003)
6. Hansen, J.: 100 pages about starting, running and marketing an online store, Stockholm AB (2005)
7. Yen, J., Langari, R.: Fuzzy Logic: Intelligence, Control, and Information. Pearson Education
8. Lee, M.K.O., Turban, E.: A Trust Model for Consumer Internet Shopping. International Journal of Electronic Commerce 6(1), 75–91 (2001)
9. Fishbein, M., Ajzen, I.: Belief, Attitude, Intention and Behavior: An Introduction to Theory and Research. Addison-Wesley, Reading (1975)
10. Nilashi, M., Bagherifard, K., Ibrahim, O., Janahmadi, N., Barisami, M.: An Application Expert System for Evaluating Effective Factors on Trust in B2C Websites. In: SciRP. Scientific Research Publications (2011)
11. Palvia, P.: The role of trust in E-Commerce relational exchange: A unified model. Information and Management 46, 213–220 (2009)
12. Zhang, X., Zhang, Q.: Online Trust Forming Mechanism: Approaches and An Integrated Model. In: Proceedings of the 7th International Conference on Electronic Commerce, ICEC 2005 (2005)

A Review of Security Risks in the Mobile Telecommunication Packet Core Network

Varin Khera[1,2], Chun Che Fung[1], and Sivadon Chaisiri[3]

[1] School of Engineering and Information Technology, Murdoch University, Australia
[2] Nokia Solution Network (NSN)
varin.khera@nsn.com, l.fung@murdoch.edu.au
[3] School of Information Technology, Shinawatra University, Thailand
sivadon@siu.ac.th

Abstract. Advances in information technology depend on the availability of telecommunication, network and mobile technologies. With the rapid increasing number of mobile devices being used as essential terminals or platforms for communication, security threats now target the whole telecommunication infrastructure that includes mobile devices, radio access network, and the core network operated by the mobile operators. In particular, the mobile core network is the most important part of the mobile communication system because different access networks are consolidated at the core network. Therefore, any risks associated with the core network would have a significant impact on the mobile network regardless of technologies of access networks are in use. This paper reviews the security risks in the mobile core network for data services by considering the confidentiality, integrity and availability (CIA) aspects, and then relates them to the ITU-T X.805 reference framework. Finally, this paper provides a recommendation on how to address these risks using the ITU-T X.805 reference framework. This paper will benefit mobile operators and network designers looking to secure the mobile packet core system.

Keywords: telecommunication, network security, ITU-T Recommendation X.805, risks mitigation.

1 Introduction

With the advancement of mobile telecommunication technologies, wireless data access is on the rise with mobile users accessing telecommunications services (e.g., Internet and cloud services) from anywhere at anytime. Such technologies are essential to the stability and future development of a nation's economy. They form the backbone supporting the communication and value-added services for individuals and organizations. In addition, they enable effective operations of government agencies and private sectors. Disruption of the telecommunication systems have serious impacts and implications to the public safety and security of the country [1].

B. Papasratorn et al. (Eds.): IAIT 2013, CCIS 409, pp. 93–103, 2013.
© Springer International Publishing Switzerland 2013

A mobile telecommunication system consists of two layered networks, namely access and core networks. Access networks are edge networks where mobile devices (i.e., mobile users) connect to the telecommunication system. In particular, the mobile core network plays the most important role of the mobile telecommunication system since every access network is attached to the core. Hence, vulnerabilities in the core network could tremendously affect the entire telecommunication network [2].

In a mobile telecommunication system, core networks are classified into circuit and packet core networks. The circuit and packet core networks are deployed for voice services (e.g., services in the public switched telephone network) and data services (e.g., services in the Internet), respectively. In this paper, we mainly review the security risks on the packet core network which is highly vulnerable to security attacks. The main objectives of this paper can be summarized as follows:

- This paper reviews the risks associated with the mobile core network regardless of the technologies applied for the access networks. Then, we classify the risks into specific domains using the confidentiality, integrity, and availability (CIA) triad which is a widely used model for designing information security policies.
- We provide a recommendation on how the reviewed risks can be mitigated using the X.805 security framework defined by the Telecommunication Standardization Sector of the International Telecommunication Union (ITU-T) [3]. Specifically, we propose a design of secured mobile packet core which is able to protect itself against the risks.

This review will be useful to mobile telecommunication operator and network designers since the risks can be considered as the benchmark to assess the operators' core networks. Furthermore, the proposed mobile packet core network design based on the ITU-T X.805 framework will be a guideline for improving the core networks. As a result, the secured core network will be able to protect invaluable information and assets belonging to the mobile users and operators.

The rest of this paper is organized as follows. Related works conducted in this area are discussed in Section 2. Section 3 describes the mobile network architecture. Then, risks associated with the mobile packet core network are presented in Section 4. The proposed improvement of the core network is presented in Section 5. Finally, Section 6 gives a conclusion and suggestion for future work on this topic.

2   Related Work

A number of studies have been conducted on the security implication of the user equipment (e.g., cellular phones) and the radio access network without focusing much on the mobile packet core network e.g., [4–7]. In [7], the infrastructure security of 3GPP relating to universal mobile telecommunications system (UMTS) network was discussed but did not investigate how risks could be associated with the core network. As the mobile core network is essentially the most important part of the mobile telecommunication system, this core network therefore forms the main focus of this paper.

Security issues on the core network were studied. Security issues in GPRS tunnel protocol (GTP) and a solution to address the issues were presented in [8]. The study in [9] proposed a honeynet solution to secure a 3G core network. In [10], a review of security for a 3G network was presented, and then a security enhancement model was proposed with primarily focus on the access domain security. In [11], some security treats on a femtocell-enabled cellular network were reviewed. A study in [2] focused on security risks on a 4G network using the X.805 framework with short explanation on how the framework could be used to understand and mitigate risks on the mobile core network as a whole.

It was also noted from the mentioned literature that security standards have not been applied to the mobile core network with an objective to correlate between standards and the risks. In addition, the literature did not discuss how to protect against different risks using recommended standards.

3   Mobile Network Architecture

Fig. 1 shows a typical mobile network consisting of three main parts, namely user equipment (UE), radio access network (RAN), and the core network. The UE is the closest to the users, for example, the user cellular phone. The UE has a radio connection to the RAN (also called the NodeB in a typical GSM network). An access network is an edge network where the UE accesses the core network. The RAN is then connected into the core network via a radio network controller (RNC) and into either the circuit-switched domain for voice services or the packet-switched domain for data services.

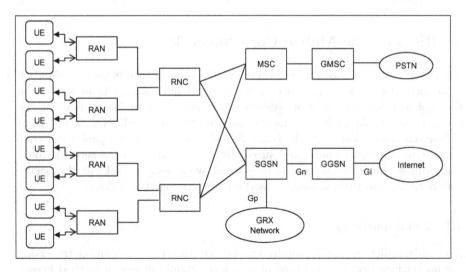

Fig. 1. Overview of the mobile communication system

In a typical 3G core network, the most important elements in the circuit-switched domain are the mobile switching center (MSC) and the gateway MSC (GMSC) which provide an external connection to an external circuit-switched network such as the public switched telephone network (PSTN). In the packet-switched domain, the serving GPRS support node (SGSN) and the gateway GPRS support node (GGSN) provide an external connection for the packet-switched network, i.e., the packet core network for data services [6]. The SGSN connects the global roaming exchange (GRX) network being a hub for GPRS connections for mobile devices. Again, this paper mainly reviews the risks on the packet core network or the packet-switched domain.

When the mobile packet core network is discussed, it is important to understand the different type of interface used at each location. We only focus three interfaces that are relevant to our work, namely Gi, Gp, and Gn. The Gi interface is the connection between the GGSN and the external network such as the Internet or the partner network. The Gp interface is the connection between the SGSN with the external GGSN for roaming partners. The Gn interface is the connection between the internal SGSN and GGSN. At the Gi interface, the protocol is purely IP based whereas the Gp and Gn protocols are carried inside the GPRS tunnelling protocol (GTP).

Mobile operators are now moving towards deploying 4G networks, commonly referred to as Long Term Evolution (LTE) [12]. LTE networks contain only the packet-switched domain and offer a large data transmission rate (over 100 Mbps). LTE introduces a significant change at the radio access network. At the core network, the system still shares many characteristics of the 3G network but without the circuit switch connection [2]. Most operators also concurrently provide the 2G, 3G, and 4G networks in which 2G and 3G networks share the same core network while a 4G network deploys a new element to the existing core network.

4   Risks on the Mobile Core Network

The mobile core network is where the different access networks are consolidated. Therefore, any risks on the core network would have a significant impact on the mobile telecommunication system regardless of technologies used for the access networks. As mobile operators concurrently provide different generations of telecommunication networks (e.g., 2G, 3G and 4G) at the packet-switched domain to their customers, any successful attacks at the core network could compromise the entire networks. In general, we classify attacks at the packet core network into three domains based on the CIA triad as follows:

4.1   Confidentiality

A confidentiality attack is usually carried out to steal information traversing the packet network [1]. This type of attack commonly utilizes a method known as a man-in-the-middle (MitM) [14]. This type of attack allows an attacker to intercept and change data traversing the network in real time. The attack can be accomplished this using the following techniques.

- *Spoofed Update PDP Context Request Attack* – An attacker can use his or her own SGSN or a compromised SGSN to send an update PDP context request to an SGSN, which is handling an existing GTP session. The attacker can then insert his or her own SGSN into the GTP session and hijack the data connection of the subscriber. This will give the attacker full view of the data and allow modification of data compromising data integrity as well.
- *Capturing Subscriber's Data Session Attack* – Since GTP are not encrypted, an attacker who has access to the path between the GGSN and SGSN such as a malicious employee or a cracker who has compromised access to the GRX can potentially capture a subscriber's data session.
- *Internal Access Attack* – Most packet switching core networks of mobile operators are not properly protected especially the internal connection through the operators access network such as the GPRS/EDGE/3G and LTE networks. This weakness opens a potential for an attacker to compromise the core network and take full control over the operator network. Then, the attack can result in disruption to a level that could lead to significant losses for the operators.

4.2   Integrity

Another common form of attack is related to integrity. In this form of attacks, data is changed or modified without the consent of the users [1]. At the mobile packet core level integrity attacks is generally accomplished by manipulating the billing information of the subscriber. This type of attacks allows an attacker to target individual subscribers and potentially exploit them for fun or bring them into an extensive social engineering scheme.

- *GPRS Overbilling Attack* – This attack can overcharge fake phone bills to mobile users. With this attack, the attacker first connects to a server on the Internet. Then, this malicious server starts sending UDP packets (e.g., packets for video/audio streaming service). The attacker then changes his IP address, but as the connection from Internet side remains opens. Once the victim connects to the Internet and is assigned an IP address previously assigned to the attacker, the server continues sending the UDP packets (i.e., the GGSN resumes packet forwarding) and the victim is charged the malicious traffic even though the victim has not generated any traffic.
- *Billing Bypass for Free Internet Usage Attack* – Based on the MitM attack, this attack allows an attacker to use an Internet connection for free and possibly offering free or low cost of a VoIP connection.

4.3   Availability

A common type of attacks on the packet core network is the denial of service (DoS) attack causing network resources to be unavailable. The attacks could result in prominent damage to the operator's network [13]. A DoS attack on the core network can be accomplished using the following techniques.

- *Border Gateway Bandwidth Saturation Attack* – In this attack, a malicious operator that is also connected to the same GRX network may have the ability to generate a sufficient amount of network traffic directed at the operators border gateway such that legitimate traffic is starved for bandwidth in and out of the operators network, thus denying roaming access to or from the operators network.
- *Domain Name System (DNS) Flooding Attack* – The DNS servers on the operator network can be flooded with either correctly or malformed DNS queries denying subscribers' the ability to locate the proper GGSN to use as an external gateway.
- *GTP Flood Disabling Roaming Users Attack* – SGSNs and GGSNs may be flooded with GTP traffic that causes them to spend their CPU cycles processing illegitimate data. This may prevent subscribers from being able to roam, to pass data out to external networks, or from being able to attach to the packet network..
- *Spoofed GTP Packet Data Protocol (PDP) Context Delete Attack* – In this attack, an attacker with the appropriate information can potentially craft a GTP PDP context delete message, which will remove the GPRS tunnel between the SGSN and GGSN for a subscriber. Crafting these types of attack will require that the attacker has certain information about the victim. The attacker can send many PDP context delete messages for every tunnel ID that are being used to deny multiple victims' services.
- *Bad BGP Routing Information Denying Access into Roaming Partners Attack* – An attacker who has control of a GRXs router or who can inject routing information into a GRX operators route tables, can cause an operator to lose routes for roaming partners thereby denying roaming access to and from those roaming partners.
- *DNS Cache Poisoning for Man in the Middle Attack* – It is possible for an attacker to forge DNS queries and/or responses that causes a given user's APN to resolve to the wrong GGSN or even none at all. If a long time-to-live (TTL) is given, this attack can prevent subscribers from being able to pass any data at all.
- *Spoofed Create PDP Context Request Attack* – It is well known that GTP inherently provides no authentication for the SGSNs and GGSNs themselves. As a result, the appropriate information of a subscriber, an attacker with access to the GRX, another operator attached to the GRX network, or a malicious insider can potentially create his or her own bogus SGSN, a GTP tunnel to the GGSN of a subscriber, and a false charging or distributed DoS (DDoS) attacks on the subscriber.
- *Gi Bandwidth Saturation Attack* An attacker may be able to flood the link from the Internet to the mobile operator with network traffic thereby prohibiting legitimate traffic to pass through causing a massive DoS.

- *Flooding Mobile System Attack* – If a flood of traffic is targeted towards the network (IP) address of a particular mobile system, that system will most likely be unable to use the GPRS network.

5 Addressing Risks with ITU-T X.805

To improve the security of the mobile telecommunication packet core network from the risks outlined in the previous section, we apply the ITU X.805 framework as the reference architecture [3]. As depicted in Fig. 2, the ITU X.805 network security model provides a set of principles including three layers (i.e., application, services, and infrastructure), three planes (i.e., end user, control, and management planes), eight security dimensions (i.e., access control, authentication, non-repudiation, data confidentiality, communication security, data integrity, availability, and privacy), and five threats/attacks (i.e., destruction, corruption, removal, disclosure, and interruption) which can be mapped to the mobile core network in order to determine if a network is vulnerable to any attacks listed in the risk domains discussed in Section 4, and to pinpoint where such weaknesses exist and how to mitigate the detected risks.

Table 1 reviews the risks outlined in Section 4 and associates them with the threats in the ITU X.805. This mapping will help identify how the risks are associated with the recommended framework. Then, we apply the eight security dimensions of the ITU X.805 recommendation to identify suggested technologies to mitigate the threats as presented in Table 2.

Finally, we present a topological view of the mobile packet core network with the recommended protection that we have derived by using the X.805 reference model and provided the description of each recommended component.

As illustrated in Fig. 3, to protect the eight security dimensions in the X.805 framework, we propose the design of secured mobile packet core network. This

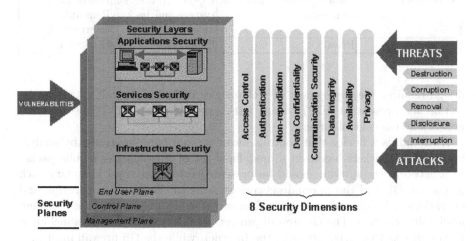

Fig. 2. ITU-T Recommendation X.805 [3]

Table 1. Mapping the Risk Domains into X.805 Threats Model

Threat	Description	Risk Domain
Destruction	Destruction of information and/or network resources	Availability
Corruption	Unauthorized tampering with an asset	Integrity
Removal	Removal or loss information or other resources	Availability
Disclosure	Unauthorized access to an asset	Confidentiality
Interruption	Network become unavailable or unusable	Availability

Table 2. Security Dimensions and Risk Mitigations

Dimension	Description	Mitigation	Threats Solved
Access Control	Only allow access to authorize system	Firewall	Destruction, Interruption
Authentication	Verifying the identity of the person or device observing or modifying data	Network Access Control system with single sign on service	Disclosure, Disruption
Non-repudiation	Provide a record that identify each individual or device that observed on modify the data	Certificate authority, identity management system	Destruction, Corruption
Data confidentiality	Data is confidential and only readable by whom it is intended	Encryption such as SSL/VPN	Disclosure
Communication Security	Data access and communication is secured	VPN / IPSec Tunnel	Interruption
Data Integrity	Data is no changed or modified	Digital certificate	Corruption
Availability	Data or access is available as needed	DDoS protection system and backup links	Destruction, Removal, Interruption
Privacy	Privacy	Encryption	Disclosure

design requires the deployment of technologies including firewall, intrusion detection and prevention (IDP) system, virtual private network (VPN) server, and network access control server.

A firewall is a device that controls incoming and outgoing traffic by analyzing the data packets based on a predefined set of rules. In the mobile packet core network, the firewall should be presented on the external boundary such as the Gi, Gi, and the internal network such as the charging, application and operations, administration and management (OAM) domain, in a form of high availability clusters. The Gi firewall protects against external attacks including DDoS attacks that originate from the Internet, while the Gp firewall must provide GTP inspection capabilities to filter traffic travelling into the mobile core

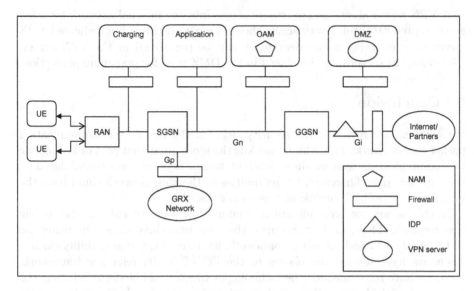

Fig. 3. Proposed secured mobile packet core network design

network from the roaming partners. Basically, the Gi and Gp firewalls act as an external defence to block against any threats coming into the packet core network. In the case of the DMZ zone (i.e., a perimeter network), the firewall for this zone can be shared with the Gi firewall. At the internal network zone (e.g., the operations support system (OSS), application, and the charging domains), a firewall must be available as the second line of defence to protect these internal systems.

The IDP system is normally the next line of defence for the mobile packet core network. The IDP system utilizes signature and entropy-based behaviour to block against attacks managing to bypass the firewall filters. This system provides the second line of defence in the most critical zone of the mobile core network. In the mobile packet network, we recommend that an IDP system should be placed behind the firewall at the Gi domain. This placement will allow the IDP system to filter any threats coming into the network from the Gi including the DMZ zone which could be compromised.

A network access management (NAM) server allows administrators to implement a single user interface to securely control every access to the network element in the mobile network. Since the mobile core network contains a large number of network elements, it is important that the access to these elements can be controlled and audited in a timely fashion. We recommend that a NAM server should be placed in the OAM domain. In addition, the NAM server must be enforced as a single interface for logging into any network elements on the mobile core network.

A VPN server allows secure remote access into the internal network by using an encrypted protocol. Every access should be passed through a dedicated VPN server since encryption and decryption can be performed at the VPN server. Therefore, the server must be placed in the DMZ zone for maximum protection.

6   Conclusion

We have mainly reviewed the security risks on the mobile telecommunication packet core network. This core network is the most important part of the mobile telecommunication system since different access networks are consolidated at the core network. Therefore, vulnerabilities in the core network could have the major impact on both mobile operators and users.

In this paper, we have identified a number of security risks in the mobile core network. Then, we have grouped the risks into three classes by using the widely used CIA triad including confidentiality, integrity, and availability classes. Then, we have related the classes to the ITU-T X.805 reference framework. Next, we have recommended the technologies which could be deployed along the framework with the objective to safeguard against the risks in the eight security domains. Finally, we have proposed the secured mobile packet core network design which is able to mitigate the risks.

This review will be useful to mobile telecommunication operators and network designers. The risks outlined in the review can be considered by the operators as the benchmark to assess their packet core networks in order to safeguard data services. Furthermore, our proposed mobile packet core network design could be applied as a guideline for improving the security of the mobile telecommunication systems. A secure telecommunication system will be able to safeguard invaluable information belonged to the mobile users and operators against the risks.

For future work, we will study a hypothetical mobile telecommunication packet core network and evaluate how attacks can be carried out on the network. Countermeasures to address the risks using the three dimensions of people, process, and technology will also be investigated and proposed.

References

1. Harmantzis, F., Malek, M.: Security Risk Analysis and Evaluation. In: IEEE International Conference on Communications, vol. 4, pp. 1897–1901 (2004)
2. Chouhan, S., Gaikwad, R.B., Sharma, N.: A Study on 4G Network and Its Security. International Journal of Computer Architecture and Mobility 1(9) (2013)
3. ITU-T Recommendation X.805: Security Architect for Systems Providing End-to-End Communication (2003)
4. Ahmadian, Z., Salimi, S., Salahi, A.: Security Enhancement against UMTS-GSM Internetworking Attacks. Elsevier Computer Network Journal 54, 2256–2270 (2010)
5. Xenakis, C., Merakos, L.: Security in third Generation Mobile Network. Elsevier Computer Communication Journal 27, 638–650 (2004)
6. Vriendt, J.D., Laine, P., Lerouge, C., Xu, X.: Alcatel: Mobile Network Evolution: A Revolution on the Move. IEEE Communication Magazine, 104–111 (April 2002)

7. Prasad, A., Wang, H., Schoo, P.: Infrastructure Security for Future Mobile Communication System. In: WPMC 2003, Yokosuka, Japan (2003)
8. Peng, X., Wen, Y., Zhao, H.: Security Issues and Solutions in 3G Core Net-work. Journal of Networks 6(5), 823–830 (2011)
9. Dimitriadis, C.K.: Improving Mobile Core Network Security with Honeynets. IEEE Security & Privacy 5(4), 40–47 (2007)
10. Xenakis, C.: Security Measures and Weaknesses of the GPRS Security Architecture. International Journal of Network Security 6(2), 158–169 (2008)
11. Bilogrevic, I., Jadliwala, M., Hubaux, J.-P.: Security Issues in Next Generation Mobile Networks: LTE and Femtocells. In: 2nd International Femtocell Workshop, Luton, UK (2010)
12. Astely, D., Dahlman, E., Furuskar, A., Jading, Y., Lindstrom, M., Parkvall, S.: LTE: The Evolution of Mobile Broadband. IEEE Communications Magazine 47(4), 44–51 (2009)
13. Ricciatoa, F., Colucciaa, A., D'Alconzo, A.: A Review of DoS Attack Models for 3G Cellular Networks from a System-design Perspective. Elsevier Computer Communications Journal 33, 551–558 (2010)
14. Meyer, U., Wetzel, S.: A Man-in-the-Middle Attack on UMTS. In: Proceedings of the 3rd ACM Workshop on Wireless Security (2004)

Efficient Code Obfuscation for Android

Aleksandrina Kovacheva

University of Luxembourg
aleksandrina.kovacheva.001@student.uni.lu

Abstract. Recent years have witnessed a steady shift in technology from desktop computers to mobile devices. In the global picture of available mobile platforms, Android stands out as a dominant participant on the market and its popularity continues rising. While beneficial for its users, this growth simultaneously creates a prolific environment for exploitation by vile developers which write malware or reuse software illegally obtained by reverse engineering. A class of programming techniques known as code obfuscation targets prevention of intellectual property theft by parsing an input application through a set of algorithms aiming to make its source code computationally harder and time consuming to recover. This work focuses on the development and application of such algorithms on the bytecode of Android, Dalvik. The main contributions are: (1) a study on samples obtained from the official Android market which shows how feasible it is to reverse a targeted application; (2) a proposed obfuscator implementation whose transformations defeat current popular static analysis tools while maintaining a low level of added time and memory overhead.

Keywords: Android, bytecode obfuscation, Dalvik, reverse engineering.

1 Introduction

Ever since the early 1990s, devices combining telephony and computing have been offered for sale to the general public. Evolving to what is presently referred to as "smartphones", their extensive usage is indisputable: a report from February 2013 estimated the total number of smartphone devices sold only in 2012 as surpassing 1.75 billion [1]. Due to their wide ranging applicability and high mobility smartphones have been preferred over stationary or laptop computers as access devices to personal information services such as e-mail, social network accounts or e-commerce websites. By the end of 2012, the mobile market was dominated with a ratio of 70% by the Android platform [1].

The huge market share as well as the sensitivity of the user data processed by most applications raise an important security question regarding the source code visibility of the mobile software. Firstly, developers have an interest of protecting their intellectual property against piracy. Moreover, an alarming 99% of the mobile malware developed in 2012 has been reported to target Android platform users and inspection reveals both qualitative and quantitative growth [2]. Hence, Android applications code protection is crucial to maintaining a high level of

B. Papasratorn et al. (Eds.): IAIT 2013, CCIS 409, pp. 104–119, 2013.

trust between vendors and users which in turn reflects in a correct functioning of the Google Play market itself.

In general, there are two main approaches towards software protection: enforcing legal software usage policies or applying various forms of technical protection to the code. This work concentrates on the latter, more precisely on a technique called *code obfuscation*. In the context of information security the term obfuscation encompasses various deliberately made modifications on the control-flow and data-flow of programs such that they become computationally hard to reverse engineer by a third party. The applied changes should be semantic preserving with ideally negligible or minor memory-time penalty.

2   Related Work

The idea of obfuscation was first suggested by Whitfield Diffie and Martin Hellman in 1976 in their paper "New Directions in Cryptography" [3] where they introduced the usefulness of obscuring cryptographic primitives in private key encryption schemes for converting them into public key encryption schemes. In 1997 C. Collberg et al. presented obfuscation together with a relevant taxonomy as a way of protecting software against reverse engineering [4]. The theoretically computational boundaries of obfuscation are examined in a work titled "On the (Im)possibility of Obfuscating Programs" by Boaz Barak et al. in 2001 [5]. In the latter, the authors give a framework for defining a perfect or *black-box* obfuscator and show that such a primitive cannot be constructed. Although in theory perfect obfuscation is proven impossible, there is a discrepancy with its practical aspects.

In applied software engineering obfuscation is used on various occasions, mainly for protection against reverse engineering, defending against computer viruses and inserting watermarks or fingerprints on digital multimedia. Usually, a software vendor does not try to hide the functionalities of their program, otherwise software would never be accompanied by user documentation which is not the case. Rather, the developer aims at making unintelligible the implementation of a selected set of functions.

To recover the original code of an application, bytecode analysis is most often used. By applying both *dynamic* and *static* techniques, in the context of Android applications, it is possible to detect an over-privileged application design, find patterns of malicious behavior or trace user data such as login credentials. Due to its simplicity over bytecode for other architectures, Dalvik bytecode is currently an easy target for the reverse engineer. The following listed set of analysis tools and decompilers is a representative of the largely available variety: androguard [6],baksmali [7], dedexer [8], dex2jar [9], dexdump [10], dexguard [11], dexter [12], radare2 [13].

Evidently, there are numerous tools to the help of the Android reverse engineer. They can be used either separately or to complement each other. The same diversity cannot be claimed for software regarding the code protection side, especially concentrating on Dalvik bytecode. Most existing open-source and commercial obfuscators work on source code level. The reason is that effective protection techniques successfully applied on Java source code have been suggested previously [14]. Furthermore, Java code is architecture-independent giving freedom to design generic code transformations. Of the here listed Dalvik bytecode obfuscation tools the first two are open-source, the last (which also modifies the source code) is commercial: `dalvik-obfuscator` [15], `APKfuscator` [16], DexGuard [17]. Unfortunately, the open-source tools have the status of a proof-of-concept software rather than being used at regular practice by application developers.

3   A Case Study on Applications

There exist an extensive set of works examining Android applications from the viewpoint of privacy invasion as can be seen in [18–21]. The here presented case study aims to show that bytecode undergoes few protection. If present, obfuscation is very limited with regards to the potential transformation techniques which could be applied, even for applications which were found to try protecting their code.

3.1   Study Methodology

To obtain a sample apps set, a web crawler was developed downloading the 50 most popular applications from each of the 34 categories available on the market. There were applications in repeating categories, thus the actual number of the examined files was 1691. The study was performed in two stages. Initially, automated static analysis scripts were run on bytecode for a coarse classification the purpose of which was profiling the apps according to a set of chosen criteria. A secondary, fine grinding examination, was to manually select a few "interesting" apps and looking through the code at hand. The following enumerated were used for apps profiling:

1. **Obfuscated versus non-obfuscated classes.** A study on the usage of `ProGuard` which is an available in the Android SDK code obfuscator was an easy target. Since this tool applies variable renaming in a known manner, the classes names and contained methods were processed with a pattern matching filter according to the naming convention i.e. looking for minimal lexical-sorted strings. A class whose name is not obfuscated, but contains obfuscated methods was counted as an obfuscated class.

2. **Strings encoded with Base64.** Several applications were found to contain "hidden" from the resources files in the form of strings encoded with Base64. Manual examination of a limited number of these revealed nothing but `.gif` and `flash` multimedia files. However, this finding suggests that it might be common practice that data is hidden as a string instead of being stored as a separate file which is why this criteria was considered relevant to the study.

3. **Dynamic loading.** Dynamic loading allows invocation of external code not installed as an official part of the application. For the initial automation phase its presence was only detected by pattern matching check of the classes for the packages:

```
Ldalvik/system/DexClassLoader
Ljava/security/ClassLoader
Ljava/security/SecureClassLoader
Ljava/net/URLClassLoader
```

4. **Native code.** Filtering for the usage of code accessing system-related information and resources or interfacing with the runtime environment was also performed. For the coarse run only detecting the presence of native code in the following packages was considered:

```
Ljava/lang/System
Ljava/lang/Runtime
```

5. **Reflection.** The classes definition table was filtered for the presence of the Java reflection packages for access to methods, fields and classes.

6. **Header size.** The header size was also checked in referral to previous work suggesting bytecode injection possibility in the `.dex` header [22].

7. **Encoding.** A simple flag check in the binary file for whether an application uses the support of mixed endianess of the ARM processor.

8. **Crypto code.** With regards to previous studies on inappropriate user private data handling as well as deliberate cryptography misuse, the classes were also initially filtered for the usage of the packages:

```
Ljavax/crypto/
Ljava/security/spec/
```

3.2 Results Review

The distribution of applications according to the percentage of obfuscated code with ProGuard is shown on table 1. On table 2 are noted the absolute number of occurrences of each factor the apps were profiled for. The automated study reveals that encoding strings in base64 is quite common practice: 840 applications containing a total of 2379 strings were found and examined, shown on table 3. To determine the file format from the decoded strings the python magic library[1] was used. Unfortunately, 1156 files which is 48.59% of the total encoded files could not be identified by this approach and using the Unix file command lead to no better results. The remaining set of files was divided into multimedia, text and others. As a final remark to table 3 is that the percentage marks the occurrences in the 1241 successfully identified files.

A set of several applications was selected for manual review, the selection criteria trying to encompass a wide range of possible scenarios. Among the files were: (1) a highly obfuscated (89.7%) malicious application[2]; (2) a very popular social application with no obfuscation and a large number of packages; (3) a popular mobile Internet browser with 100% obfuscated packages; (4) an application

---

[1] https://github.com/ahupp/python-magic

[2] Detected by the antivirus software on the machine where the download occurred.

Table 1. Obfuscation ratio. The row with # marks the absolute number of applications with obfuscated number of classes in the given range. The row with % marks the percentage this number represents in the set of the total applications.

OBF	100%	(100 − 80]	(80 − 60]	(60 − 40]	(40 − 20]	(20 − 0)	0%	Total
#	82	291	196	166	283	423	250	**1691**
%	4.85	17.21	11.59	9.82	16.74	25.01	14.78	**100%**

Table 2. Profiling the set of applications according to the given criteria: OBF (total obfuscated classes), B64 (apps containing base64 strings), NAT (native code), DYN (dynamic code), REF (reflection), CRY (crypto code), HEAD (apps with header size of 0x70), LIT (apps with little endian byte ordering). The row with # marks the absolute numbers of occurrences, % marks the percentage this number represents in the set of the total applications.

	OBF	B64	NAT	DYN	REF	CRY	HEAD	LIT
#	41.839	840	629	224	1519	1236	1691	1691
%	46.74	49.68	37.20	13.25	89.83	73.09	100	100

Table 3. Classification of the base64 encoded strings. Categories are denoted as follows: TXT for text, MUL for multimedia, OTH for other.

	# files	%total	DATA TYPE			
unknown	1156	48.59	non-identified data			
			type	#	%	category
			ASCII text	56	4.51	TXT
			GIF	48	3.87	MUL
			HTML	3	0.24	OTH
known	1241	51.41	ISO-8859 text	1	0.08	TXT
			JPEG	33	2.66	MUL
			Non-ISO extended-ASCII text	24	1.93	TXT
			PNG	522	42.06	MUL
			TrueType font text	548	44.17	MUL
			UTF-8 Unicode text	1	0.08	TXT
			XML document	2	0.16	OTH

which androguard (DAD) and dexter failed to process; (5) an application which is known to use strings encryption and is claimed to be obfuscated as well; (6) an application containing many base64 encoded strings; (7-10) four other applications chosen at random.

With the exception of application (4) all files were successfully processed by the androguard analysis tool. The source code of all checked obfuscated methods was successfully recovered to a correct Java code with the androguard plugin for Sublime Text[3]. The control-flow graphs of *all* analyzed files was

---

[3] http://www.sublimetext.com/

recovered successfully with `androgexf.py`. However, in some applications the excessive number of packages created an inappropriate setting for adequate analysis thus the graphs were filtered by pattern-matching the labels of their nodes. Having the graphs of all applications simplified revealed practices such as implementation of custom strings encryption-decryption pair functions and having their source code implementation hidden in a native library (seen in two of the analyzed files). Reviewing the graph of application (4) was a key towards understanding why some tools break during analysis: they simply do not handle cases of Unicode method or field names (e.g. 文章:`Ljava/util/ArrayList;`). On the other hand, `baksmali` did fully recover the mnemonics of the application, Unicode names representing no obstacle.

Regarding the permissions used in the malicious application, it is no surprise that it required the `INTERNET` permission. In fact, being at-first-sight a wallpaper application, it had as much as 27 permissions including install privileges, writing to the phone's external storage and others. This result only comes as confirmation to what previous studies have already established as user privacy invasive practices [20].

3.3 Study Conclusion

The main conclusion of both automated and manual inspection is that even in cases where some tools hindered recovering the bytecode mnemonics or source code, there is a way round to obtain relevant information. Where a given tool is not useful, another can be used as complement. Reversing large applications may be slowed down due to the complexity of the program graph, but with appropriate node filtering a reasonable subgraph can be obtained for analysis. To prevent information extraction by static analysis some applications made use of Java reflection or embedding valuable code in a native library. Apart from using ProGuard to rename components and decrease program understandability, no other code obfuscation was found. Using Unicode names for classes and methods could be regarded as an analogical type of modification: it merely affects program layout not the control flow.

3.4 Remarks

A number of considerations need to be taken into account when reviewing the results of the performed study. (1) All applications studied were available through the official Google Play market as of March 2013. (2) Only freely available applications were processed: the results will highly likely differ if identical examinations were performed on payed applications. (3) The set of popular applications in the Google Play market differs with the country of origin of the requesting IP address: the download for this study was executed on a machine located in Bulgaria.

4   Implementing a Dalvik Bytecode Obfuscator

This section suggests an implementation of a Dalvik bytecode obfuscator including four transformations whose main design accents fall on fulfilling the generic and cheap properties.

In the context of this work the term "generic" denotes that the transformations are constructed in aspiration to encompass a large set of applications without preliminary assumptions which must hold for the processed file. On Android this can be a challenge since an application has to run on a wide range of devices, OS versions and architectures. Thus, it is crucial that any applied code protection would not decrease the set of application running devices. When a transformation is characterized as "cheap", this is in referral to previously published work by Collberg et. al. on classifying obfuscating transformations [4]. By definition, a technique is cheap if the obfuscated program $\mathcal{P}'$ requires $\mathcal{O}(n)$ more resources than executing the original $\mathcal{P}$. Resources encompass processing time and memory usage: two essential performance considerations, especially for mobile devices. Following is a description of the general structure of the Dalvik bytecode obfuscator[4] as well as details on the four transformations applied.

4.1   Structure Overview

The input of the tool is an APK file which can be either processed by ProGuard i.e. with renamed classes and methods, or not modified at all. Auxiliary tools used during the obfuscation are the pair `smali` assembly and `baksmali` disassembly. The application is initially disassembled with `baksmali` which results in having a directory of `.smali` files. These files contain mnemonics retrieved from the immediate bytecode interpretation. Three of the transformations parse, modify the mnemonics and assemble them back to a valid `.dex` file using `smali`. One transformation modifies the bytecode of the `.dex` file directly. After the modifications have been applied, the `.dex` file is packed together with the resource files, signed and is verified for data integrity. This last step yields a semantically equivalent obfuscated version of the APK file. Figure 1 summarizes the entire obfuscation process.

Adopting this workflow has the advantage of accelerating the development process by relying on a `.dex` file assembler and disassembler pair. However, a disadvantage is that the implemented obfuscator is bound by the limitations of the used external tools.

4.2   Transformations

The tool can apply four transformations designed such that all of them affect both the data and control flow. The transformations targets are: calls to native libraries, hardcoded strings, 4-bit and 16-bit numeric constants. Native

---

[4] `https://github.com/alex-ko/innocent`

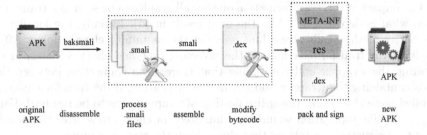

Fig. 1. Workflow of the obfuscator

calls are redirected through external classes in methods that we call here "wrappers". Strings are encrypted and numeric constants are packed in external class-containers, shuffled and modified. The fourth modification injects dead code which has a minor effect on the control flow, but makes the input APK resistant to reverse engineering with current versions of some popular tools which is why it is called "bad" bytecode injection.

Adding Native Call Wrappers. While native code itself is not visible through applying static analysis, calls to native libraries cannot be shrunk by tools such as ProGuard. The reason is that method names in Dalvik bytecode must correspond exactly to the ones declared in the external library for them to be located and executed. This transformation does not address the issue with comprehensive method names since this depends on the developer. However, another source of useful information is the locality of the native calls i.e. by tracking which classes call particular methods metadata information for the app can be obtained. To harden the usage tracking process one could place the native call in a supplementary function, what is referred here as a native call wrapper. The exact sequence of steps taken is on the following schematic figure:

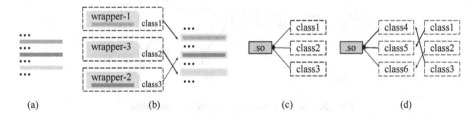

Fig. 2. Adding native call wrappers

Let us have a class containing three native calls which are highlighted on (a). For each unique native method a corresponding wrapper with additional arguments is constructed redirecting the native call. To complicate the control flow, the wrappers are scattered randomly in external classes from those located originally. As a final step each native call is replaced with an invocation of its respective wrapper as shown in (b).

The impact of this transformation on the call graph can be seen as a transition from what is depicted in (c) to the final result in (d). Initially, the locality of the native method calls give a hint on what the containing class is doing. After applying the transformation once, the reversing time and effort is increased by locating the wrapper and concluding that there is no connection between the class containing the wrapper and the native invocation. If the transformation is applied more than once, the entire nesting of wrappers has to be resolved. Usually, a mobile application would have hundreds of classes to scatter the nested wrapping structures: a setting that slows down the reversing process.

Packing Numeric Variables. The idea behind this transformation stems from what is known in literature as opaque data structures [23]. The basic concept is to affect data flow in the program by encapsulating heterogeneous data types in a custom defined structure.

The target data of this particular implementation are the numeric constants in the application. The bytecode mnemonics are primarily scanned to locate the usages and values of all 4-bit and 16-bit constants. After gathering those, the obfuscator packs them in a 16-bit array (the 4-bit constants being shifted) in a newly-created external class as shown on (a) in the schematic figure below. Let us call this external class a "packer". The numeric array in the packer is then processed according to the following steps. Firstly, to use as little additional memory as possible, all duplicated numeric values are removed. Next, the constants are shuffled randomly and are transformed in order to hide their actual values. Currently, three transformations are implemented: XOR-ing with one random value, XOR-ing twice with two different random values and a linear mapping. Then, a method stub to get the constant and reverse the applied transformation is implemented in the packer. Finally, each occurrence of a constant declaration is replaced with an invocation to the get-constant packer method.

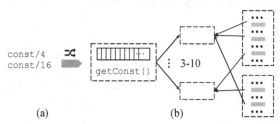

(a)   (b)

Fig. 3. Packing numeric variable constants

The transformation thus put represents not much of added complexity to the program. To further challenge the reverser, the packer class creates between 3 and 10 replicas of itself, each time applying anew the shuffling and the selection of the numeric transformation to the array. This means that even if the obfuscated application has several packer classes which apply, for example, the XOR-twice transformation, in each of them the two random numbers will differ as well as the data array index of every unique numeric value. Designed like this, the transformation has the disadvantage of data duplication. However, an advantage that is possible due to this reduplication is removing the necessity that a single class containing constants is calling the get-constant method of the same packer which is shown on (b) in the figure above.

To summarize, control flow is complicated by multiple factors. Firstly, additional classes are introduced to the application i.e. more data processing paths in the program graph for the reverser to track. Then, in each packer class the array constant values will diverge. Lastly, different packers are addressed to retrieve the numeric constants in a single class and the reverser would have to establish that the connection between each of the different packer calls is merely data duplication.

Strings Encryption. The decision to include this transformation in the tool is motivated by the fact that none of the here cited open-source tools implements strings encryption at the moment of submission. Moreover, the transformation is designed in such a way that it aspires to add more control flow complexity than what is currently found to be implemented [11] and instead of using a custom algorithm (usually simply XOR-ing with one value) the strings here are encrypted with the RC4 stream cipher [24].

The figure on the right gives an overview to how the transformation works. The classes containing strings are filtered out. A unique key is generated for and stored inside each such class. All strings in a class are encrypted with the same class-assigned-key. Encryption yields a byte sequence corresponding to each

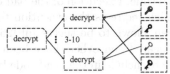

Fig. 4. Strings encryption

unique string which is stored as a data array in a private static class field. This results in removing strings from the constant pool upon application re-assembly thus preventing from visibility with static analysis. A consideration to use static class fields for storing the encrypted strings is the relatively small performance impact. Decryption occurs during runtime, the strings being decoded once upon the first invocation of the containing class. Whenever a given string is needed, it is retrieved from the relevant class field.

Analogically to previous transformations, adding control flow complexity is at the cost of duplication. The decryption class creates between 3 and 10 semantically equivalent replicas of itself in the processed application as shown in the figure. Each class containing strings chooses randomly its corresponding decryption class.

To summarize, there are several minor improvements of the here suggested implementation over what was found in related works. Encrypting the strings in each class with a unique key slows down automatic decryption because the keys are placed at different positions and need to be located separately for each class. Designing the transformation by using a decryption-template approach allows in principal the developer to modify this template: they can either choose to strengthen potency and resilience or change easily the underlying encryption/decryption algorithm pair. Finally, the added control flow complexity is increased by the supplementary decryption classes.

Injecting "Bad" Code. The proposed here transformation has as main purpose to defy popular static analysis tools without claiming to be highly resilient. In fact, it is shown that a simple combination of known exploits is enough to cause certain tools to crack and produce an output error. There are two defeat target tool types: decompilers and disassemblers performing static analysis. The used techniques are classified in previous works as "preventive" [4] for exploiting weaknesses of current analysis tools.

To thwart decompilers an advantage is taken from the discrepancy between what is representable as legitimate Java code and its translation into Dalvik bytecode. Similar techniques have been proposed for Java bytecode protection [25]. The Java programming language does not implement a `goto` statement, yet when loop or switch structures are translated into bytecode this is done with a `goto` Dalvik instruction. Thus by working directly on bytecode it is possible to inject verifiable sequences composed of `goto` statements which either cannot be processed by the decompilers or do not translate back to correct Java source code.

To thwart disassemblers several "bad" instructions are injected directly in the bytecode. Execution of the bad code is avoided by a preceding opaque predicate which redirects the execution to the correct paths. This technique has already been shown to be successful [26]. However, since its publishing new tools have appeared and others have been fixed. The here suggested minor modifications are to include in the dead code branch: (1) an illegal invocation to the first entry in the application methods table; (2) a packed switch table with large indexes for its size; (3) a call to the bogus method we previously created such that it looks as if it is being used (not to be removed as dead code).

4.3   Evaluation of the Modified Bytecode

To verify the efficiency of the developed tool a set of 12 test applications was selected among the huge variety. The apps profiling is given in Appendix A. The performance tests of the modified applications were executed on two mobile devices: (1) HTC Desire smartphone with a customized Cyanogenmod v7.2 ROM, Android v2.3.7; (2) Sony Xperia tablet with the original vendor firmware, Android v4.1.1.

During the development process all transformations were tested and verified to work separately. On table 4 are given the results of their combined application. The plus sign should be interpreted as that the transformations have been applied consequently (e.g. w+o+p means applying adding wrappers then obfuscating strings then packing variables).

With the exception of the bad code injection on the facebook application, every application undergoing the possible combinations of transformations was installed successfully on both test devices. An observation on the error console logs for the facebook application suggests that the custom class loader of this app conflicts with the injected bad code [27]. The rest of the transformations did not make the app crash. For the Korean ebay app no crash occurred, but not all of the UTF-8 strings were decrypted successfully i.e. some messages which should

Table 4. Testing the obfuscated applications on HTC Desire and Sony Xperia tablet. The transformations abbreviations are as follows: w adding native wrappers, o obfuscating strings, p packing variables, b adding bad bytecode. The black bullet indicates successful install and run after applying the series of transformations.

APP	w	w+o	w+o+p	w+o+p+b
com.adobe.reader.apk	•	•	•	•
com.alensw.PicFolder.apk	•	•	•	•
com.disney.WMPLite.apk	•	•	•	•
com.ebay.kr.gmarket.apk	•	•	•	•
com.facebook.katana.apk	•	•	•	○
com.microsoft.office.lync.apk	•	•	•	•
com.rebelvox.voxer.apk	•	•	•	•
com.skype.android.access.apk	•	•	•	•
com.teamlava.bubble.apk	•	•	•	•
cz.aponia.bor3.czsk.apk	•	•	•	•
org.mozilla.firefox.apk	•	•	•	•
snt.luxtraffic.apk	•	•	•	•

have been in Korean appeared as their UTF-8 equivalent bytes sequence. The most probable reason is that large alphabets are separated in different Unicode ranges and smali implements a custom UTF-8 encoding/decoding[5] which might have a slight discrepancy with the encoding of python for some ranges. Finally, the Voxer communication app did not initially run with the injected bad code. This lead to implementing the possibility to toggle the verification upon bytecode injection. By setting a constant in the method as verified its install-time verification can be suppressed. Enabling this feature let the Voxer app run without problems. However, verifier suppression is disabled by default for security considerations.

Besides the upper mentioned, no other anomalies were noted on the tested applications. No noticeable runtime performance slowdown was detected while testing manually. The memory overhead added by each transformation separately is shown on Appendix B. Because the applications differ significantly in size, for a better visual representation only the impact on the least significant megabyte is shown.

Finally, some of the popular reverse engineering tools were tested against the modified bytecode. Two possible outcomes were observed: either the tool was defeated i.e. did not process the app at all due to a crash, or the analysis output is erroneous. Tools which crashed were: baksmali, apktool, DARE decompiler, dedexer, dex2jar. Tools with erroneous output were: androguard, JD-GUI.

4.4 Limitations

To be effective, the transformations had to comply with the Dalvik verifier and optimizer [28]. Moreover, the workflow used by the obfuscator relies on external

---

[5] https://code.google.com/p/smali/source/browse/dexlib/src/main/java/org/jf/dexlib/Util/Utf8Utils.java

tools which imply their own constraints. Hence, it is worth noting the limitations of the proposed transformations.

Native Call Wrappers is applied only to native methods which have no more than 15 registers. The reason is that `smali` has its own register implementation distinguishing between parameter and non-parameter registers and is working only by representing methods with no more than 15 non-parameter registers. In case more registers need to be allocated, the method is defined with a register range, not a register number. Defined so to ease the editing of smali code, this has its restrictions on our transformation.

Packing Numeric Variables is applied only to the 4-bit and 16-bit registers, because there is a risk of overflowing due to the applied transformation when extended to lager registers. Clearly, a transformation shifts the range of the possible input values. Regarding the simple XOR-based modifications, the scope is preserved but a linear mapping shrinks the interval of possible values. Also, packing variables was restricted only to numeric constant types because in Dalvik registers have associated types i.e. packing heterogeneous data together might be a type-conversion potentially dangerous operation [29].

5   Conclusion

This work accented on several important aspects of code obfuscation for the Android mobile platform. To commence, we confirmed the statement that currently reverse engineering is a lightweight task regarding the invested time and computational resources. More than 1600 applications were studied for possible applied code transformations, but found no more sophisticated protection than variable name scrambling or its slightly more resilient variation of giving Unicode names to classes and methods. Some applications used strings encryption during runtime. Yet, these applications themselves had hardcoded strings visible with analysis tools.

Having demonstrated the feasibility of examining randomly selected applications, a proof of concept open-source Dalvik obfuscator was proposed. Its main purpose is introducing a reasonable slowdown in the reversing process. The obfuscator performs four transformations all of which target both data flow and control flow. Various analysis tools were challenged on the modified bytecode, showing that the majority of them are defeated.

Android is merely since five years on the market, yet because of its commercial growth much research is conducted on it. The evolution of the platform is a constantly ongoing process. It can be seen in its source code that some of the now unused bytecode instructions were former implemented test instructions. Possible future opcode changes may invalidate the effects our transformations. Moreover, analysis tools will keep on getting better and to defeat them newer, craftier obfuscation techniques will need to be applied. This outwitting competition between code protectors and code reverse engineers exists ever since the topic of obfuscation has been established of practical importance. So far, evidence proves this game will be played continuously.

Acknowledgements. This paper is a derivation of the author's thesis work which was supervised by Prof. Alex Biryukov and Dr. Ralf-Philipp Weinmann while in candidature for a master degree at the University of Luxembourg. The author wishes to thank them for their guidance, especially Dr. Ralf-Philipp Weinmann for his valuable advice and support.

References

1. Gartner News (February 2013, press release),
   http://www.gartner.com/newsroom/id/2335616
2. Kaspersky Lab: 99% of all mobile threats target Android devices,
   http://www.kaspersky.com/about/news/virus/2013/
   99_of_all_mobile_threats_target_Android_devices
3. Diffie, W., Hellman, M.: New directions in cryptography. IEEE Transactions on Information Theory IT-22(6), 644–654 (1976)
4. Collberg, C., Thomborson, C., Low, D.: A Taxonomy of Obfuscating Transformations, Technical Report 148, Department of Computer Science, University of Auckland, New Zealand (1997)
5. Barak, B., Goldreich, O., Impagliazzo, R., Rudich, S., Sahai, A., Vadhan, S.P., Yang, K.: On the (Im)possibility of Obfuscating Programs. In: Kilian, J. (ed.) CRYPTO 2001. LNCS, vol. 2139, pp. 1–18. Springer, Heidelberg (2001)
6. Androguard project home page, https://code.google.com/p/androguard/
7. Smali/Baksmali project home page, https://code.google.com/p/smali/
8. Dedexer project home page, http://dedexer.sourceforge.net/
9. Dex2jar project home Page, https://code.google.com/p/dex2jar/
10. Dexdump, Android SDK Tools,
    http://developer.android.com/tools/help/index.html
11. Bremer, J.: Automated Deobfuscation of Android Applications,
    http://jbremer.org/automated-deobfuscation-of-android-applications/
12. Dexter project home page, http://dexter.dexlabs.org/
13. Radare2 project Home Page, http://radare.org/y/?p=download
14. Collberg, C., Thomborson, C., Low, D.: Manufacturing Cheap, Resilient, and Stealthy Opaque Constructs (1998)
15. Schulz, P.: Dalvik-obfuscator project GitHub page,
    https://github.com/thuxnder/dalvik-obfuscator
16. Strazzere, T.: APKfuscator project GitHub page,
    https://github.com/strazzere/APKfuscator
17. DexGuard main page, http://www.saikoa.com/dexguard
18. Felt, A.P., Chin, E., Hanna, S., Song, D., Wagner, D.: Android Permissions Demystified. University of California, Berkeley (2011)
19. Gommerstadt, H., Long, D.: Android Application Security: A Thorough Model and Two Case Studies: K9 and Talking Cat. Harvard University (2012)
20. Hornyack, P., Han, S., Jung, J., Schechter, S., Wetherall, D.: These aren't the droids you're looking for: retrofitting android to protect data from imperious applications. In: Proceedings of the 18th ACM Conference on Computer and Communications Security (2011)
21. Enck, W., Octeau, D., McDaniel, P., Chaudhuri, S.: A Study of Android Application Security. In: Proceedings of the 20th USENIX Security Symposium (2011)
22. Strazzere, T.: Dex Education: Practicing Safe Dex, Blackhat, USA (2012)

23. Collberg, C., Nagra, J.: Surreptitious Software: Obfuscation, Watermarking, and Tamperproofing for Software Protection (2009) ISBN-13: 978-0321549259
24. Cypherpunks (mailing list archives), RC4 Source Code, http://cypherpunks.venona.com/archive/1994/09/msg00304.html
25. Batchelder, M.R.: Java Bytecode Obfuscation, Master Thesis, McGill University School of Computer Science, Montréal (2007)
26. Schulz, P.: Dalvik Bytecode Obfuscation on Android (2012), http://www.dexlabs.org/blog/bytecode-obfuscation
27. Reiss, D.: Under the Hood: Dalvik patch for Facebook for Android (2013), http://www.facebook.com/notes/facebook-engineering/under-the-hood-dalvik-patch-for-facebook-for-android/10151345597798920
28. Android Developers Website, http://developer.android.com/index.html
29. Bornstein, D.: Dalvik VM Internals (2008), https://sites.google.com/site/io/dalvik-vm-internals

Appendix

A Profiles of the Applications Selected for Testing

Table 5. Profiles of the test applications. The label abbreviations are identical to those in the case study of applications. The black bullet marks a presence of the criteria. The label MISC stands for "miscellaneous" and indicates notable app features. In the facebook app, CCL stands for the custom class loader.

APP	OBF	NAT	DYN	REF	CRY	MISC
com.adobe.reader.apk	0%	●	○	●	●	SD card
com.alensw.PicFolder.apk	100%	●	○	●	○	camera
com.disney.WMPLite.apk	5%	●	○	●	●	graphics
com.ebay.kr.gmarket.apk	0%	●	○	●	●	UTF-8 text
com.facebook.katana.apk	84%	●	●	●	●	CCL
com.microsoft.office.lync.apk	0%	●	○	●	●	phone calls
com.rebelvox.voxer.apk	0%	●	○	●	●	audio, SMS
com.skype.android.access.apk	0%	●	○	●	○	audio, video
com.teamlava.bubble.apk	0%	●	○	●	●	graphics
cz.aponia.bor3.czsk.apk	0%	●	○	●	○	GPS, maps
org.mozilla.firefox.apk	0%	●	●	●	●	internet
snt.luxtraffic.apk	0%	○	○	○	○	GPS, maps

B Memory Overhead Results

Table 6. Measuring the memory overhead of the transformations

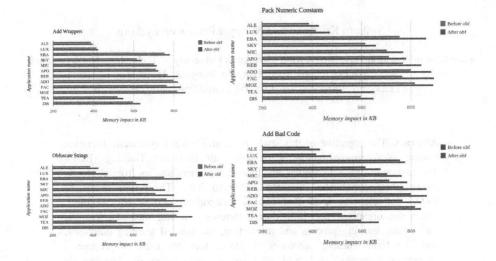

Identifying Factors Influencing Hybrid Self-regulated and Collaborative Learning: Toward an End-User Training Framework

Sirikorn Krompho and Nalinpat Porrawatpreyakorn

Faculty of Information Technology, King Mongkut's University of Technology North Bangkok
1518 Pracharat 1 Road, Bangsue, Bangkok, Thailand
sirikorn.k@nrru.ac.th, nalinpatp@kmutnb.ac.th

Abstract. The objective of this study is to undertake a systematic literature review to determine factors associated with End-User Training (EUT). The review analyzes 52 studies identified for primary studies from academic digital libraries published between 2003 and 2013. The results reveal 77 factors influciencing EUT that can be categorized into seven categories, which are organizational, individual difference, training methods, learning techniques, learning process and interaction, immediate learning outcomes, and long-term learning outcomes. These factors are used to propose a conceptual framework of hybrid self-regulated and collaborative learning for EUT that aims at improving performance of EUT.

Keywords: End-User Training, Self-Regulated Learning, Collaborative Learning, Factors.

1   Introduction

Nowadays Information Technology (IT) and the use of Information System (IS) in organizations are growing rapidly. In terms of software, End-User Training (EUT) is used for training and learning applications or ISs. Factors influencing EUT can be grouped into five categories, which consist of individual difference, needs assessments, training goals, training methods, and learning techniques [1]. However, it is important to study other factors that may be related to the hybrid of self-regulated learning and collaborative learning for EUT before designing and developing the EUT programs.

In this study, self-regulated learning is defined as self-managed learning behavior to acquire knowledge and skill for improving learning outcome. Collaborative learning is defined as collaborative knowledge sharing to achieve learning goal and facilitate transfer of training.

Accordingly, this review focuses on prior studies of EUT published between 2003 and 2013 to identify key success factors that influence hybrid self-regulated and collaborative learning for EUT, and to determine how to evaluate the effectiveness of EUT programs. This will be achieved through conducting Systematic Literature Review (SLR).

B. Papasratorn et al. (Eds.): IAIT 2013, CCIS 409, pp. 120–130, 2013.

2   Review Method

This study undertakes an SLR process based on the methods proposed by [2] and [3]. Initially, a review protocol was defined. The protocol provided a plan for the review in terms of the method to be followed, including the research questions, search strategy, inclusion and exclusion criteria, quality assessment, the data to be extracted, and data synthesis.

2.1   Research Questions

In our review, to investigate the effectiveness, evaluation and factors that influence EUT, we define three research questions as follows.

RQ1. What are training processes, training strategies, and training methods for end-user training and how are they applied?

RQ2. What are key success factors influencing hybrid self-regulated and collaborative learning for end-user training?

RQ3. What are measurements of hybrid self-regulated and collaborative learning for End-User Training?

2.2   Inclusion and Exclusion Criteria

In this phase, the criteria were identified to evaluated studies following the review by [2]. The inclusion criteria were as follows:

• The studies that were published between 2003 and 2013;
• Publications that describe empirical studies of any particular study design in EUT applied in any organization; and
• If several publications reported the same study, only the most complete publication was included.

The studies that met the following criteria were excluded from this review:

• Studies that did not report on the EUT;
• Theoretical studies related to the EUT; and
• Studies which have only an abstract available.

2.3   Data Sources and Search Strategy

Systematic search used keywords and search terms derived from the research questions. Strategies used to generate search terms in this review included:

• Major terms derived from the research question, i.e., population, intervention and outcomes;
• Keywords from the studies found;
• Alternative spellings and synonyms of key terms;
• Boolean OR was used with relevant terms; and
• Boolean AND was used to combine search terms from population, intervention and outcomes to limit search.

The designed search string for preliminary search was:

("end-user training" OR "training" OR "user training")AND ("training method" OR "factors") AND ("self-regulated learning" OR "collaborative learning") AND (year $\geq$ 2003 AND year $\leq$ 2013).

The search was conducted on seven digital libraries, namely: ACM Digital Library, SCOPUS, IEEE Xplore, ScienceDirect, ISI Web of Science, Emerald, and Google Scholar. Summary of digital library search is presented in Table 1.

Table 1. Digital library search

Digital library	Relevant	Not relevant	Total
ACM Portal	15	14	27
SCOPUS	13	46	59
IEEE Xplore	5	34	39
ScienceDirect	11	14	25
ISI Web of Science	1	10	11
Emerald	8	16	24
Google Scholar.	19	120	139
Totals	72 (52 excluding duplicates)	252	324

2.4   Selection of Primary Studies

Publication selection is a multistage process. At stage 1, the focus was on identification of relevant studies from the digital library search. At this stage, 324 studies that appeared to be completely irrelevant were excluded. Relevant citations from stage 1 were store in EndNote software to manage the number of reference that can be obtained from the literature search. The full list of studies was then import to Excel. At stage 2, initially selected primary studies were reviewed covering the title of each publication, the keywords associated with publication, and the abstract. At stage 3, the studies were reviewed again by applying the inclusion and exclusion criteria. At this stage, another 148 studies were excluded, which left 132 studies for the detailed quality assessment.

2.5   Quality Assessment

In the quality assessment phase, each primary study was assessed according to the 11 quality criteria based on a systematic review of empirical studies [3] presented in Table 2. Each of the 132 studies that remained after stage 3 was assessed with criteria covering three main issues: rigor, credibility, and relevance. We accepted a study graded "yes" or "1" on studies that pass our quality assessment.

Table 2. Summary of the quality assessment criteria [3]

Main issues	Quality criteria	Description
Minimum Quality Threshold	1. Is the paper based on research? 2. Is there a clear statement of the aims of the research? 3. Is there an adequate description of the context in which the research was carried out?	The publication appropriately describes the aims and the detail of research.
Rigor	4. Was the research design appropriate to address the aims of the research? 5. Was the recruitment strategy appropriate to the aims of the research? 6. Was there a control group with which to compare treatments? 7. Was the data collected in a way that addressed the research issue? 8. Was the data analysis sufficiently rigorous?	The publication appropriately research design and data analysis.
Credibility	9. Has the relationship between researcher and participants been considered to an adequate degree? 10. Is there a clear statement of the findings?	The publication describes a clear relation between researchers and participants and clearly presents findings.
Relevance	11. Is the study of value for research or practice?	The publication describes values for research and/or practice.

2.6   Data Extraction and Synthesis

In this step, a data extraction form was design based on [2] and [3] to extract data from the publications. The 52 publications that passed the quality assessment were reviewed to record details into the form for further analysis. The results from all the finding of primary studies were tabulated and summarized to answer the research questions. Tabulated results are also useful to identify current research gaps. These results are presented in the next section.

3   Results and Discussion

The following sections present the findings, discuss the results in the context of the research questions, identify gaps and point directions toward future research. Totally, 52 studies remained after the quality assessment process and data were extracted to answer our three research questions.

3.1   Research Question 1

Our first research question is "What are training processes, training strategies, and training methods for End-User Training and how are they applied?" Training and learning process can be developed for specific training methods involves with technology-support learning [4] and technology-mediated learning [5, 6] . It was found that individuals learn in different ways. Self-regulated learning strategies let to better outcomes in learning to use systems [7]. Training and learning strategies are an important part of the training method, which is composed of types of IT tools and types of trainees [8]. Learning techniques that applied to End-User Training are behavior-modeling method [9] , vicarious and enactive learning [5].

3.2   Research Question 2

Our second research question is "What are key success factors influencing hybrid self-regulated and collaborative learning for End-User Training?" In relevance to this question, some studies proposed a number of other factors related to EUT. They can be grouped into seven categories, which are organizational, individual difference, training methods, learning techniques, learning process and interactions (i.e., virtual interaction), immediate learning outcomes, and long-term learning outcomes Summary of factors influencing to EUT from the review are presented in Table 3.

Organizational factors refer to factors that are related to the improvement of organizational performance through training. Individual difference factors refer to the difference of capability of each individual that affects to EUT. At present, training methods consist of training methods based on social cognitive theory and technology-mediated learning to improve learning outcomes. Learning techniques factors refer to human learning behaviors. Learning process and interactions refers to the enhancement of learning system emphasizing on individual aptitude that can increase learner's satisfaction. Immediate learning outcomes refer to perceived knowledge and skill after training. Finally, long-term learning outcomes refer to the expected outcomes of the training that may also lead to further transfers of skill and knowledge acquired from the training.

Table 3. Factors of EUT from the review

Categories	Factors	Studies
Organizational	Organizational support, Perceived benefits/cost, Organizational readiness, External pressures , Firm's management support, Supervisory support, Training needs/requirements, Training organization, and organizational training efforts	[4, 10-16]
Individual differences	Self-efficacy, Computer self-efficacy, Mastery orientation, Computer anxiety, Learning goal orientation, Learning styles, Attitudes towards the system, Pre-training motivation, Prior experience, Motivation to Transfer, Self-regulated learning, Outcome expectancies, Motivation perspective, Traits	[5, 7, 9, 10, 12-15, 17-37]
Training methods	Instructor-led training, Online training, Technology-mediated Learning, Web-based training, Exploration-based training, Behavior modeling training, Technology training, Simulator, Mentor, and Hybrid	[4, 5, 7, 9, 14, 19, 20, 27, 30, 31, 36, 38-43]
Learning techniques	behavior-modeling method, self-regulated learning, vicarious learning, enactive learning, cooperative or collaborative learning	[5, 7, 9, 30, 32, 33]
Learning process and interaction	learner interface, interaction, learning climate, faithfulness of technology use, meta-cognitive activity, faithfulness, attitude, attitude-respect of technology, learning effects, assessment skills, assessment process, learning process, training process	[6, 18-20, 24, 25, 30, 31, 34]
Immediate learning outcomes	satisfaction, learning performance, technology self-efficacy in ERP system usage, learning achievement, declarative knowledge, procedural knowledge, level of knowledge, skill, cognition, affection	[5, 7, 18-20, 22, 30, 44]
Long-term learning outcomes	perceived ease of use, perceived usefulness, enjoyment, intention to use, transfer of training, adoption, perceived skill retention, transfer implementation intentions, transfer-enhancing activities, technical support, system usage, post-training support, training utilization, performance expectancy, effort expectancy, learning and skill transfer	[5, 12, 17, 18, 27-30, 34, 40, 45-49]

3.3   Research Question 3

Our last research question is "What are measurements of hybrid self-regulated and collaborative learning for End-User Training?" According studies relevant to this question, end-user training evaluation classifying into five levels, which consist of technology (usefulness of technology i.e., the delivery and the presentation of training materials and communication tools), reaction (the satisfaction toward training i.e., relevance of the course to the trainee's job and quality of instruction), skill acquisition (acquisition of knowledge or skills), skill transfer (the ability to apply skill learned at work for improving job performance), and organizational effect (improvements in individual or organizational outcomes and trainers) [49]. These five levels help to explicitly distinguish between skill acquisition and skill transfer [44]. In addition, training effectiveness involve post-training support [46], and measurement of learning process [5].

4   A Proposed Framework

A proposed conceptual framework of hybrid self-regulated and collaborative learning for EUT consists of three processes, which are pre-training, training and learning, and post-training as presented in Fig. 1. The proposed framework aims at supporting software/application learning by self-regulation and collaboration.

In Fig. 1, the pre-training process is composed of the analyses of the characteristics of the software and of the end-users participating in the training. The analyses of factors, including computer self-efficacy and other individual's factors affecting computer self-efficacy, are to determine the training goals and the factors for the training and learning process.

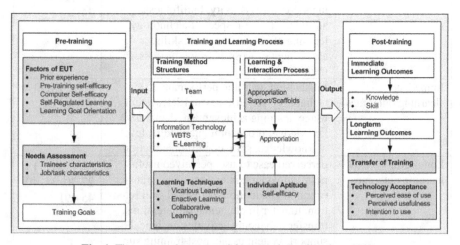

Fig. 1. The proposed conceptual framework (applied from [30])

The training and learning process is composed of training methods involving organizing team and information technologies appropriate for the training. For example, training may utilize technology to support the learning techniques such as vicarious learning and collaborative learning. The learning and interaction process utilizes a support system for appropriation by prioritizing individual aptitude.

The post-training process involves the improvement of learning methods and interaction processes based on immediate learning outcomes and long-term learning outcomes. The technology acceptance model is finally used to evaluate the proposed hybrid self-regulated and collaborative learning framework.

5   Conclusion

This paper presents an SLR on factors influencing hybrid self-regulated and collaborative learning for EUT. In conclusion, 324 studies were identified from the literature search, of which 52 satisfied the quality assessment. The results show 77 influential factors that help when developing training support tools to increase the effectiveness of IT/IS applications and their impacts on the work of personnel within organizations. These factors are groups into seven categories and used to propose a conceptual framework of hybrid self-regulated and collaborative Learning for EUT. The framework aims at contributing to the improvement of EUT performance. The next step of this study is to build the framework.

Acknowledgements. The authors would like to thank the Higher Education Research Promotion (HERP) of the Higher Education Commission of Thailand for supporting this work in the form of a scholarship.

References

1. Sirikorn, K., Nalinpat, P., Montean, R.: A Conceptual Model of Factors Influencing in Hybrid Self-Regulated and Collaborative Learning for End-User Training. In: The 6th National Conference and 2nd Internatinal Conference on Applied Computer Technology and Information Systems 2013, Nonthaburi,Thailand, pp. 144–149 (2013)
2. Turner, M., et al.: Does the technology acceptance model predict actual use? A systematic literature review. Information and Software Technology 52(5), 463–479 (2010)
3. Dybå, T., Dingsøyr, T.: Empirical studies of agile software development: A systematic review. Information and Software Technology 50(9), 833–859 (2008)
4. LeRouge, C., Webb, H.: Managing training in a technology context. In: Proceedings of the 2003 SIGMIS Conference on Computer Personnel Research: Freedom in Philadelphia–Leveraging Differences and Diversity in the IT Workforce 2003, pp. 98–103. ACM, Philadelphia (2003)
5. Gupta, S., Bostrom, R.P.: Achieving end-user training effectiveness through web-based training systems: An empirical study, Hyderabad (2009)
6. Sein, M.K., Nordheim, S.: Learning processes in user training: the case for hermeneutics. In: Proceedings of the 2010 Special Interest Group on Management Information System's 48th Annual Conference on Computer Personnel Research on Computer Personnel Research 2010, pp. 105–111. ACM, Vancouver (2010)

7. Gravill, J., Compeau, D.: Self-regulated learning strategies and software training. Information & Management 45(5), 288–296 (2008)
8. Coulson, T., et al.: ERP training strategies: conceptual training and the formation of accurate mental models. In: Proceedings of the 2003 SIGMIS Conference on Computer Personnel Research: Freedom in Philadelphia–leveraging Differences and Diversity in the IT Workforce 2003, pp. 87–97. ACM, Philadelphia (2003)
9. Chen, C.C., Ryan, T., Olfman, L.: The efficacy of behavior modeling: A comparison of face-to-face and online asynchronous software-training methods. In: Proceedings of the 37th Annual Hawaii International Conference on System Sciences. IEEE (2004)
10. Arasanmi, C.N., Wang, W.Y., Singh, H.: Motivational Determinants of Training Utilisation in Enterprise Systems (2012)
11. Chan, S.C., Ngai, E.W.: A qualitative study of information technology adoption: how ten organizations adopted Web-based training. Information Systems Journal 17(3), 289–315 (2007)
12. Govindarajulu, N.: Transfer climate in end-user computing: The influence of trainee characteristics and supervisory support. Journal of Advances in Management Research 6(1), 87–98 (2009)
13. Olfman, L., Bostrom, R.P., Sein, M.K.: A best-practice based model for information technology learning strategy formulation. In: Proceedings of the 2003 SIGMIS Conference on Computer Personnel Research: Freedom in Philadelphia–Leveraging Differences and Diversity in the IT Workforce 2003, pp. 75–86. ACM, Philadelphia (2003)
14. Scott, J.E., Walczak, S.: Cognitive engagement with a multimedia ERP training tool: Assessing computer self-efficacy and technology acceptance. Information & Management 46(4), 221–232 (2009)
15. Norton, A.L., et al.: Delivering training for highly demanding information systems. European Journal of Training and Development 36(6), 646–662 (2012)
16. Rondeau, P.J., Ragu-Nathan, T., Vonderembse, M.A.: The Impact of IS Planning Effectiveness on IS Responsiveness, User Training, and User Skill Development within Manufacturing Firms (2010)
17. Chatzoglou, P.D., et al.: Investigating Greek employees' intention to use web-based training. Computers & Education 53(3), 877–889 (2009)
18. Cheng-Hua, W., Lu-Wen, L., Yi-Ying, C.: The effect of ERP software interface design and cognitive function on performance of user learning. In: 2011 IEEE International Conference on Service Operations, Logistics, and Informatics, SOLI (2011)
19. Choi, D.H., Kim, J., Kim, S.H.: ERP training with a web-based electronic learning system: The flow theory perspective. International Journal of Human-Computer Studies 65(3), 223–243 (2007)
20. Chou, S.-W., Liu, C.-H.: Learning effectiveness in web-based technology-mediated virtual learning environment. In: Proceedings of the 38th Annual Hawaii International Conference on System Sciences, HICSS 2005. IEEE (2005)
21. De Waal, B.M.E., Batenburg, R.: What makes end-user training successful? A mixed method study of a business process management system implementation. International Journal of Knowledge and Learning 8(1-2), 166–183 (2012)
22. Gravill, J.I., Compeau, D.R., Marcolin, B.L.: Experience effects on the accuracy of self-assessed user competence. Information & Management 43(3), 378–394 (2006)
23. Gripenberg, P.: Computer self-efficacy in the information society Design of learning strategies, mechanisms and skill areas. Information Technology & People 24(3), 303–331 (2011)

24. Hardin, A.M., Looney, C.A., Fuller, M.A.: Self-efficacy, learning method appropriation and software skills acquisition in learner-controlled CSSTS environments. Information Systems Journal (2013)
25. Johnson, R.D., Gueutal, H., Falbe, C.M.: Technology, trainees, metacognitive activity and e-learning effectiveness. Journal of Managerial Psychology 24(6), 545–566 (2009)
26. Johnson, R.D.: An empirical investigation of sources of application-specific computer-self-efficacy and mediators of the efficacy-performance relationship. International Journal of Human-Computer Studies 62(6), 737–758 (2005)
27. Liegle, J.O., Janicki, T.N.: The effect of learning styles on the navigation needs of Web-based learners. Computers in Human Behavior 22(5), 885–898 (2006)
28. Machin, M.A., Fogarty, G.: Perceptions of Training-Related Factors and Personal Variables as Predictors of Transfer Implementation Intentions. Journal of Business and Psychology 18(1), 51–71 (2003)
29. Sánchez, R.A., Hueros, A.D., Ordaz, M.G.: E-learning and the University of Huelva: A study of WebCT and the Technological Acceptance Model. Campus-Wide Information Systems 30(2), 5–5 (2013)
30. Gupta, S., Bostrom, R.P., Anson, R.: Do I matter?: the impact of individual differences on training process. In: Proceedings of the 2010 Special Interest Group on Management Information System's 48th Annual Conference on Computer Personnel Research on Computer Personnel Research, pp. 112–120. ACM, Vancouver (2010)
31. Soh, P., Subramanian, A.M.: Is Usage a Missing Link in Explaining the Perceived Learning Outcome of Technology-Mediated Learning. IEEE Transactions on Engineering Management 55(1), 50–66 (2008)
32. Tavakolizadeh, J., Ebrahimi-Qavam, S.: Effect of teaching of self-regulated learning strategies on self-efficacy in students. Procedia - Social and Behavioral Sciences 29, 1096–1104 (2011)
33. Yusuf, M.: Investigating relationship between self-efficacy, achievement motivation, and self-regulated learning strategies of undergraduate Students: A study of integrated motivational models. Procedia - Social and Behavioral Sciences 15, 2614–2617 (2011)
34. Marshall, B., Mills, R., Olsen, D.: The Role Of End-User Trainin. In: Technology Acceptance. Review of Business Information Systems (RBIS) 12(2), 1–8 (2008)
35. Mun, Y.Y., Im, K.S.: The role of personal goal and self-efficacy in predicting computer task performance. In: Advanced Topics in End User Computing, p. 65 (2005)
36. Noguera, J.H., Watson, E.F.: Effectiveness of using an enterprise system to teach process-centered concepts in business education. Journal of Enterprise Information Management 17(1), 56–74 (2004)
37. Eyitayo, O.T.: Do students have the relevant ICT skills they need to do their research projects. In: Proceedings of the 2011 Conference on Information Technology Education, pp. 287–292. ACM, West Point (2011)
38. Vucinich, C.L.: Online training @ duke: technology training - anytime, anywhere. In: Proceedings of the 38th Annual ACM SIGUCCS Fall Conference, pp. 127–130. ACM, Norfolk (2010)
39. Sperl, G.: Establishing and delivering training for the Zimbra collaboration suite. In: Proceedings of the 37th Annual ACM SIGUCCS Fall Conference 2009, pp. 163–166. ACM, St. Louis (2009)
40. Henneke, M., Matthee, M.: The adoption of e-Learning in corporate training environments: an activity theory based overview. In: Proceedings of the South African Institute for Computer Scientists and Information Technologists Conference. ACM (2012)

41. Palumbo, J., Becchi, M., Way, S.: ULearn more: transitioning to a learning management system for staff at American University. In: Proceedings of the 40th Annual ACM SIGUCCS Conference 2012, pp. 189–192. ACM, Memphis (2012)
42. Kaplan-Mor, N., Glezer, C., Zviran, M.: A comparative analysis of end-user training methods. Journal of Systems and Information Technology 13(1), 25–42 (2011)
43. Palvia, S.C.J., Palvia, P.C.: The effectiveness of using computers for software training: an exploratory study. Journal of Information Systems Education 18(4), 479 (2007)
44. Sein, M.K., Simonsen, M.: Effective training: applying frameworks to practice. In: Proceedings of the 2006 ACM SIGMIS CPR Conference on Computer Personnel Research: Forty Four Years of Computer Personnel Research: Achievements, Challenges the Future 2006, pp. 137–146. ACM, Claremont (2006)
45. Marler, J.H., Liang, X., Dulebohn, J.H.: Training and effective employee information technology use. Journal of Management 32(5), 721–743 (2006)
46. Snoddy Jr S., Novick, D.G.: Post-training support for learning technology. In: Proceedings of the 22nd Annual International Conference on Design of Communication: The Engineering of Quality Documentation. ACM (2004)
47. Sujatha, H., Murthy, H.S.: End-user training on the utilization of electronic information sources in fisheries sciences institutions in South India. The Electronic Library 28(5), 741–754 (2010)
48. Velada, R., et al.: The effects of training design, individual characteristics and work environment on transfer of training. International Journal of Training and Development 11(4), 282–294 (2007)
49. Mahapatra, R., Lai, V.S.: Evaluating end-user training programs. Commun. ACM 48(1), 66–70 (2005)

Effect of Training Sample on Reconstructing 3D Face Shapes from Feature Points

Ashraf Y.A. Maghari[1], Ibrahim Venkat[1], Iman Yi Liao[2], and Bahari Belaton[1]

[1] School of Computer Sciences, Universiti Sains Malaysia, Penang, Malaysia
myashraf2@gmail.com
[2] School of Computer Science, University of Nottingham Malaysia Campus

Abstract. Statistical learning models are recognized as important emerging methodologies in the area of data reconstruction. The learning models are trained from a set of examples to reach a state where the model will be able to predict the correct output for other examples. PCA-based statistical modeling is a popular technique for modeling 3D faces, which can be used for 3D face reconstruction. The capability of 3D face leaning models in depicting new 3D faces can be considered as the representational power (RP) of the model. This paper focuses on examining the effect of the sample size (number of training faces) on the accuracy of the 3D face shape reconstruction from a small set of feature points. It also aims to visualize the effect of the training sample size on the RP of PCA-based models. Experiments were designed and carried out on testing and training data of the USF Human ID 3D database. We found that although the representational power increases with a larger training sample size, the accuracy of reconstruction is limited by the number of the feature points used. This means that by reconstructing faces from a limited number of feature points, a definite number of examples are sufficient to build a satisfactory 3D face model.

Keywords: 3D face Reconstruction, Sample size, statistical face modeling, PCA, Regularization.

1   Introduction

The problem of reconstructing 3D objects, such as human faces, from 2D image coordinates of a small set of feature points is a partially solved problem. In addition to the interpolation between the sparse points, the 2D projection of 3D points into the image plane is considered as an underconstrained problem [1]. The presence of 3D scanning technology leads to create a more accurate 3D face model examples [2]. Examples-based modeling allows a more realistically face reconstruction than other methods [3], [4]. Reconstructing a complete 3D face shape vector from a few number of feature points is considered as an ill-posed problem. In order to solve this problem, prior knowledge about the face shape objects is required. 3D Morphable Model (3D MM) [5] provides a prior knowledge about the object class of the face shapes such that any new face shape can be estimated from a few number of feature points. In order to estimate the complete face shape from a limited number of feature points, Tikhonov

B. Papasratorn et al. (Eds.): IAIT 2013, CCIS 409, pp. 131–140, 2013.
© Springer International Publishing Switzerland 2013

regularization can be utilized [6]. The regularized algorithm that uses the 3D Morphable Model has been presented in [1] and [7]. However, they did not study how the training sample affects the reconstruction. This study aims to explain how a training sample size affects the accuracy of 3D face shape reconstruction from a small set of feature points. It also visualizes the effect of the sample size on the Representational Power (RP) of the PCA-based model. RP of the PCA-based model has been studied by [8] in terms of the accuracy of representing new face shapes. However, no experiments were conducted to find out how a sample size affects the accuracy of reconstructing training and testing 3D face shapes from a few number of feature points. Also, the RP of the models was not visualized in terms of displaying represented 3D face shapes. USF Human ID 3D database which contains 100 face scans has been used to train and test PCA-model.

The current study is organized as follows: Statistical 3D face modeling is introduced in Section 2, whereas in Section 3 the Representational Power of PCA models have been explained. The Experiments are explained in Section 4. The findings and the discussion are reported in section 5. The last section summarizes the paper.

2   Statistical 3D Face Modeling

Statistical learning models are trained from a set of examples to reach a state where the model will be able to predict the correct output for other examples. Principle Component Analysis (PCA) can be considered as standard statistical model where a representation of face shapes are provided such that any realistic face can be a linear combination of face vectors (e. g. 3DMM [5]). The 3D shapes are aligned with each other in such a way that 3D-3D correspondence for all vertices are obtained [5]. The p number of vertices corresponding to each face is defined by concatenating the xyz coordinates of the face surface to a single vector s_i with the dimension $n = 3 \times p$ as:

$$s_i = (x_{i1}, y_{i1}, z_{i1}, ..., x_{ip}, y_{ip}, z_{ip})^T , \tag{1}$$

where $i = 1,...,m$ (number of face shapes). Let $X = [x_1, x_2, ..., x_m]^T \in R^{m \times n}$ is the data matrix with each vector $x_i = s_i - s_0$ is centered around the mean s_0. PCA is then applied on the covariance matrix. As a result of the analysis, a new shape vector $s_{rec} \in R^n$ can be expressed as

$$s_{rec} = s_0 + E\alpha = s_0 + \sum_{i=1}^{m} \alpha_i e_i , \tag{2}$$

where $E = (e_1, e_2, ..., e_m)$ is the matrix of scaled basis vectors, α_i is the coefficient of the scaled basis vector e_i. Since E is an orthogonal matrix, the PCA-coefficients α of a vector $x = s - s_0 \in R^n$ can be derived from Eq. (2) as

$$\alpha = E^T x . \tag{3}$$

2.1   3D Face Shape Reconstruction from Feature Points

Prior knowledge about object classes such as 3D faces can help to solve the ill-posed problem of reconstructing a complete 3D face from small set of feature points. PCA-based models are holistic models that can be employed as prior knowledge to represent 3D face objects in order to obtain meaningful reconstruction results. However, in our case where the training data set are relatively small and there is too much missing feature in the testing data, the PCA model cannot be adapted to the particular set of feature points resulting in overfitting. Therefore, regularization can be used to enforce the result to be plausible according to the prior knowledge [9].

Given a number of feature points $f \ll p$, our problem is to find the 3D coordinates of all other vertices. Assume that $s_f \in R^l (l = 2f)$, s_{0f} is the corresponding points on s_0 (the average 3D face shape) and $x_f = s_f - s_{0f}$ is related to A such that

$$x_f = Ar + \varepsilon, \qquad A : R^m \mapsto R^l, \tag{4}$$

where $r \in R^m$ is the model parameter, $A \in R^{l \times m}$ is the corresponding subset of the matrix of scaled basis vectors $E^T \in R^{n \times m}$ and $\varepsilon \in R^l$ can be considered as measurement errors with unknown properties. Eventually, the goal is to estimate r as accurate as possible, given A and x_f. A simple least square technique can be used to solve the inverse problem as

$$r = (A^T A)^{-1} A^T x_f. \tag{5}$$

In this study, the selected feature points x_f captures only a very small portion of the original 3D face shape x. Hence, regularization is used as a constraint that utilizes the possible features in the holistic model to produce plausible results. The standard Tikhonov regularization enables an approximate solution which can be written as

$$r_{reg} = (A^T A + \lambda I)^{-1} A^T x_f. \tag{6}$$

As the original data matrix X is a multivariate normal distribution, and the errors in x_f are assumed to be independent with zero mean and same standard deviation σ of the original data, the Tikhonov-regularized solution is the most probable solution according to Bayes' theorem [6]. In order to ensure that the solution will be in the boundary of the learning model, the stabilizing item was chosen to be the inverse of the diagonal eigenvalue matrix W. The model parameter α can be estimated as

$$\hat{\alpha} = (A^T A + \lambda W^{-1})^{-1} A^T x_f. \tag{7}$$

Then, a new face shape srec can be obtained by applying $\hat{\alpha}$ to Eq. (2). Jiang et al. [10] have used the same regularization equation in an iterative procedure in order to converge to a stable solution. Similar to [11], the shape coefficients in this paper are calculated directly using Eq. (7).

2.2   Reconstruction of Testing and Training Face Shapes

The 3D face shapes in the database are already aligned with each other as explained by [5]. Therefore, we first selected a number of feature vertices from one reference 3D face. Then, the indices of the selected vertices were used to directly select the correspondences of the feature vertices from the other training/testing face shapes. The feature vertices were formed by salient points such as nose-tip and eyes corners. We used only the xy coordinates of the feature points to calculate the 3D shape coefficients α using Eq. (7). This procedure serves to set the ground to conduct further studies wherein 3D shapes can be reconstructed from 2D images. The resulting α is incorporated in Eq. (3) to reconstruct the complete 3D face shape. The reconstructed face can be compared with original face by using Eq. (8).

3   Representational Power of PCA Models

The Representational Power (RP) of the PCA-based model was defined in [8] in terms of the capability in depicting a new 3D face of a given input face image. The capability of the PCA model can be measured by evaluating the quality of face representation with respect to its ground-truth. The sum of the Euclidean distances over all vertices of the shapes weighted by the number of vertices was used to compare 3D surfaces:

$$Ed_w = \frac{\sum_{i=1}^{n}\sqrt{(s_i - s_{ri})^2}}{n} , \tag{8}$$

where Ed_w is the weighted Euclidean distance, s is the probe face shape, s_r is the represented face shape, and n is the number of vertices of the face shape. Fig. 1 demonstrates the relationship between the sample size and the average of Ed_w of all testing faces (RP-mean). It shows that the average representation error (RP-mean) of the PCA-model decreases with a larger training-sample size. Further details regarding the RP are provided in [8].

Furthermore, the current work demonstrates the advantage of RP in terms of visualizing the quality of reconstruction (see Fig. 2). A new face shape is projected to PCA-based models learned from different dataset sizes. As one can see in Fig. 2, the face representation gets less noisy and more realistic when Ed_w decreases. This means that the PCA model that represents a new 3D face with less Ed_w has more RP. However, this relation depends on projecting all face vertices to the PCA-models trained with different sample sizes. In this case the inverse system is overdetermined whereas the face shape vectors have the dimension 227916 which is very large compared with the degrees of freedom of the PCA-models (10 - 90). When 3D shapes are reconstructed from small set of feature points, the inverse system is undetermined. Therefore, this work studies the effect of sample size on reconstructing 3D faces from a small set of feature points.

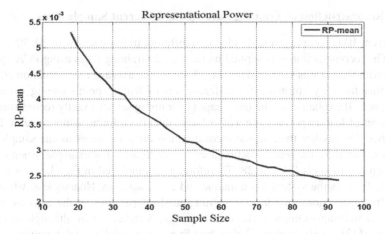

Fig. 1. The relation between the sample size and the average representation error (RP-mean) of the PCA-model [8]

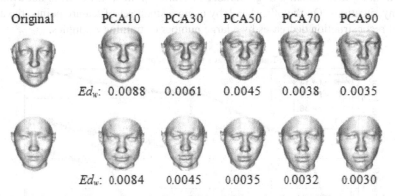

Fig. 2. Projecting the leftmost face shape to PCA models trained with different sample sizes. The Ed_w that represent the projection errors are shown below the shapes. PCA10 means the training set has 10 examples; PCA30 means the training set has 30 examples and so on.

4 Experiments

To assess the effect of the training sample size on the accuracy of 3D face shape reconstruction, we varied the number of examples in the training set. Then we selected sets of $f = 14, 25, 38$ and 78 2D feature points from the reference 3D face. These feature points were formed using salient points such as nose-tip and eyes corners. The accuracy of reconstruction was evaluated by calculating the Ed_w (Eq. (8)) of the resulted 3D face compared with that of the original 3D face shape. The USF Raw 3D Face Data Set [5] was used in the evaluation since it contains 3D faces that can be numerically compared with the reconstructed 3D face shapes. It was used for both training and testing purposes. The USF database contains 100 3D faces obtained by using Cyberware head and face 3D color scanner. Each face shape has 75972 vertices saved in a text file, one line per vertex and 3 points each line.

4.1   Reconstruction of Training Faces Using Different Sample Sizes

The current 100 examples were divided into different training sets with 20, 30, ..., 100 faces. The reconstruction was applied on the first 20 training faces using PCA models trained with the various sample sizes. Fig. 3 shows the average reconstruction error of 20 training faces by optimal λ for different sets of feature points among variety of training sets. It explains that the face shapes of training set are exactly reconstructed if the number of feature points f is equal or larger than the training sample size m. However when f is smaller than m, the reconstruction error increases as the sample size increases, and, thus, the reconstruction accuracy decreases. For example, when $f = 14$, the dimension of sf is $l = 2f = 28$. Therefore, as exemplified in Fig. 3, when sample size $m < 28$ faces the system has a unique and exact solution. Nonetheless, when $m > 28$, the reconstruction error increases dramatically depending on the increase in the number of training examples. The results in Fig. 3 indicate that although many researchers ([12], [13]) confirmed that building a powerful model requires a large amount of 3D faces, yet a large number of feature points is needed to reconstruct the exact training face. Such a large number of feature points, however, is not available in many situations. On the other hand, by using a small set of feature points, the accuracy of reconstruction decreases by a large number of training examples.

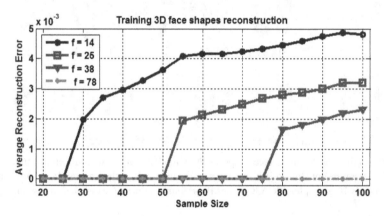

Fig. 3. Average reconstruction error of training faces form different sets of feature points among variation of sample sizes

Fig. 4 visualizes examples of reconstructed training faces for different sample sizes using 14 feature points. The figure demonstrates that the reconstruction error increases with a large sample size (e.g., 80 and 100), while the smaller sample size (e.g., 20 and 40) produces a more accurate reconstruction. For example, the exact 3D face has been reconstructed by using only 20 training face shapes. This is because the dimension of the feature point vector ($14 \times 2 = 28$) is greater than 20 (degrees of freedom).

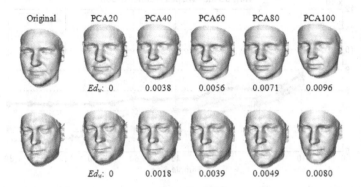

Fig. 4. Reconstruction of training 3D face shapes from 14 feature points using different sample sizes. The results depend on the optimal λ which produces the minimum Ed_w.

4.2   Reconstruction of New Faces Using Different Sample Sizes

To assess the effect of sample size on reconstructing new 3D faces, we varied the number of training examples from 5 to 80 as a sequence of 5, 10, 15, ..., 80. Then the remaining 20 of the 100 3D faces were used for testing. Fig. 5 shows the average reconstruction error of 20 testing faces for three different sets of feature points using various sample sizes. The figure shows that as the number of training examples increases the accuracy of reconstruction increases until $m > f$. Then, the accuracy of reconstruction is relatively the same in all cases and is further associated with slight improvements depending on the sample size and the number of feature points. This indicates that a large training sample size may be needed to build a powerful statistical model. This finding is consistent with the comments made by [12], [13]. Furthermore, the findings revealed that the number of feature points should also be considered in building statistical reconstruction models. The sample size, however, should not be excessively larger than the number of feature points; an extremely larger sample size may unfeasible because it consumes time and exerts no more positive effect on the reconstruction accuracy.

On contrary, a small sample size (e.g. 20 faces) may hardly reconstruct new 3D faces even by using a large set of feature points for the reconstruction. The visualized results in Fig. 6 show examples of reconstructed faces for optimal λ using different sample sizes. It demonstrates that by small sample sizes (e. g. 20, 40), the reconstructed face shape is excessively smooth (closer to the mean face and farther from the ground truth) while the larger sample sizes (e.g. 60, 80, and 99) produce more accurate faces with relatively same accuracy.

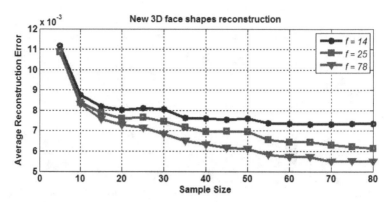

Fig. 5. Reconstructing new 3D faces from sets of feature points using different sample sizes

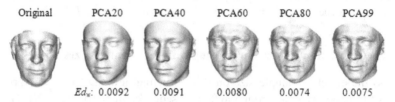

Fig. 6. Reconstruction of novel 3D face shapes from 25 feature points using different sample sizes. The results depend on the optimal λ which produces the minimum Ed_w.

5   Findings and Discussion

For reconstructing training 3D faces, the training faces were exactly recovered with a number of feature points greater than or equal the sample size. However, when a smaller constant number of feature points were used, the accuracy of reconstructed faces decreased as the training sample size increased (Fig. 3). This means that, even if the representational power of the PCA-based model increases by a larger data set [8], reconstructing the exact training faces by small set of feature points becomes more difficult.

On the other hand, when new 3D faces are reconstructed, the reconstruction accuracy can be optimally increased by a larger data set to a specific degree when it cannot increase any more. Furthermore, in some cases the reconstruction accuracy may decrease because the number of feature points becomes extremely smaller than the degree of freedom of the model. Therefore, when building a statistical model for the purpose of reconstructing 3D faces from feature points, the number of feature points has to be considered. Else, with a larger sample size the computation of the reconstruction system can be increased and the accuracy may be negatively affected. On contrary, a small sample size (e.g. 20 faces) may hardly reconstruct new 3D faces even by using a large set of feature points for the reconstruction.

Furthermore, in practice the number of facial feature points (landmarks) on the 2D face image is limited; it is impractical to select a very large number of feature points. As a conclusion of this paper and according to the recent study on the effect of facial feature points on the 3D face reconstruction [14], a minimum number of feature points that can be used for reconstruction should not be much smaller than half of the training examples, i.e., the dimension of the feature point vector should not be much smaller than the degree of freedom of the model. An optimal reconstruction may be achieved if the dimension of the feature point vector is larger than the number of training faces (degree of freedom of the model). Generally, the reconstruction accuracy depends on the size of the 3D face database as well as the available number of 2D facial points.

Moreover, according to the extensive experiment on the USF database, a minimum number of 80 training faces may produce a plausible 3D face reconstruction by using more than 25 feature points.

6   Conclusion

The effect of training sample size used for building a PCA-based model has been studied. The accuracy of reconstruction was evaluated with a series of experiments by analyzing the 3D face database obtained from University South Florida (USF). The current USF Human ID 3D database has 100 faces. For reconstructing training 3D faces, all the 100 faces were used for training and testing. However, for reconstructing new 3D faces, 80 faces have been used for training and 20 for testing. Tikhonov regularization algorithm was employed to reconstruct 3D faces from small sets of feature points using various PCA-based models trained with different sample sizes. The extensive experimental results showed that if the testing face is from the training set, then a limited number of points can only reconstruct the exact solution if the sample size is smaller than the number of points used. If the testing face does not belong to the training set, it may hardly reconstruct the exact 3D face using 3D PCA-based models. However, it could reconstruct an approximate face depending on the sample size and the number of feature points. Although the representational power of the PCA model increases with a larger training sample size, the accuracy of reconstruction, however, is limited by the number of the feature points used. This means that by reconstructing faces from a small set of feature points, a limited set of examples is sufficient to build a satisfactory 3D face model.

Acknowledgments. The first author would like to thank Ministry of Higher Education, Malaysia for supporting him with the MIS scholarship. This research is also partly supported by RU Grant 1001/PKCOMP/817055 (Universiti Sains Malaysia).

References

1. Blanz, V., Mehl, A., Vetter, T., Seidel, H.-P.: A Statistical Method for Robust 3D Surface Reconstruction from Sparse Data. In: Proceedings of the 2nd International Symposium on 3D Data Processing, Visualization, and Transmission. IEEE Computer Society (2004)
2. Luximon, Y., Ball, R., Justice, L.: The 3D Chinese head and face modeling. Computer-Aided Design 44, 40–47 (2012)

3. Widanagamaachchi, W.N., Dharmaratne, A.T.: 3D Face Reconstruction from 2D Images. In: Digital Image Computing: Techniques and Applications, DICTA 2008, pp. 365–371. IEEE (2008)

4. Martin, D.L., Yingfeng, Y.: State-of-the-art of 3D facial reconstruction methods for face recognition based on a single 2D training image per person. Pattern Recogn. Lett. 30, 908–913 (2009)

5. Blanz, V., Vetter, T.: A morphable model for the synthesis of 3D faces. Proceedings of the 26th Annual Conference on Computer Graphics and Interactive Techniques, pp. 187-194. ACM Press/Addison-Wesley Publishing Co (1999)

6. Vogel, C.R.: Computational methods for inverse problems. SIAM (2002)

7. Blanz, V., Vetter, T.: Reconstructing the Complete 3D Shape of Faces from Partial Information (Rekonstruktion der dreidimensionalen Form von Gesichtern aus partieller Information. it+ti - Informationstechnik und Technische Informatik 295–302 (2002)

8. Maghari, A., Liao, I., Belaton, B.: Quantitative analysis on PCA-based statistical 3D face shape modeling. In: Computational Modelling of Objects Represented in Images III, vol. null, pp. 13–18. CRC Press (2012)

9. Knothe, R., Romdhani, S., Vetter, T.: Combining PCA and LFA for surface reconstruction from a sparse set of control points. In: Proceedings of the Seventh International Conference on Automatic Face and Gesture Recognition, pp. 637–642 (2006)

10. Jiang, D., Hu, Y., Yan, S., Zhang, L., Zhang, H., Gao, W.: Efficient 3D reconstruction for face recognition. Pattern Recognition 38, 787–798 (2005)

11. Maghari, A.Y., Venkat, I., Liao, I.Y., Belaton, B.: PCA-based Reconstruction of 3D Face shapes using Tikhonov Regularization. Int. J. Advance. Soft Comput. Appl. 5 (2013)

12. Kemelmacher-Shlizerman, I., Basri, R.: 3d face reconstruction from a single image using a single reference face shape. IEEE Transactions on Pattern Analysis and Machine Intelligence 33, 394–405 (2011)

13. Jose, G.-M., Fernando De la, T., Nicolas, G., Emilio, L.Z.: Learning a generic 3D face model from 2D image databases using incremental Structure-from-Motion. Image Vision Comput. 28, 1117–1129 (2010)

14. Maghari, A.Y.A., Liao, I.Y., Belaton, B.: Effect of facial feature points selection on 3D face shape reconstruction using regularization. In: Huang, T., Zeng, Z., Li, C., Leung, C.S. (eds.) ICONIP 2012, Part V. LNCS, vol. 7667, pp. 516–524. Springer, Heidelberg (2012)

Use of Multi-agent Based Platform
for Providing Document-Centric Interoperability
in the Realm of E-government

Muhammad Faran Majeed[1,2], Vatcharaporn Esichaikul[1], and Mah e No[3]

[1] Computer Science & Information Management,
School of Engineering & Technology, Asian Institute of Technology, Thailand
{muhammad.faran.majeed,vatchara}@ait.ac.th
[2] Department of Computer Science, Shaheed Benazir Bhutto University,
Sheringal, Dir (Upper), Khyber Pakhtunkhwa, Pakistan
[3] CECOS University of IT & Emerging Sciences, Peshawar,
Khyber Pakhtunkhwa, Pakistan
mahenouali@yahoo.com

Abstract. E-government has become basic ingredient for good governance. Through e-government different services are provided to different stakeholders that include business community, employees of different
government departments and especially to the citizens. E-government is
implemented by a huge number of countries in the world. Some of them
are developed but most of them are developing countries and working
on improving e-government services. Developing countries have different
systems working in different departments like some have legacy systems
and some have new. The problem is interoperability between these systems. This research contains an architecture that can provide a way to
cope the problem of interoperability. Through which different systems
will be able to exchange document-centric information.

Keywords: e-government, interoperability, document-centric, multi-agent
system, information exchange.

1 Introduction

1.1 E-government

E-government is not a new field. In its beginning, it emerged in a different form
like a couple of decades or may be before that when the integration of IT started
in the government [16]. But there are profound claims that use of IT started
within government in 1970s [1]. With the passage of time the focus of using IT
in government changed from providing services to citizens using digital means
[4]. E-government can be defined through different aspects. One of the general
definitions of e-government in [16] is "use of web technologies and applications
along with other information technologies by the government in such a way that;
it helps to improve access and delivery of information and services; help build

B. Papasratorn et al. (Eds.): IAIT 2013, CCIS 409, pp. 141–149, 2013.

the efficiency, service quality, effectiveness or transformation". If we look at this
definition, it seems to be more precise and broader, and has discussed improvements in the form of effectiveness, efficiency, service quality, and transformation.
These terms are thoroughly discussed in [9] and have thrown a dense light of
literature over obtaining of these improvements through a good methodology
and planning initiative.

The influential circle of e-government is very wide like; its Government-to-
Business (G2B) when there is a service for the private businesses by the government, Government-to-Employee (G2E) when government provide certain set
of services to the employees, Government-to-Citizens (G2C) when services are
solely provided to the citizens and Government-to-Government (G2G) when
there is any service being provided within the governmental departments.

G2G further has different components like it can be intergovernmental service
exchange or intra-governmental service exchange. When there is intergovernmental service exchange then the services can be provided among different departments of different governments and when there is intra-governmental service
exchange then services are provided among the departments of same government
component. The main focus of this research is G2G. It is because different departments in government have different systems deployed on different platforms
which can include legacy systems or new sophisticated systems [2], [4], [7], [10].
Providing symmetric services over heterogeneous platforms is the requirement
for better e-governance [14].

1.2   Interoperability

E-government has achieved a great importance in the new millennium. Today
almost every government is striving to get good benefits of e-government by implementing it. But e-government also faces issues like other technologies faced
in their infancy. Although e-government is not in its infancy anymore but it
still has certain issues that are of much importance. Those issues include trust,
security, system integration, language differences, and interoperability [18]. Interoperability is the issue if answered can put answers to other many issues like
trust, system integration, language difference etc.

A good interoperability mechanism can provide a best way of communication
among service provider and consumer and is not limited to only this concept.
Likewise mechanism can be developed for mutual integration of different departments and bureaus. Interoperability has great impact on technological improvement [18]. Products that provide interoperability in a good manner whether for
government and business or consumer and provider can be best used for sharing
and exchange of information. Now most of the IT companies are focusing on
products that are interoperable with products of other companies.

EU has been working on interoperability issue since long ago [EU 1991 Software Directive (Directive 91/250)]. It was included in 2005 EU Action Plan to develop a European Interoperability Framework (EIF) for European e-government
strategy [13]. The basic notion of interoperability is to make IT systems work together. One of the best definitions of interoperability by EU Software Directive is

"the ability to exchange information and mutually to use the information which has been exchanged". EIF has defined three elements of interoperability distinctively:

1. *Technical interoperability*: involves agreement on standards for information exchange through computer system linkage.
2. *Semantic interoperability*: involves surety of sharing the same meaning when information is exchange between linked computer systems.
3. *Organizational interoperability*: involves organization of infrastructures and business processes for information exchange.

But Thomas Lee et al. added two extra elements i.e. data interoperability: as an agreement on definition and representation of information exchange; and process interoperability: as an agreement on business rules for activities that take place between two parties. Just like elements there are different levels of interoperability defined in [2].

1.3   Software Agent and Multi-Agent System (MAS)

Software Agent. Literature review of the software agent and agent-based technology demonstrated that agent and agent-based technology can be used for doing plenty of tasks. As mobile agent and agent-based technology can perform different works so it can be described through multiple angles, like software that works as an interceder for another computer system, software program or human [11] or a program that coordinates with other software agents to perform same task or some other [8]. [comprehensive information can be found at www.soi.city.ac.uk/~eduardo/agents]. As discussed earlier, an agent can perform different tasks so it can be viewed from different angles in a programming perspective: like it can be programmed to adapt to the changing environment or to provide the information of an environment to one from which it started and many more.

Multi-Agent System (MAS). A simple definition of multi-agent system (MAS) is defined in [8] as "an architectonics for providing the co-ordination facility to autonomous entities". MAS makes the agent able to move, adapt, interact, coordinate, and survive autonomously.

Adaptation is a feature that makes the agent based technology defter. Agent can bring behavioral change according to the changing environment with regard to adaptation to new environment. [thorough information can be seen at www.cs.cmu.edu/~softagents/muri/adaptability.html]. It is believed that it is the capability of the adaptability that makes the agent intelligent. Without this intelligence, agent cant adapt according to its environment. As discussed by [8], adaptability puts intelligence in the agent which helps to improve the efficiency by looking at the resources. Like agent can sense about the platform on which it is running so if the platform is a device which needs less processing so that battery power can be saved. A number of agent-based systems are flourished that contain the adaptability feature in an agent like Jade [thorough information can be seen at `www.jade.cselt.it`], Grasshopper [thorough information can be seen at `www.grasshopper.de`], Aglet [thorough information can be found at `aglet.sourceforge.net`], and Cougar [thorough information can be found at `cougaar.org`] etc.

Myriad architectures are devised for providing communication between MASs. One of them is by Object Management Group (OMG) by a name of Mobile Agent System Interoperability Facility (MASIF). Another one is from IEEE named as Foundation for Intelligent Physical Agent (FIPA). According to Milojicic et al., MASIF does the support the feature of mobility in the mobile agent and also mobile communication of agents [5]. But if we look at the FIPA architecture, it is known that this architecture supports many of the features of agent not limited to mobility and communication like interoperability, adaptability, coordination, and security etc. [17].

2   Motivation

Through a thorough literature survey of e-government, it is found that interoperability is one of the main issues of e-government [12]. The interoperability can be of any type in the notion of e-government but so far there is not a single architecture that can be claimed the good one for data integration and document-centric approach. A lot of work has been done for providing metadata standards and semantic interoperability [6], [7] but there is not a fair research done on data integration for document-centric interoperability [3], [10]. So the notion of the research is to provide an architecture that can support data integration among different set of services over heterogeneous systems. Its because today more than 190 countries have moved to e-government and among these most are developing. In developing countries, most of the departments are running their legacy systems and some have new technologies. So there is no interaction among these systems because there doesn't exist interoperability mechanism that makes the system integrated so that information can be shared in real-time. According to the *Abridged E-government Strategy of Pakistan (July, 2012)*, interoperability among different applications is in the basic portfolio of the strategy that needs to be handled in such a way that the systems are not affected and can still support the data integration over document-centric environment.

3   Problem Statement

The digital means that government uses to provide services to citizens are referred to as "e" (electronic) and combination of the alphabet "e" with a word "government" gives e-government. A government having implemented e-government concepts consists of different information systems in different departments for providing G2G services. And for these information systems there exist different frameworks for providing interoperability at different levels [10], [14]. Existing frameworks like HKSARG Interoperability Framework [15] and

Australian Government Technical Interoperability Framework mostly provide interoperability mechanisms at metadata level and semantic level by use of simple XML schemas and use of ontologies. And also these mechanisms are for homogenous systems mostly. So if there is any change in the platforms (software/hardware), these mechanisms do not provide full capability support for providing interoperability. As discussed in [12], one of the basic challenges in interoperability is to overcome the heterogeneity of systems that are deployed in different departments of government. So required is a mechanism that can support heterogeneous systems over diverse technology through different channels for providing exceptional G2G services.

4   Related Work

As described earlier, a lot of work on issue of interoperability has been done but still this issue requires a fair amount of research. Its because interoperability resides at different levels of e-government system integration. Following are some of the Interoperability Frameworks (IFs) for providing different types of interoperability:

4.1   HKSARG Interoperability Framework [14]

Hong Kong is one of the two Special Administrative Regions (SARS) of China. In 1998 Hong Kong government announced Digital 21 Strategy [15] for ICT in Hong Kong. In this strategy, HKSARG had also devised the interoperability framework development and implementation. So in 2003, OGCIO developed an interoperability framework (IF) for e-government.

IF is based on the XML schema design and dissemination of information through XSD defined templates. These schemas can be project schemas or common schemas. The development of these schemas is under the CECID of The University of Hong Kong. Schemas re-regulate the business process modeling by providing interoperability at semantic level. Although HKSARG IF provides interoperability at semantic level but doesn't address the issue of heterogeneity in terms of difference in systems architecture.

4.2   Australian Government Technical Interoperability Framework
[from http://agimo.gov.au/files]

Australian Government Technical Interoperability Framework (AGTIF) is developed by Interoperability Framework Working Group (IFWG) under the supervision of the Chief Information Office Committee (CIOC).

The basic notion of developing AGTIF is to provide interoperability between agencies for information exchange. The framework consists of setting out common language, conceptual model and standards. There are three domains discussed in IF; business process domain: includes all those elements that provides the facilitation of interaction between agencies like legal, commercial, policy, and organizational; information domain: includes elements for common content interpretations for documentation used between different agencies, these elements are processes, data dictionaries, industry specific libraries, and code lists; technical domain: includes elements for delivering contents according to specific agency. The only problem with AGTIF is that it does not provide a mechanism through which the architecture can respond to the changing environment. Like if there is a run time change in any standard then it is not supported.

5 Proposed Architecture

The proposed architecture has an idea solely based on embedding agent-oriented technology in e-government. Through agent-oriented technology, distributed artificial intelligence can be easily embedded. The idea is to reflect the change immediately if occurs in any of the systems connected. Architecture is as follows:

5.1 Architecture and Components

Legacy System. Suppose on one hand there is a legacy system which consists of basic framework. This is an old system that does not support new features of data integration over different set of documents but can support embedding of some technologies like XML, ontologies, and Multi-Agent Systems.

New System. A system that consists of new technologies and supports data integration but differs in lower level architecture from that of the legacy system so interoperability is an issue. This system also supports technologies like XML, ontologies and Multi-Agent Systems.

5.2 Components

Framework has different components that can be seen in Figure-1 and is described below:

- Hard format form: a hard form that is submitted by citizens to government department. The entry of this information is through digital means like PC. It is on legacy system.
- E-form: an e-form over a website where the information can be added directly. This website provides an interface for users and is connected to repository/database at backend to store data entered. It is on new system.
- Repository/Database: the repository/database is the central repository where all the information is kept. This information is about the department for which it is established.
- Knowledgebase: knowledgebase is the repository of current running XML schemas or ontologies. Whenever a change will be required first the knowledgebase will be updated.

- XML Schemas: schemas designed for providing platform independency among different types of information entered and that information related to certain documents remains same.
- Ontology: ontology here provides consistency for terms used for providing information to the system.
- Multi-Agent System (MAS): the basic entity in this architecture. Whole architecture depends upon MAS because MAS provides the actual interoperability, data integration, scalability, and information exchange. It consists of mobile agents that can move between different MASs easily.

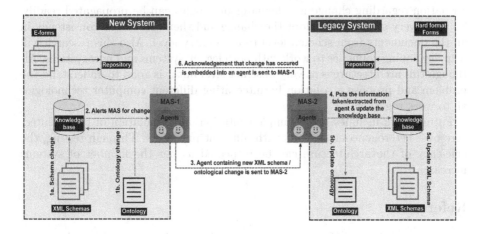

Fig. 1. Components of Proposed Architecture

5.3   Working Mechanism of Architecture

First of all MASs are deployed on both legacy and new systems. When there is a change in the XML schema on new system, MAS-1 is alerted from the knowledgebase of the new system that a change has occurred. MAS-1 takes the new XML schema, embeds it into an agent and sends the agent to the address of MAS-2 system. The transport protocols for information exchange are already defined in [8]. So there is no need to discuss them here. When MAS-2 receives the agent, it reads the information change from agent header and comes to know about the new XML schema. It informs the knowledgebase to immediately stop working on current schema and asks for updation. When knowledgebase at legacy system updates the DTD (Document Type Definition) it informs MAS-2 that the change has been completed. MAS-2 sends an agent to MAS-1 with the acknowledgement that the change has been completed. Same procedure will be used for change in ontologies as well. So whenever there will be a change in data or document format which will require change in XML schema or ontology, it'll immediately be reflected in both systems. This mechanism will not be limited to only two systems rather it can be overrated to many systems.

6   Conclusion and Future Work

G2G in E-government is the basic pillar for providing other services like G2B, G2E and G2C. If government departments are not linked together then exchange of information becomes onerous and sometimes impossible. But if these departments are linked having based upon heterogeneous systems and platforms but not interoperable then issue of data exchange remains same. For that purpose interoperability mechanisms can help them to work with both old technologies and new technologies. The proposed architecture works by integrating different technologies like XML, ontologies, and multi-agent system. Through which information regarding change in schema or ontologies can be propagated readily. So that every system can adopt the change and there should be consistency in all the documents from schema level to data entry level. Also this research will help developing countries to work with both legacy systems and new systems. Although this architecture is at very abstract level but it is good to understand the problem and propose a solution by integrating different computer technologies all to work together.

Future work includes proper implementation and simulation of the architecture over heterogeneous systems with different platforms. Through testing, the efficiency of the architecture can be inspected as per the number of systems increases.

References

1. Kraemer, K.L., et al.: Local Government and Information Technology in the United States, p. 12. OECD Informatics Studies, Paris (1978)
2. Lee, T., et al.: XML Schema Design and Management for E-government Data Interoperability. E-government Electronic Journal 7(4), 381–391 (2009)
3. Snasel, V., Pokory, J., Richta, K. (eds.): Dateso, pp. 39-48 (2011) ISBN 978-80-248-2391-1
4. Ho, A.T.-K.: Reinventing Local Government and the E-government. Initiative PA Review 4(62), 434–444 (2002)
5. Milojicic, D., Breugst, M., et al.: MASIF: The OMG mobile agent system interoperability facility. Personal and Ubiquitous Computing 2, 117–129 (1998)
6. Davies, J., Harris, S., et al.: Metadata Standards for Semantic Interoperability in Electronic Government. In: International Conference on Theory and Practice of Electronic Governance, Cairo (2008)
7. Salhofer, P., Stadlhofer, B., Tretter, G.: Ontology Driven e-government. Electronic Journal of e-government 7(4), 415–424 (2009), http://www.ejeg.com
8. Mehmood, A., et al.: Adaptive Transport Protocols in Multi Agent System. In: 5th International Conference on Information Technology: New Generations (2010)
9. Batini, C., et al.: GovQual: A quality driven methodology for E-government project planning. Government Information Quarterly 26, 106–107 (2009)
10. Nagarajan, M., et al.: Semantic Interoperability of web services-challenges and experiences (2006)
11. Lange, D.B.: Mobile Objects and Mobile Agents: The Future of Distributed Computing? In: Jul, E. (ed.) ECOOP 1998. LNCS, vol. 1445, pp. 1–12. Springer, Heidelberg (1998)

12. Goldkuhl, G.: The challenges of Interoperability in E-government: Towards a conceptual refinement. Accepted to the pre-ICIS, SIG eGovernment Workshop, Paris (2008)
13. European Review of Political Technologies (2005)
14. Gottschalk, P.: E-government Interoperability: Frameworks for Aligned Development. IGI Global, Norway (2009)
15. HKSARG. Digital 21 Strategy (2008), http://www.info.gov.hk/digital
16. Gronlund, A., Horan, T.A.: Introducing e-gov: History, Definitions, and Issues. Communication of the Association for Information Systems 15, 713–729 (2004)
17. Foundation for Intelligent Physical Agents, FIPA Abstract Architecture Specification, SC00001L (2002), http://www.fipa.org/specs/fipa00004
18. Muller, B., Wiertz, R.: eGovernment, Interoperability and Innovation. In: 5th European Conference on e-Government, University of Antwerp, Belgium, June 16–17 (2005)

Analysis of Optimization Techniques to Improve User Response Time of Web Applications and Their Implementation for MOODLE

Priyanka Manchanda

Department of Computer Science and Information Technology,
Jaypee Institute of Information Technology,
Sector 128, Noida, UP - 201304, India
pmanchanda1992@gmail.com

Abstract. Analysis of six optimization techniques grouped under three categories (hardware, back-end, and front-end) is done to study the reduction in average user response time for Modular Object Oriented Dynamic Learning Environment (Moodle), a Learning Management System which is scripted in PHP5, runs on Apache web server and utilizes MySQL database software. Before the implementation of these techniques, performance analysis of Moodle is performed for varying number of concurrent users. The results obtained for each optimization technique are then reported in a tabular format. The maximum reduction in end user response time was achieved for hardware optimization which requires Moodle server and database to be installed on solid state disk.

Keywords: Optimization, SSD, HTTP, Moodle, Nginx, caching, DNS.

1 Introduction

The Internet has seen a significant growth of web based applications over the last few years. These have now become an inseparable part of numerous industries like airline, banking, business, computer, education, financial services, healthcare, publishing and telecommunications. They are preferred because of their zero installation time (as they run on a browser), availability of centralised data, their global reach, and their availability (24 hours a day, 7 days a week). According to [1], in June 2011 an average US user spent 74 minutes a day using web applications as compared to 64 minutes a day in June 2010.

In current scenario, improvement in the user response time is the most important issue for enhancing the performance of web applications. With reference to [2], a delay of one second in the performance of web applications can impact customer satisfaction by up to 16%.

Web applications make use of a wide range of technologies including JavaScript, Apache, CSS, HTML, MySQL, PHP and protocols like HTTP headers. Optimizing the way they use these technologies can significantly improve user response time. Furthermore, the browser and hardware capabilities can be employed to reduce the user response time.

B. Papasratorn et al. (Eds.): IAIT 2013, CCIS 409, pp. 150–161, 2013.
© Springer International Publishing Switzerland 2013

Many research groups and authors have addressed this problem and reported their solutions. These include teams such as Yahoo Exceptional Performance Team [3], book authors [4] and research papers [5].

In this contribution, six optimization techniques grouped under three categories are analysed. Further, implementation of these six techniques is done for the Modular Object Oriented Distance Learning Environment (Moodle) [6]. The efficiency of these techniques is studied by comparing the original and the improved average user response time.

2   Performance Analysis of Moodle

Performance Analysis for Varying Number of Concurrent Users

Moodle is a free source Learning Management System (LMS) which is used by thousands of educational institutions around the world to provide an organized interface for e-learning. As of June 2013, it has 83059 currently active sites that have been registered from 236 countries [7]. Moodle LMS is written in PHP and uses XHTML 1.0 Strict, CSS level 2 and JavaScript for its web user interface[5].

With reference to [8], it has been reported that Moodle can support 50 concurrent users for every 1GB RAM. An experiment was performed to verify this result.

Experimental Setup

The experiment was perfomed on a machine with the following specifications:

Hardware: Intel® Core™i5-2310 CPU @2.90GHz x 4 processor, 8GB Hard disk and 1GB RAM.
Operating system: Ubuntu 12.10
Web server: Apache v2.2.22 and PHP v5.4.6 for Moodle v2.5 for Ubuntu 12.10
Database software: MySQL v5.5.31 for Ubuntu 12.10

- The experiment was performed using Apache JMeter 2.9, an open source load testing tool by the Apache Software Foundation [9].
- The test script was generated by using the JMeter Script Generator plugin for Moodle by James Brisland [10].
- The bandwidth of the network was set to 1024 kbps (1 Mbps) using JMeter.
- The load testing of Moodle was done for a chat activity.
- The sequence of pages visited on Moodle was :

   Login to site -> View Course -> View Chat page -> View Chat window -> Initialize Chat -> Initialize Initial Update

- After initializing chat the following tasks were performed five times for each concurrent user : Post Chat Message -> Initialize Update

- To test the performance of Moodle in the worst case scenario the ramp-up period, that is the amount of time for creating the total number of threads, was set to zero so as to ensure immediate creation of all the threads by JMeter.

Table 1. Average Response Time and Throughput for load testing Moodle on 1GB RAM and 8GB HARD DISK

No. of Concurrent Users	Average Response Time(s)	Throughput (per m)
10	3.671	147.6
20	8.874	129
30	15.303	99.6
40	129.786	16.8
49	243.469	11.4
50	364.480	7.8
51	Database Overload	Database Overload

While load testing Moodle for 51 concurrent users, it was observed that the connection to the database was aborted due to database overload and the testing process was killed by JMeter.

3   Hardware Optimization

Employing Solid State Disk

The performance of the web applications can be highly enhanced by using a solid state disk drive to reduce the latency of the input and output operations carried out by the server.

A Solid State Disk, or SSD is a high performance plug and play data storage device which uses integrated circuit assemblies as memory to store data persistently [11]. An SSD incorporates solid state flash memory and emulates a hard disk drive to store data [12]. However, unlike the traditional electromechanical disks like hard disk and floppy disks, an SSD is a flash-based and DRAM-based storage device which does not contain any moving parts [13].

An experiment was performed by replacing the Hard Disk Drive(HDD) of the Moodle Server with a 128GB Kingston Solid State Disk Drive.

Experimental Setup
To conform to the experiment performed in section 2 and to compare the performance of Moodle on HDD vs. SSD, the space allocated to Moodle server and database collectively was 8GB of 128GB SSD and the RAM size was limited to 1GB. The experiment was performed on a machine with following specifications:

Hardware: Intel® Core™i5-2310 CPU @2.90GHz x 4 processor, 8GB Solid State disk and 1GB RAM.
Operating system: Ubuntu 12.10
Web server: Apache v2.2.22 and PHP v5.4.6 for Moodle v2.5 for Ubuntu 12.10
Database software: MySQL v5.5.31 for Ubuntu 12.10
Bandwidth: 1024 Kbps (1 Mbps)

The experiment was performed for the chat activity mentioned in section 2 using Apache JMeter 2.9.

Table 2. Average User Response Time on HDD vs SSD(in s)

No. of concurrent users	Average Response Time on HDD(s)	Average Response Time on SSD (s)	Reduction in Response time %
10	3.671	0.349	90.49
20	8.874	1.048	88.19
30	15.303	1.938	87.34
40	129.786	3.438	97.35
50	364.480	5.274	97.83
60	Database Overload	5.97	-
70	Database Overload	6.492	-
80	Database Overload	8.009	-
90	Database Overload	8.085	-
100	Database Overload	9.797	-
110	Database Overload	13.759	-
120	Database Overload	16.828	-
130	Database Overload	22.991	-
140	Database Overload	30.187	-
150	Database Overload	36.119	-
151	Database Overload	39.141	-
152	Database Overload	Database Overload	-

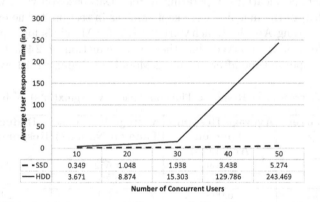

Fig. 1. Average user response time (in s) for Moodle on HDD vs. SSD

From Table 2, it is concluded that the number of concurrent users supported by Moodle installed on SSD for 1 GB RAM is increased to **151** as compared to **50** concurrent users for Moodle installed on HDD with 1 GB RAM. Also, there is a reduction of **87% to 98%** in average user response time after installing Moodle server and database on SSD.

4   Back-End Optimization

Switching to LNMP Stack from LAMP Stack

The Moodle web application runs on the LAMP stack which is a software bundle comprising of Linux based operating system, Apache HTTP server, MySQL database software and PHP object oriented scripting language. LNMP stack is almost similar to LAMP, except the change of web server from Apache to Nginx.

Apache is a process-based server, while nginx is an event-based asynchronous web server and is more scalable than Apache. In Apache, each simultaneous connection requires a thread which incurs significant overhead whereas nginx is event-driven and handles requests in a single (or at least, very few) threads [14].

The performance of Moodle or any web application that runs on Apache and frequently encounters heavy load, can be boosted by replacing Apache by Nginx. An experiment was performed to compare the performance of Moodle installed on Apache vs. Nginx web server.

Experimental Setup
Since it was observed in Section 3 that the performance of Moodle is highly enhanced by installing it on SSD, the experiment was performed on a machine with Moodle installed on 128 GB Solid State Disk and 4GB RAM.

All the other specifications (Operating system, Database software, Web server and Bandwidth) of the machine were kept same as in section 3. The experiment was performed using Apache BenchMark 2.4 [15] for Moodle's login page.

From Table 3, it is observed that there is a reduction of **24% to 34%** in average user response time after installing Moodle on Nginx v1.4.1 web server.

Table 3. Average User Response Time on Apache vs Nginx(in s) Web Server

No. of concurrent users	Average Response Time on Apache(s)	Average Response Time on Nginx(s)	Reduction in Response time %
50	2.209	1.652	25.22
100	4.505	3.359	25.43
150	6.098	4.630	24.07
200	8.192	5.408	33.98
250	10.729	7.156	33.30

5   Front-End Optimization

For any web application, only 10% to 20% of the end user response time is spent downloading the HTML document from the web server to the client's browser. The other 80% to 90% is spent in performing the front end operations, i.e., in downloading the other components of web page [4].

A set of specific rules for speeding up the front end operations carried by a web application is presented in Ref. [4]. Four of the most efficient techniques which showed significant reduction in user response time for Moodle Learning Management System are described in this section.

5.1 Browser Caching by Using Far Future Expires Header

Browsers and proxies use cache to reduce the number and size of the HTTP requests thereby speeding up the web applications. A first-time visitor may have to make several HTTP requests, but by using a Far Future Expires header the developer can significantly improve the performance of web applications for returning visitors. A server uses the Expires header in HTTP response to inform the client that it can use the current copy of a component until the specified time [4].

Moodle sends requests with an Expires Header which is set in past (**20th Aug 1969 09:23 GMT**). An experiment was performed by changing it to future date of **16th Apr 2015 20:00 GMT**. Also max-age directive was used in Cache control header so as to set the cache expiration window to 10 years in future and the pragma header was unset to enable caching.

Given below are the lines which were added to the headers.conf file of Apache2 Web Server:

```
<FilesMatch".(ico|pdf|flv|jpg|jpeg|png|gif|js|css|swf|php|html)$">
Header set Expires "Thu, 16 Apr 2015 20:00:00 GMT" Header set
Cache-Control " max-age=315360000" Header unset Pragma
</FilesMatch>
```

The experimental setup is the same as section 3 and the experiment was performed using Apache Jmeter 2.9. From Table 4, it is observed that there is a reduction of **70% to 80%** in average user response time after implementing Far Future Expires Header Optimization Technique.

Table 4. Average user response time (in s) with and without caching for 10 iterations

No. of concurrent users	Average Response Time Without Expires Header(s) (no caching)	Average Response Time with Expires Header(s) (caching)	Reduction in Response time %
10	0.625	0.144	76.96
20	1.839	0.408	77.81
40	5.061	1.210	76.09
60	7.086	1.778	74.91
80	8.124	2.426	70.14
100	9.882	3.071	68.92

5.2   Reduce DNS Lookups

The Internet uses IP addresses to find webservers. Before establishing a network connection to a web server, the browser must resolve the hostname of the web server to an IP address by using Domain Name Systems (DNS). The latency introduced due to DNS lookups can be minimized if the DNS resolutions are cached by client's browser [4]. The response time for Moodle's login page of Institutional Moodle websites of 13 universities situated in six continents of the world was recorded for two cases: With DNS Cache and Without DNS Cache. The experiment was performed for a client located in IIT Bombay, India with 128GB SSD, 4GB RAM, Intel® Core^{TM}i5-2310 CPU @2.90GHz x 4 processor and 2 Mbps average download speed.

Table 5. Average user response time (in s) With and Without DNS Cache for 1 user

Continent	Country	University	Response time With DNS Cache(s)	Response time Without DNS Cache(s)	Reduction in Response time(%)
Asia	India	IIT, Bombay [16]	2.357	1.426	39.50
Asia	India	IIT, Madras [17]	2.516	1.612	35.93
Asia	Singapore	SIM University [18]	1.381	1.055	23.61
Asia	Japan	Sojo University, Kumamoto [19]	6.223	3.116	49.93
Europe	Spain	Graduate School of Management, Barcelona [20]	3.138	1.813	42.22
Europe	UK	University of Nottingham [21]	4.174	2.041	51.10
North America	US	UCLA, California [22]	4.600	3.657	20.50
South America	Argentina	Pontifical Catholic University of Argentina, Buenos Aires [23]	2.534	1.710	32.52
South America	Colombia	University of Grand Colombia, Bogot, D.C. [24]	2.341	1.438	38.57
Africa	Egypt	Oriflame University [25]	5.497	4.288	21.99
Africa	South Africa	Virtual Academy of South Africa [26]	4.936	2.588	47.57
Australia	Australia	Australian National University [27]	4.525	3.559	21.35
Australia	Australia	Monash University [28]	4.947	4.141	16.29

From Table 5 it is concluded that there is a reduction of **16% to 51% depending on the geographical location** of Moodle server, if the resolved hostname for a web page is found in DNS cache.

Another experiment was carried out on the same client to compare the performance of Moodle by changing the number of DNS cache entries, DNS cache expiration period and HTTP keep alive timeout for Mozilla Firefox 21.0 browser. The following three scenarios were tested for 100 iterations of Moodle's login page of Moodle websites of six universities situated in six continents of the world using iMacros 9.0 Firefox extension [29] and HttpFox addon for Firefox [30].

```
Scenario 1 (S1):
DNS Cache Entries = 20
DNS Cache Expiration Period = 60 seconds
HTTP Keep Alive Timeout = 115 seconds

Scenario 2 (S2):
DNS Cache Entries = 512
DNS Cache Expiration Period = 3600 seconds
HTTP Keep Alive Timeout = 115 seconds

Scenario 3 (S3):
DNS Cache Entries = 512
DNS Cache Expiration Period = 3600 seconds
HTTP Keep Alive Timeout = 0 second
```

Table 6. Average user response time (s) for 1 user, 100 iterations for above Scenarios

Continent	University	Response time for S1	Response time for S2	Difference (s) between S1 & S2	Response time for S3	Difference(s) between S2 & S3
North America	UCLA, USA [22]	173.984	**169.284**	4.7	178.69	9.406
Asia	IIT, Madras, India [17]	108.93	**105.677**	3.253	110.548	4.871
Australia	Australian National University [27]	347.361	**344.961**	2.400	354.336	9.375
Africa	Oriflame University, Egypt [25]	244.035	**240.246**	3.789	256.08	15.834
Europe	University of Nottingham, UK [21]	153.71	**150.213**	3.497	156.76	6.547
South America	University of Grand Colombia, Colombia [23]	142.241	**135.908**	6.333	146.763	10.855

From Table 6, it is observed that the end user response time is minimum under Scenario 2. Hence, it can be concluded that the performance of a web application can be enhanced by reducing DNS Lookups, which was achieved by:

- Increasing the number of DNS cache entries,
- Increasing DNS expiration period, and
- Using a Network that supports HTTP keep-alive mechanism

5.3 Gzip Components

Gzip compression of web pages can significantly minimize the latency introduced due to transfer of the web page files from web server to client's browser. Starting with HTTP/1.1, web clients indicate support for compression with the Accept-Encoding header in the HTTP request [4].

```
Accept-Encoding: gzip, deflate
```

After the web server sees this header, it compresses the response using one of the methods listed by the client. The web server uses the Content-Encoding header in the response to inform the client about the compressed response [4].

```
Content-Encoding: gzip
```

An experiment was performed on the client mentioned in section 5.2 for Moodle installed on the machine with specifications as mentioned in section 4 using Web Developer Extension for Mozilla Firefox 21.0 [31].

It is observed that Gzip compression reduces the response size by **75%-77%**.

Table 7. Response Size of Moodle pages with and without compression of components

Moodle Page	No. of Files Requested	Response Size without Compression(KB)	Response size with Com-pression(KB)	Reduction in Response Size (%)
Index	42	926	215	76.78
Login	13	597	138	76.88
View Course	42	804	187	76.74
View Forum (with 1 post)	41	802	187	76.68
View Blog (with 10 posts)	35	889	218	75.48
View Calendar	42	861	207	75.96
View Participants (20 per page)	40	806	188	76.67
1 page quiz with 5 questions	49	847	198	76.62
View Assignments	43	804	187	76.74

5.4   Optimize AJAX

AJAX (Asynchronous JavaScript and XML) is a collection of technologies, primarily JavaScript, CSS, DOM and asynchronous data retreival which is used to exchange data with a server, and update parts of a web page - without reloading the whole page. Though AJAX allows the server to provide instantaneous feedback to the user, it does not guarantee that the user won't have to wait for the asynchronous JavaScript and XML responses. The performance of the web application can be improved by optimizing the AJAX requests. The techniques mentioned in section 5.1, 5.2 and 5.3 are collectively used to optimize the ajax components of Moodle.

The AJAX components are made cacheable by modifying the expires header which is defined in **OutputRenderers.php** file located in **lib** directory of main Moodle directory. An experiment was performed on the client mentioned in section 5.2 for Moodle installed on the machine with specifications as mentioned in section 4 using Firebug Extension 1.11.4 for Mozilla Firefox 21.0 [32].

Modifications made to expires header in OutputRenderers.php file

Default:
@header('Expires: Sun, 28 Dec 1997 09:32:45 GMT'); Line 3345

Modified:
@header('Expires: Sun, 28 Dec 2020 09:32:45 GMT'); Line 3345

There is a reduction of an average of 23.54% in user response time after optimizing the AJAX components.

Table 8. Average User Response Time (s) before and after optimizing AJAX

Activity	Response Time before optimizing AJAX(s)	Response Time after optimizing AJAX(s)	Reduction in Response Time(%)
Drag and Drop Sections	309	227	26.54
Drag and Drop Activities	2.17	1.62	25.35
Drag and Drop Files	201	175	12.94
Drag and Drop Blocks	440	354	19.55
AJAX Chat Box	36	24	33.33
Average			**23.54**

6   Conclusion

In this presented paper, six methods to optimize web applications have been analysed and tested for Moodle LMS. These methods can be further used to optimize other essential web applications including webmail, online retail sales, online auctions, wikis and e-learning. It is observed that Moodle shows faster response time under heavy traffic, if it is loaded on a solid state disk. This technique can be used to scale high traffic web applications.

The caching mechanism can be used by the client's browser to optimize the front-end operations that can reduce the end-user response time by up to 80%. This mechanism can be used for content that changes infrequently, that is, application's static assets like graphics, style sheets and scripts. In addition to application's static assets, DNS resolutions can be cached by client's browser and can reduce the end-user response time by up to 50%.

The six web optimization techniques discussed in this paper were successfully tested for the Moodle LMS which showed a maximum reduction of 98% in average user response time by using the hardware optimization technique used in (Section 3). These best practices can be further applied to a novel or existing web application to improve its performance by reducing end user response time and thereby increasing the number of concurrent users and throughput.

Acknowledgement. The author would like to thank the members of Department of Computer Science, Indian Institute of Technology, Bombay, India for their kind support and encouragement.

References

1. French, C.N.: Mobile Apps Put the Web in Their Rear-view Mirror (June 20, 2011), from Flurry Blog: http://blog.flurry.com/bid/63907/Mobile-Apps-Put-the-Web-in-Their-Rear-view-Mirror (accessed June 4, 2013)
2. Borg, A.: Web Site Performance: When Seconds Count(December 17, 2009), from technewsworld.com: http://www.techhnewsworld.com/story/68918.html (accessed June 4, 2013)
3. Yahoo Exceptional Performance Team, http://developer.yahoo.com/performance
4. Souders, S.: High Performance Web Sites. O'Reilly Media (2007)
5. Horat, D., Arencibia, A.Q.: Web Applications: A Proposal to Improve Response Time and Its Application to MOODLE. In: Moreno-Díaz, R., Pichler, F., Arencibia, A.Q. (eds.) EUROCAST 2009. LNCS, vol. 5717, pp. 218–225. Springer, Heidelberg (2009)
6. Project Moodle, http://moodle.org
7. Moodle Statistiscs, https://moodle.org/stats/
8. Joint Information Systems Committee, Regional Support Centre, West Midlands Moodle Wiki, http://wiki.rscwmsystems.org.uk/index.php/Moodle
9. Apache JMeter, http://jmeter.apache.org/
10. Moodle-jmeter-script-generator, https://github.com/kabalin/moodle-jmeter-script-generator

11. Solid State Drive by Wikipedia.org,
    http://en.wikipedia.org/wiki/Solid-state_drive
12. Wong, G.: SSD Market Overview. In: Micheloni, R., Marelli, A., Eshghi, K. (eds.)
    Inside Solid State Drives (SSDs). Springer Series in Advanced Microelectronics,
    vol. 37, pp. 1–18. Springer Science+Business Media, Dordrecht (2013)
13. Martin, D.: Is SSD Technology Ready for the Enterprise? (January 14, 2009),
    from Wikibon.com:
    http://wikibon.org/wiki/v/Is_SSD_Technology_Ready_for_the_Enterprise?
    (accessed June 11, 2013)
14. Apache vs nginx, http://www.wikivs.com/wiki/Apache_vs_nginx
15. ab - Apache HTTP server benchmarking tool,
    http://httpd.apache.org/docs/current/programs/ab.html
16. Indian Institute of Technology, Bombay : Moodle,
    https://moodle.iitb.ac.in/login/index.php
17. Indian Institute of Technology, Madras : Moodle,
    http://www.cse.iitm.ac.in/moodle/
18. Singapore Institute of Management University, Singapore : Moodle,
    http://cp.unisim.edu.sg/moodle/
19. Sojo University, Nishi-ku, Kumamoto, Japan : Moodle,
    http://md.ed.sojo-u.ac.jp/
20. Graduate School of Management, Barcelona, Spain : Moodle,
    http://moodle.gsmbarcelona.eu/
21. University of Nottingham, Nottingham, UK : Moodle,
    https://moodle.nottingham.ac.uk/login/index.php
22. University of California, Los Angeles : Physics and Astronomy Dept. Moodle,
    http://reserve.pna.ucla.edu/
23. Pontifical Catholic University of Argentina, Puerto Madero, Buenos Aires, Argentina : LirWeb Moodle,
    http://www.lirweb.com.ar/
24. University of Grand Colombia, Bogot, D.C., Colombia : Moodle,
    http://virtual.ulagrancolombia.edu.co/login/index.php
25. Oriflame University : Moodle, http://www.oriflame-eg.com/uni/moodle/
26. Virtual Academy of South Africa: Moodle, http://www.virtualacademy.co.za/
27. Australian National University: Moodle, http://moodle.anu.edu.au/
28. Monash University: Moodle, http://moodle.vle.monash.edu/
29. iMacros, http://www.iopus.com/iMacros/
30. HttpFox Addon for Mozilla Firefox 21.0,
    https://addons.mozilla.org/en-us/firefox/addon/httpfox/
31. Web Developer Extension for Mozilla Firefox 21.0,
    https://addons.mozilla.org/en-US/firefox/addon/web-developer/
32. Firebug 1.11.4 Extension for Mozilla Firefox 21.0,
    https://addons.mozilla.org/en-US/firefox/addon/firebug/

Event-Driven Implementation of Layer-7 Load Balancer

Takayuki Sasajima and Shin-ya Nishizaki

Department of Computer Science, Tokyo Institute of Technology
2-12-1-W8-69, Ookayama, Meguro, Tokyo 152-8552, Japan
nisizaki@cs.titech.ac.jp

Abstract. A single-page application is a web application which is retrieved with a single page load, and has become popular recently. In such web applications, real-time interaction is offered by long polling of HTML requests, typically the Comet model. However, such communication between a client and a server is inefficient because of the TCP handshake and HTTP header overhead. In order to improve this kind of inefficiency, WebSocket is proposed as a web technology providing full-duplex communications between web browsers and servers. In this paper, we design and implement a load balancer suitable for Web applications using the WebSocket protocol, which enables us to get improved performance with respect to simultaneous connectability. Usually, load balancers handle TCP packets in the transport layer, or L4, of the network. Our load balancer is designed as a relay in the application layer, or L7, in order to provide a finer distribution of the network load. We implement the load balancer on an event-driven web application framework, Node.js. We evaluate the implementation of efficiency of the load balancer.

1 Introduction

1.1 Load Balancing in Networking

Load balancing [2,4] is a computer networking method to distribute workload across multiple computing resources, typically, computer servers, in order to maximize throughput and minimize response time. Recently, several kinds of load balancers have been proposed, and they can be divided into two groups: L4 load balancers and L7 load balancers. L4 and L7 means network layers in the OSI model (Table 1).

Table 1. OSI Model

Layer		Example
L7	Application layer	HTTP, FTP, DHCP
L6	Presentation layer	MIME
L5	Session layer	TLS/SSL, NetBIOS, PPTP
L4	Transport layer	TCP, UDP
L3	Network layer	IP, ARP, ICMP
L2	Data link layer	PPP
L1	Physical layer	IEEE 802.11, USB, Bluetooth

B. Papasratorn et al. (Eds.): IAIT 2013, CCIS 409, pp. 162–172, 2013.
© Springer International Publishing Switzerland 2013

Today's most widely used method of load balancing is based on information on the 4th layer, the *transport layer*, more specifically, the contents of TCP and/or UDP packets. Such a load balancer distributes packets by seeing their source IP addresses and port numbers. On the other hand, there are load balancers which use information on the 7th layer, the *application layer*. For example, an L7 load balancer for web servers analyzes the contents of packets of the HTML protocol. A comparison between the L4 and L7 load balancing methods is summarized as follows.

— Generally speaking, performance of the L4 load balancing is better than that of the L7 load balancing, because packet analyzing of L4 load balancing is much simpler than that of L7 load balancing.
— L4 load balancers can maintain keep-alive sessions to back-end servers.
— L7 load balancers can distribute loads to back-end servers and fix an appropriate server to each connection, monitoring information in the 7th layer, such as parameters attached to URLs in clients' requests.
— L7 load balancers can distribute load to back-end servers, classifying by use. For example, L7 load balancers for HTML can determine packet distribution using the user-agent information in HTML packets.

One of the clear differences between L4 and L7 load balancing is the initial part of the communication between a client and a server via a load balancer. In L4 load balancing, a server is selected after an L4 load balancer receives a SYN packet from a client (Fig. 2). On the other hand, in L7 load balancing, a server is selected after an L7 load balancer receives an HTTP request packet from a client (Fig. 3).

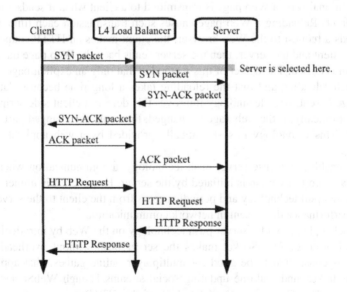

Fig. 1. Packet Flow of L4 Load Balancer

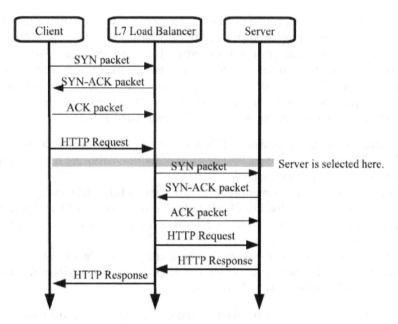

Fig. 2. Packet Flow of L7 Load Balancer

1.2   Push Technology in Web

In the traditional way, a Web page is transmitted to a client when it sends a request to a Web server. Reloading a Web page causes such transmission each time. Once the client sends a request to the Web browser, the client makes an HTTP connection between the client and the server, then the server sends back the Web page data, and the connection is closed. The defect of this method is that only an explicit page transition causes such reloading and that the reloading takes a long time because data for the whole page is sent. Ajax technology improves this defect: a client-side script sends a request periodically; if the web page is changed, then only the changed part is sent to the client. This technology is systematically provided by a web application model *Comet* [3].

Comet enables us to use server push technology, a communication where the request for a given transaction is initiated by the server. However, it is implemented by the traditional pull technology and periodic access from the client to the server, which causes a performance decrement in network communication.

WebSocket [11] provides server push technology on the Web by introducing a new TCP-based protocol. WebSocket makes the server push without overheads, unlike Comet. It is considered to be good for multiplayer online games, chat applications, live sports ticker, and realtime updating social streams.Though WebSocket is more sophisticated than Comet, it is independent of the HTTP protocol, and therefore, communication infrastructure for web communication, such as L7 load balancers, has to be extended to the WebSocket protocol.

1.3   Purpose of This Paper

In WebSocket communication, a client gets data on a web page, including an HTML description and JavaScript codes, and then establishes a connection with a WebSocket server in execution of the JavaScript codes. If the HTTP server and the WebSocket server are installed on different machines, an L4 load balancer cannot distinguish the HTTP request packets from the WebSocket packets, and consequently, the load balancer cannot distribute the servers' loads appropriately. We therefore deduce that L4 load balancing is necessary for WebSocket communication.

Unfortunately, the WebSocket protocol was recently standardized and L7 load balancing has not yet been well studied. In this paper, we propose L7 load balancing, ready for the WebSocket protocol.

2   Design of Our Load Balance

The WebSocket protocol keeps a full duplex connection as long as necessary; on both the client-side and server-side, the connection should be held. As a result, many connections can be simultaneously handled by the L7 load balancer. Its performance must be proportionally scaled up with respect to the number of simultaneous connections. There are two options for scheduling for simultaneous HTTP communication:

— Multi-thread based style
— Event-driven style.

It has been a debatable topic which option has better performance when there are a large number of simultaneous connections. Ousterhout [7] showed the superiority of the event-driven style over the multi-thread style in 1996. In 2003, Rob von Behren et al.[1] supported the primacy of the multi-thread style over the event-driven style, improving a multi-thread library. In 2007, Pariag [8] argued that the event-driven style is superior to the multi-thread style, improving implementations of both the styles. According to the research [7,8], we can summarize the feature of the event-driven style as follows.

— Though we should be careful about synchronization and locks in the multi-thread based style, such care is not necessary in the event-driven style because a program in the event-driven style is executed in a single thread.
— We can expect high performance improvement by reducing blocking I/O.
— Though each program written in the event-driven style is executed in a single thread, multi-processing makes full use of a multi-core CPU's performance.

Since our purpose is improvement of performance under numerous simultaneous connections, we adopt the event-driven style.

2.1   Overview of Our Load Balancer

Our system is composed of two processes: a *load balancer* and a *server health check-er*. The load balancer has three major parts:

— **HTTP Processor**, which receives HTTP requests from clients and distributes them to HTTP servers (we call them *slave servers* in the following),
— **WebSocket Processor**, which handles WebSocket's communication,
— **Server-Health-Checker Controller**, which communicates with the server health checker process and receives a notification if some change occurs in one of its slave servers.

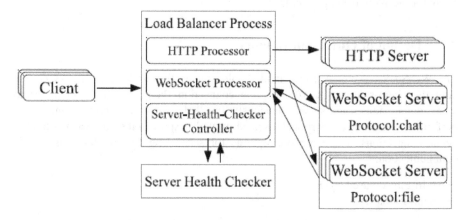

Fig. 3. Overview of Our System

An example of our system's configuration is presented in Fig.4. In this configuration, two kinds of WebSocket sub-protocol are provided; one is the sub-protocol `chat' and the other is `file'. For each sub-protocol, a group of WebSocket servers is assigned.

Communication between clients and servers passes through the load balancer process. The load balancer processes requests of HTTP and WebSocket.

HTTP Load Balancing. The outline of the load balancing for HTTP requests in our system is described as follows:

1. The load balancer receives an HTTP request.
2. The HTTP schedule module described below chooses an HTTP server from the server pool. If there is no HTTP server to be chosen, the load balancer returns an er-ror response of HTTP status code "Internal Server Error"(HTTP Status Code 500)
3. The HTTP request and the HTTP packets following it are relayed to the chosen HTTP server.
4. If the load balancer cannot receive a reply from the HTTP server, then the load ba-lancer replies with an error response "Internal Server Error" to the client, similarly to Step 2. If the load balancer receives a reply from the HTTP server, it relays the received reply to the client.

In 2, the HTTP schedule module chooses an HTTP server from a set of active HTTP servers whose validity is verified by the Server Health Checker. The HTTP schedule module chooses an HTTP server based on the round-robin scheduling algorithm [10].

WebSocket Load Balancing. A connection between the load balancer and Web-Socket servers is established in the following procedure:

1. The load balancer receives a WebSocket request.
2. An object called a *session object*, which controls the connection between the client and a WebSocket server, is generated.
3. The *dispatch module*, which is explained below, chooses a WebSocket server from the server pool. If a WebSocket server is not available, the load balancer refuses the request for a WebSocket connection from the client.
4. The load balancer makes a connection with the selected WebSocket server. If the connection is not established successfully, the connection request is refused.
5. Once the connection is established, it is registered in the session object. The load balancer sends back an acknowledgment of the connection request to the client and registers the connection between the load balancer and the client to the session object.

The *dispatch module* selects a group of WebSocket servers from the server pool for each WebSocket connection request from the server. Its selection policy is given in the two kinds of style: one is based on path names and other on sub-protocols. For example, let us assume that there are two groups of servers: Group 1 is assigned to "chat" and Group 2 to "file". If the path name of the connection request is "/chat/3", then the connection request is distributed to Group 1 because the path name contains the substring "/chat". After the dispatch module selects a WebSocket servers' group, a WebSocket schedule module chooses a server from the group. The schedule module chooses a server from the servers' group based on the *minimum connection policy* by which it selects a server with the minimum number of connections.

Server Health Checking. Server Health Checking in our system is implemented in the following two parts: a server health checker process and a server-health-checker controller in the load balancer process (see Fig. 4.).

The server health checker process communicates with the WebSocket servers and checks their condition. The information on the condition of the WebSocket servers is passed to the server-health-checker controller. The controller manages the information in order to select an appropriate server from the servers' pool. The reasons the server health checker process is separated from the load balancer process are:

− the load of the load balancer process should be reduced
− the servers' condition should be collectively managed if several load balancer processes are conducted simultaneously.

Relaying WebSocket Packets. The load balancer process relays the WebSocket packets from the clients without analyzing the contents of the sockets, except of a *closing frame*. The WebSocket handshake has the *closing handshake*, which is provided since the TCP closing handshake (FIN/ACK) is not always reliable end-to-end, especially in the presence of intercepting proxies and other intermediaries [11].

If the load balancer process receives a closing frame from a client, then the load balancer process sends the closing frame to the WebSocket server. If the load balancer process receives a closing frame from the WebSocket server, then it sends a closing frame back to the client and disconnects the TCP connections between the WebSocket server and the client.

3   Evaluation

We conducted an experiment in the machine environment which consisted of four machines as servers and load balancers, and one machine for a client. The specifications of the two kinds of machines were as follows.

Table 2. Specification of machines used in the evaluation

Servers and Load Balancers		Clients	
OS	Ubuntu 10.04 LTS (32bit)	OS	Ubuntu 11.10 (32bit)
CPU	Intel Core 2 Duo 2.4 GHz	CPU	Intel Core i7-3930K
Memory	4GB	Memory	8GB
HDD	500GB	HDD	1TB

Ideally, we should evaluate our load balance based on actual traffic load. However, the WebSocket protocol is comparatively new, and accordingly, efficient number of experiences is not known yet. Therefore, we evaluate the load balancer in a simple communication setting.

In our experiment, we assumed that the Web server makes an echo: if the server receives a string from a client, then it returns the string to the client.

We conducted an experiment in order to investigate throughput for several configuration of servers in Fig. 7.

— Line "s1" in Fig. 7 represents the variation in the number of connections using one server. We know that the CPU resources are exhausted at around 5,000 connections, and around 5,000 requests can be processed per second.
— Line "lb-s2" in Fig. 7 is the result for an experiment using two servers. In this case, we know that around 10,000 connections are handled.
— Line "lb-s3" in Fig. 7 is the result for an experiment using three servers. In this case, we know that only 14,000 connections are handled. We know this because the capacity of the load balancer exceeds that of the servers.

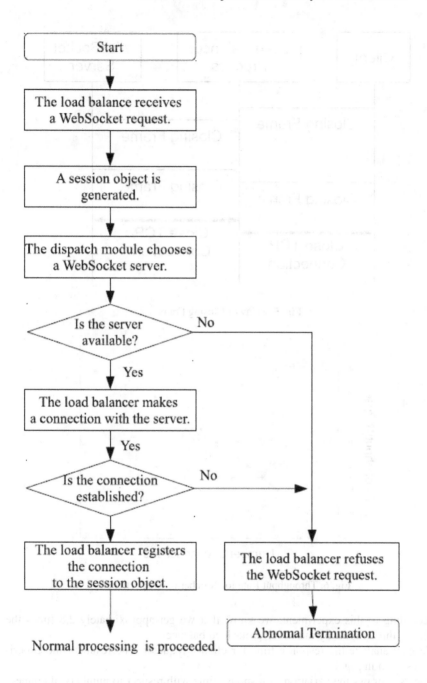

Fig. 4. Establishing Connection between Load Balancer and WebSocket Servers

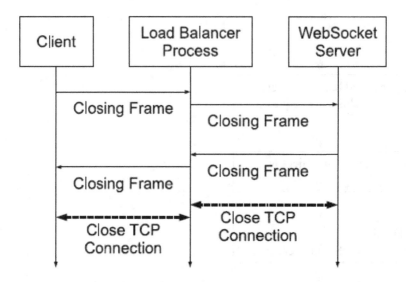

Fig. 5. Relay of Closing Frame

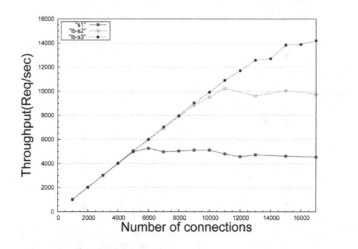

Fig. 6. Throughput Rate for Number of Connections

According to this experiment, we know that we get approximately 2.8 times the number of throughputs by introducing our load balancer.

We next analyze the response time for clients' requests. The result of the experiment is shown in Fig. 8.

Line "s1" draws the variation of response time with respect to numbers of connections with one server.

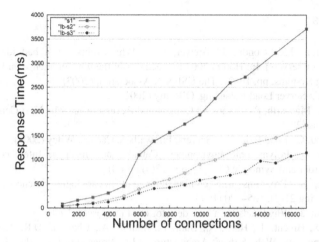

Fig. 7. Response Time Rate for Number of Connections

Line "lb-s2" ("lb-s3") is the case in which load is distributed to two servers (three servers respectively) using the load balancer. We know that the use of the load balancer eases the bottleneck. The slope of the line s1 for more than 6000 connections is 23.7%. The slope of the line lb-s2 for more than 12000 connections is 11.7¥%. The latter is half of the former, which is considered the result of load balancing by double servers.

However, if the number of connections is less than 5000, the load balancing is not as effective as is the case with more than 6000 connections, which is because the handling cost of multiple servers is comparatively higher than the processing load of each server.

4   Conclusion

In this paper, we designed an L7 load balancer for WebSocket communication, which distributes processing loads to back-end servers appropriately based on information of WebSocket packets. We implemented the load balancer on an event-driven web application framework, Node.js, and evaluated the increase in efficiency of the load balancer.

There are many issues to be solved. One of the most important is further evaluation of the design of the load balancer. We experimented with the load balancer using only three back-end servers. In practical situations, we should carry out experiments with many more back-end servers. We chose event-driven scheduling rather than multi-threading, which should be compared through experimental performance evaluation. Besides the evaluation, we also considered introducing redundancy into our load balancer, since such redundancy does not exist at present.

Acknowledgements. This work was supported by Grants-in-Aid for Scientific Research (C) (24500009).

References

1. von Behren, J.R., Condit, J., Brewer, E.A.: Why events are a bad idea (for high-concurrency servers). In: HotOS 2003 Proceedings of the 9th Conference on Hot Topics in Operating Systems, pp. 19–24. The USENIX Association (2003)
2. Bourke, T.: Server Load Balancing. O'Reilly (2001)
3. Crane, D., Maccarth, P., Tiwari, S.: Coment and Reverse Ajax: The Next Generation Ajax 2.0. APress (2008)
4. Kopparapu, C.: Load Balancing Servers, Firewalls & Caches. Wiley (2002)
5. Nishizaki, S.: Polymorphic Environment Calculus and Its Type Inference Algorithm. Higher-Order and Symbolic Computation 13(3) (2000)
6. Nishizaki, S.: Programs with continuations and linear logic. Science of Computer Programming 21(2), 165–190 (1993)
7. Ousterhout, J.: Why treads are a bad idea (for most purposes) (1996)
8. Pariag, D., Brecht, T., Harji, A., Buhr, P., Shukla, A., Cheriton, D.R.: Comparing the Performance of Web Server Architectures. In: Proceedings of the Second ACM SIGOPS/EuroSys European Conference on Computer Systems (2007)
9. Sasajima, T., Nishizaki, S.: Blog-based distributed computation. In: Liu, B., Ma, M., Chang, J. (eds.) ICICA 2012. LNCS, vol. 7473, pp. 461–467. Springer, Heidelberg (2012)
10. Silberschatz, A., Galvin, P.B., Gagne, G.: Operating System Concepts. John Wiley & Sons (2010)
11. RFC455 – The WebSocket Protocol (2011)

RFID Privacy and Security Risks: Italian Case Study

Maria Concetta De Vivo, Alberto Polzonetti, and Pietro Tapanelli

School of Science and Technology,
Computer Science Division, University of Camerino, Camerino, Italy
{concetta.devivo,alberto.polzonetti,pietro.tapanelli}@unicam.it

Abstract. Radio Frequency Identification (RFID) technology can be used in different areas such as in occupational safety and health. This article discusses the development of the RFID technology and its legal implications in the context of the Italian law. This is one of the most advanced European Union law when legal framework for RFID systems is considered. The paper will also face the important problem of the workplaces security. When implementing certain types of systems the workplaces security can be a critical issue to be addressed. In these systems the workplace security laws can affect the RFID legal framework application. Provisions of data protection can be weakened in order to fully apply workplace security laws. The article will conclude with useful legal guidelines that must be followed when implementing an RFID system for applications with workplaces security issues.

Keywords: RFID, privacy, security, workplace, data protection.

1 Introduction

The term RFID denotes any RF device that is used to identify an object or a person. An RFID system consists of as tag, a reader and a computer to which the reader is connected. An RFID tag is small wireless device. It is generally connected to an antenna. The appearance is that of a small sticker which can vary in size. An RFID tag can communicate data in response to requests from an RFID reader. This usually consists of antennae and electronic circuit. There are different versions of RFID readers some with separated antennae and circuit while some have these components integrated. Computers can have very small dimensions and usually is a build-in part of RFID reader.

The use of RFIDs is continuously increasing and today RFID market is $6.37 million with a total amount of 2.93 billion tags sold. RFIDs are increasingly used in applications demanding high security and safety such as transit, healthcare, banking, smart houses, smart environment [1], works of art authentication, passports [2]. Thus it is very important to understand the use of the RFID technology and its legal implications in the context of laws after subject.

This paper investigates the use of RFID systems in the context of the Italian law where privacy is ensured by the Data Protection directive, transposed by the Italian Code (legislative decree no. 196/2003) while security by the Workers' Statute (law no. 300/1970). Although the use of RFID systems for monitoring, identifying and

B. Papasratorn et al. (Eds.): IAIT 2013, CCIS 409, pp. 173–183, 2013.

tracking employees is not permitted exceptions are allowed. For instance when the system is shown to be objectively necessary and required for the company strategy monitoring of workers can be performed. This requires the agreement between the company and various institutional bodies. Monitoring can be also allowed when this is necessary for the heath and safety of the workers.

This papers analyzing the difficult matters of deciding when RFID systems that monitor the employee activities are allowed.

2   Remote Control of Employees' Activity : Italian Cases

The first paragraph of the article 4 of the Italian law no. 300/1970 (henceforth the Workers' Statute) prohibits the installation of audio-visual and other equipment that can be used in order to remotely control the activities of employees [3]. Although this paragraph seems to forbid the use of any monitoring technology, the second paragraph of the same law allows the monitoring of employees in the following two cases:

1. The company requires a system that is proven to be necessary for its strategy and for production purposes;
2. The company requires the monitoring for workplaces security. Even if the system has a side effect of monitoring the workers this is allowed.

This law is completed by a ministerial report. This specifies that a company can use monitoring technology for organization and production purposes when the "human dignity" is not affected [4]. The legislative decree no. 196/2003 (hereinafter the Privacy Code) must also be considered. It adds to the article 4 the concept of privacy protection. Thus when building an RFID system we need to comply with both Workers' Statute and the Privacy Code.

When monitoring of employees is legal the second paragraph of the article 4 states that the company must reach an agreement with its internal trade unions. In the case there is no trade union the company must reach an agreement with the internal committee of employees. If the agreement with the trade union and committee of workers is not achieved or these bodies do not exist the company must request the possibility of monitoring the workers to the "Inspettorato del lavoro" (Labour Office of Province). The article 4 of the Workers' Statute tells specifically about worker's activity. For instance, this includes the working time and the pause time that is the time between entering and leaving the work place. In contrast, to stress the different concept, the article 3 talks about employment that is only the working activity. It does not include activities such as coffee time and lunchtime.

The article 4 also states that "other equipment" cannot be used in order to monitor employees' activity. The term "other equipment" is so general that can include potentially any kind of technology in order to keep the law up to date with any technological advance. Generally speaking "other equipment" could include any systems for workstation security. It is therefore necessary that any equipment (that is not exclusively designed to monitor workers' activity) must perform a careful balancing between the workers' dignity and occupational safety and health in the workplaces.

With respect to the use of the monitoring technologies there are different doctrines. One is in favor of the use of monitoring technology as long as it does not violate the article 4, paragraph 2 of Workers' Statute [5]. A different doctrine is against any use of such devices [6] while another perhaps, with a more liberal spirit, states that monitoring systems can be always used when they are crucial for the organization needs. More precisely, the company should not ask the permission of any committee [7]. For instance, nowadays PCs have become essential for the organization needs, thus the article 4 should be not applied [8].

Currently we are moving into the direction of so-called "defensive controls". These are monitoring controls performed after some events have happened inside the company. The Italian Supreme Court has established that there are not absolute defensive controls. In other words, whether or not there is the need of absolute controls must be assessed in each single case depending on the monitoring purposes. The Italian Supreme Court mentioned some examples of defensive controls in the Cass. 3 April 2002, n. 4746: "certainly allowed outside the scope of the application of the rule on direct controls to detect illegal conduct (access to restricted areas such as illegal conduct) of the employee (so-called defensive controls) such as, for example, access control systems to restricted areas or, indeed, the apparatus to detect unwarranted calls.".

3   Occupational Safety and Health

The key figures concerned with occupational safety and health are the following ones, according to Italian legislative decree no. 81/2008 (hereinafter TUSL). They are listed in a top-down way considering also their active role.

— Employer: he is the person who signed the employment contract. Otherwise he can be the person who has the responsibility of his own organization or each single production unit because he can exercise decision-making powers. More precisely, he can manage the employees. Furthermore, three sub-definitions of employer can be listed. The employer can be:
  • the person who formally signs employment contract, as specified by the article 2082 of the Italian civil code;
  • the employer's delegate, who is delegated by the employer for some company functions;
  • the employer de facto, who in practice has decision-making powers.
  Therefore is possible that in a company there are more than one employer. For instance if we consider several production units, owned by the same property, we will have a different employers (responsible for each single unit) even if, formally, there is a sole company chief.

  The employer must prepare the risk assessment and police document that identifies the hazards and the control measures to safeguard employees' security and health. Moreover, the employer has to attend to the implementation of this document.

— Manager: he is the person who, for his professional and power skills, have to put in practice the employer's directives for organizing and supervising the employees' activity. More precisely, the manager is independently of any delegation (which may be or not) and he uses to play an active role in the company management, included the management of issues related to occupational safety and health. It is not necessary an employment contract (with this position) to qualify a person as a manager, but it is sufficient a "simply" situation in which this person puts in practice crucial decisions for the company. In this way there are similar skills and similar responsibilities with employer.
— Individual in charge: he is a person who has to supervise the work activity and ensure the implementation of the directives received. More precisely, he checks the correct employment performance by workers and he also exercises some management functions for his professional competence and within the limit of his functional hierarchy. Therefore, the individual in charge, according to the definition provided by TUSL, has an intermediate function: the junction between managers and employees. Indeed, the individual in charge, as the manager, is directly responsible for the failure of risk assessment and police implementation. However, in absence of any express delegation with full powers and decision-making autonomy, the individual in charge can never obtain obligations and responsibilities as the employer (or manager).
— Employee: he is a person who does a specified type of work, regardless of his employment contract, in a private or public organization, with or without salary, also in order to learn a craft, an art or a profession excluding domestic and family services. In this category, regarding occupational safety and health as provided by TUSL, we have to list also:
  • worker-members of a cooperative or corporation;
  • associate members;
  • beneficiaries for job training or guidance;
  • students from education institutions and universities;
  • participants in training courses in which they use chemical, physical and biological laboratories or equipment. This qualification is limited for all the training period;
  • volunteers.
— Responsible for occupational safety and health: he is a person, with specific professional skills, defined by the article 32 of TUSL. He is nominated by the employer, from whom depends, to coordinate the entire process of a company for occupational safety and health.

Defined those key figures, we can say that the entire topic of occupational safety and health determines not only rights and duties, but also helps to identify a unique group where all company key-figures (above-mentioned) are co-responsible in order to achieve the highest quality standards.

Obviously there are also dangerous jobs where the hazards cannot be eliminated from the beginning. In this case those hazards can and should be limited, for example, minimizing the number of workers involved in specified operations or some preventative measures can be improved to guarantee hygiene in specific locations using appropriate equipment (a first aid stations or an acoustic system of warning, for instance). It means that there is a reasonableness limit which cannot be exceeded because, eliminating from the beginning some hazards, we would get the impossibility of execution of some job performances.

This leads us to understand how the worker's security, in the Italian legal system, is not itself an absolute value but it is a preeminent value compared to other constitutional values. The only absolute value, in this case, is that all the people are equal and they had to be protected with the same approach. More precisely, the occupational safety and health topic must be compared with other constitution principles. For instance, in our Constitutional fundamental charter we find principles of full development of the individual, free choice of employment, freedom of movement, freedom of information and protection of public order [9].

In this delicate topic the main tendency, also at supranational level, is to level up the best practices necessary to increase occupational safety and health: so it is definitely acceptable the implementation of quality standards, which are useful to limit hazards, through the use of RFID technology. For these reasons, in compliance to the balance of above-mentioned principles and to the importance of workers' safety, it is acceptable a "voluntary" standardization upwards (for instance we could find a precious allied in the international bodies for certification of processes and/or products, such as ISO standards).

4   In Depth with "Defensive Controls"

The idea of defensive controls has been developed by Italian courts and also positively appreciated by Italian doctrine. This definition allows to overcome an interpretative obstacle and permits the introduction of devices suitable for workers' monitoring but only if these devices are installed to suppress unlawful conducts. Indeed, the idea of defensive controls has led to the development of polyvalent protection both for the employer and employee when the unlawful conduct must be avoided. Without a doubt, the same idea is not oriented to censor or to cancel any workers' guarantee of dignity and privacy. More precisely, it is necessary to speak about a process ruled by the "information idea" where the employee takes part to the employer's decision. In this way the contribution of trade unions becomes fundamental: therefore we are coming back to the provision of the article 4 of the Workers' Statute where the trade unions' role is active [10].

To understand how Italian courts are interpreting the defensive control, it is necessary to quote a recent decision of the Italian Supreme Court. The court has ruled that a layoff decided by the control of some employee's e-mail can be considered legal, respecting the article 4 of Workers' Statue. The same court, based on uncontested fact, has however ruled that "the employer has implemented ex post controls, after the unlawful conduct of his employee, because he had uncovered evidence to recommend the notification of a job complaining. [...] In this case the employer has used some control activities over ICT network. This conduct is not the direct monitoring of the execution of the employment performance [...]. The so-called defensive control, in other words, was not about the correct fulfillment of the obligations raised from the employment contract, but it was oriented to ascertain the employee's conduct that put in danger the same image of the company." (Cass. 23 February 2012, n. 2722).

At this point it is clear how many difficulties are arising from this topic: these uncertainties, for this part only connected to occupational safety and health, make very difficult, if not impossible, to determine when there are crossed the border of defensive controls. The employer's conduct must be controlled always with the support of trade unions and, specifically, in compliance with article 4, paragraph 2, of Workers' Statute.

5   New Technologies, Privacy and Controls

The "information idea" and the collaboration between employer and employee are becoming the central themes. We have seen how it is important the application of Workers' Statue and, in this paragraph, we are facing how the privacy legal framework can be useful to add defenses for personal data processing of employees. It is strictly connected to the paper topic because the development of any system (in this papaer is about RFID, but it could be also an NFC system), necessary to improve occupational safety and health, has to respect the data protection legal framework. In Italy, to adopt both European Union's directives 95/46/CE and 2002/58/CE, there is the legislative decree no. 193/2003 (hereafter Privacy Code).

Indeed the processing of personal data, also in workplaces, must necessary consider the provisions contained in the Italian Privacy Code. The relations between Privacy Code and Workers' Statute are very closed. More precisely, the Title VIII - Labour and Social Security (of Privacy Code), clears the field from any doubts when, both in the articles 113 and 114, refers to provisions of the articles 8 and 4 of law no. 300/1970 (Workers' Statute) [11].

Moreover we have to consider the most important decisions ruled by Italian courts and by the Italian privacy guarantor. The evolution of technologies, applied for occupational safety and health, has been constantly increased during last years. For this reason it is important to underline some decisions that have been pointed out the attention to RFID systems. It was a step-by-step way towards the RFID technologies, in fact the early decision never mentioned this kind of technology. However, these decisions are fundamental to stress the basic principle that must be followed.

For instance, connected to telephone line monitoring, the Italian Supreme Court (Cass. 3 April 2002, n. 4746) analyzed what was really the object of control. Indeed, if the object of control is the workers' activities it will apply the article 4 of the Statute (so we have the option specified by the article 4, paragraph 2, of Workers' Statute). On the other hand if the control is oriented to determine an unlawful use of working objects (so the employer is not monitoring the workers' activity), the article 4 will not apply and this system can be installed and used without any permission. The court specifies that:

— the control cannot be extended to the call content;
— the last three digits must be obscured;
— there must be an adequate privacy policy.

In sum, the criteria of proportionality (and adequacy), purpose, necessity and legality, that are the cornerstones of the entire Italian Privacy Code and European data protection legal framework, must always kept in mind.

The Italian privacy guarantor ruled with several acts (we cannot talk about sentences because the Italian privacy guarantor is an administrative authority but its decisions are anyway binding) about the data treatment combined with the evolution of technology related to the topic addressed in this paper. One relevant case was about a control system implemented by a roofing cement industry. The company management used this system, based on fingerprints detection, in order to calculate salaries. When the Italian privacy authority was invested by the case he ruled against the use of this system. More precisely, the guarantor stated doubts about the system security (it seemed vulnerable by data breaches) and he detected that the privacy policy was totally inadequate (one more time there is the "information idea"). Furthermore the authority ruled that the data treatment was certainly disproportionate and unnecessary in respect to the purpose. Indeed, in order to calculate the employees' salary should have been used a "simple" magnetic badge, without processing and archiving biometric data such as fingerprints [12].

In another case, also connected with biometrics issues, the Italian guarantor ruled in favor of using fingerprints accesses system implemented by a milling industry (processing of grain). In this circumstance the fingerprints was "detected and converted into a template encrypted smart card" and the card was in the exclusive availability of the single employee. Moreover the worker had to put the smart card into a card reader and his finger on a specific reader: the association of the two codes would open the plant doors. The Italian guarantor considered the data treatment technologically appropriate, proportionate and necessary as well. More precisely, the aim was to regulate the access to particular plant areas and only authorized personal could be admitted [13].

Following the same basic principles there is the general act of Italian guarantor entitled "Guidelines for the data treatment of private employee". This is not a case based act, but it is a general document that systematically regulate every given topic: indeed, the biometric data processing require that all fingerprints, once translated in a mathematical model and putted over a smart card, shall be deleted after 7 days (automatic deletion must be provided to avoid oversights by staff). This document confirms what the guarantor ruled with above-mentioned pronounces based on explicit cases and he adds also a specific prevision about data retention. This is a one more millstone that show the importance of personal data processing related to technology evolution.

In addiction, there is another recent decision of the Italian privacy guarantor (dated 4 October 2011) regarding vehicle tracking systems implemented by a logistic company. Also this decision is very important because of its several obiter dicta that are able to underline some principles applicable to all types of personal data processing in workplaces with the presence of new technologies. Indeed, the Italian guarantor makes explicit reference to the balancing of interests (an principles) involved. Talking about localization of vehicles with GPS systems, in order to admit this type of monitoring system, the Italian authority, in section 2.3, ruled positively about its installation. He stated that if the employer (both private and public) follows the guarantees provided by the article 4, paragraph 2, law no. 300/1970 (Workers' Statute), the GPS monitoring system can be installed. In this case the management of his company, the topic of occupational safety and health and the trade union's involvement are all well balanced to make lawful this personal data processing and the installation of this system. Furthermore, specifies the authority, it is not necessary neither the workers' consent.

In conclusion, even if there are not specific pronounces or law about RFID technology, we can disclose that also an RFID system can be lawful installed especially in relation to improve the occupational safety and health. However the employer has to respect the basic principles listed above and the others, more detailed, showed below.

6   "Smart Labels" (RFID): The Italian Privacy Guarantor Established the Warranties for Their Use

There is a not recent document of the Italian privacy guarantor strictly related to RFID technology: it is a guideline useful to improve an efficient management of a retail distribution. It seems to be, for these reasons, far from occupational safety and health topic, but the Italian authority is also focused on the basic principles of personal data processing: in this way, even if there are different aims, we can affirm that the results are the same [14]. This document, in sum, states that the use of RFID system (but we could say any kind of technology) become relevant according to the data protection law when third parties' personal data are in. In fact, if smart labels are connect to some goods there will not be any issues, but when there are some personal data processes the data controller has to follow all the provisions up to know identified [15].

According to these guidelines, the employer has to start from the cornerstones of the data protection law when he needs to install an RFID system useful to process personal data of his employees. For this reason it is important also in relation to all the RFID systems suitable to improve workplaces security. The Italian authority lists these principles:

— principle of necessity (article 3 of Italian Privacy Code): RFID systems have be configured in order to avoid the use of personal data. These system have not to identify people (personal data subjects) unless it is strictly necessary for the purpose;
— principle of legality (article 11, paragraph 1, lett. a), of Italian Privacy Code): personal data processing is permitted only in compliance with privacy law. More precisely, the data controller always needs the privacy policy and, when required, the data subject consent. Furthermore, a specific notification, for very delicate data processing, has to be notified to the Italian privacy guarantor;
— principle of purpose and quality of personal data (art. 11, paragraph 1, lett. b), c), d) e e), of Italian Privacy Code): the controller may process personal data only for one or more specified and lawful purposes. Personal data must also be archived only for the time strictly necessary for these purposes. Moreover, personal data should also be relevant, accurate, not excessive and updated as well;

– principle of proportionality (art. 11, paragraph 1, lett. d) of Italian Privacy Code): personal data processing have not to be disproportionate according to the specified and lawful purpose.

In relation to the point no. 3 the employees' consent it is not required. In fact, the use of RFID system has to be considered as a measure included into the employment contract and for this reason it benefits of the exemption provided by the article 24, paragraph 1, lett. b) of the Italian Privacy Code. Furthermore, the employees' consent it is not necessary in according to the exemption of the article 24, paragraph 1, lett. a) of the Italian Privacy Code. Indeed, the personal data processing takes place to improve the legal obligation provided by the Legislative Decree no. 81/2008 (TUSL) and strictly related to occupational safety and health issues [16].

7   Data Retention

Defined the legal framework that must be followed to install an RFID system, it is necessary to face some issues related to data retention.

RFID systems need the archiving of personal data generated by tags records. For this reason the above-mentioned principle of proportionality becomes one more time the key point. Indeed, the temporary storage must be proportionate to one or more specific and lawful purposes decided by the employer. In fact, the data retention have to be limited for twenty-four hours subsequent to record registration. Only in some specific cases it can be provide for a longer term: for instance, in case of holidays or if personal data are required by police or judicial authorities. Even a longer data retention period can be established. This happens in some specific cases that are not listed by the law: in this way there is a discretionary fringe, but the Italian privacy guarantor recommends to not exceed over a period of seven days [17].

In all other cases, longer than a week, in which the employer wish to storage personal data, he has to notify a request to the Italian guarantor that, verified the security requirements of the RFID system, can allow an exception in order to authorize this long-lasting limit.

Nevertheless time limits above-mentioned, the RFID system must be configured in order to delete personal data automatically. It is necessary to make personal data unreadable or unusable and it is necessary also to avoid carelessness of staff that can forget to cancel data.

8   Conclusions

Personal data, occupational safety and health and Information and Communication Technology are strictly connect and RFID systems include the sum of these three main topics. All of these are contributing to improve the workplaces security but these are also oriented to care about the employees privacy as a fundamental principle (also provided by the article 8 of the Charter of Fundamental Rights of the European Union).

For this reason, to develop lawfully an RFID system in Italy, it is necessary to be in compliance with the Workers' Statute and with the data protection legal framework. To do that the employer has to follow the above-mentioned previsions about workers' activity controls (in accordance with its article 4, paragraph 2). Furthermore, the employer has to follow more delicate provisions regarding personal data processing. More precisely, to develop an RFID system lawfully, the employer has to achieve these followings points:

— Trade Unions involvement: if there is not any trade union, the employer has to involve the internal committee or (following the article 4, paragraph 2, of Workers' Statute) he has to notify a request to the "Inspettorato del lavoro" (Labour Office of Province);
— Adequate privacy policy given to the employees: it is necessary that the employees have knowledge about the RFID system. The article 13 of Italian Privacy Code states how the privacy policy has to be drafted by the employer;
— Identification of data subject: it is necessary that each RFID tag does not contain personal information. The most lawful solution is to give impersonal RFID tags containing data which are not strictly related to employees. In this case, the identification (association tag - employee) has to be able only in another phase: for instance, in case of employees' illegal conducts, judicial authorities requests, hazards and any other law provisions which require employees' personal identification. Moreover, all tags and readers have to be clearly visible and they don't have to be hidden. If it is impossible, or very hardly, to make visible these items (because of their size), the employer has to use images to disclosure readers with the purpose for which the system is established: the CCTV code of practice can be used as well because there are not specific provisions provided by law to disclosure an RFID system. Finally, the RFID system cannot constantly monitor the employees' position: for instance, to regulate accesses to some specific workplaces can be used "proximity readers", limiting their activity to entrances;
— Data retention: even if the maximum retention period can leap over a week, it is advisable the retention will not go beyond this limit;
— Security measures: the Italian Privacy Code provides some measures about security of personal data processing (articles 31, 33, 34, 35 and Appendix B). In order to achieve easily this aim, ISO/IEC 27000-series can be used to draft an efficient security policy;
— Persons in charge of processing personal data: three different persons in charge have to be listed, for three different processing areas of personal data, by the employer: a) the person who can access and process personal data relating to the RFID system functions. More precisely, he manages access levels for each impersonal tag, determining which tag is allowed in specific working areas; b) the person who can access and use the information only to perform the association tag - employee; c) the person who can access both types of personal data and he is therefore potentially able to associate employees to each entrance crossed during their activity.

References

1. Cook, D., Das, S.: Smart Environments: Technology, Protocols and Applications, p. XI - foreword. Wiley - Interscience, Hoboken (2005)
2. De Angelis, F., Gagliardi, R., Marcantoni, F., Polzonetti, A.: Ambienti Intelligenti a supporto della Sicurezza Personale in Congresso Nazionale AICA Smart Tech and Smart Innovation (AICA 2011), Turin (2011)
3. Zoli, C.: Il controllo a distanza del datore di lavoro: l'art. 4, l. n. 300/1970, tra attualità ed esigenze di riforma, Riv. it. dir. lav., vol. 04, p. 485 - foreword (2009)
4. Bellavista, A.: Il controllo sui lavoratori, Giappichelli, Torino (1995)
5. Toffoletto, F.: Nuove tecnologie informatiche e tutela del lavoratore, Giuffrè, Milano (2006)
6. Frezzi, M.: Le nuove frontiere del controllo sui lavoratori (il chip RFID),
   http://www.di-elle.it/index.php?url=/consultazione/
   approfondimenti_4/le_nuove_frontiere_del_controllo_sui_
   lavoratori_793/view/793/
7. Pisani, C.: I controlli a distanza dei lavoratori, in DLRI (giornale di Diritto del Lavoro e di Relazioni Industriali), p. 138 - foreword (1987)
8. Cass. Sez. V pen. 1/6/2010 n. 20722, L'ambito di applicazione dell'art. 4 dello Statuto dei Lavoratori tra finalità difensiva e caratteristiche delle apparecchiature di controllo, in Orient. giur. lav., con nota di Lorenzo Cairo, p. 323 - foreword (2010)
9. Ichino, P.: Il contratto di lavoro, in Trattato di Diritto civile e commerciale, a cura di Schlesinger P., Milano, p. 58 - foreword (2003)
10. Tullini, P.: Comunicazione elettronica, potere di controllo e tutela del lavoratore, in Rivista italiana di diritto del lavoro, vol. I, p. 323 - foreword (2009)
11. Pradelli, A.: Nuove tecnologie: privacy e controlli del datore, in Diritto e pratica del lavoro, vol. 7, p. 471 - foreword (2007)
12. The Italian data protection authority, Companies: The use of biometrics for time and attendance and working time, document n. 1664257 of 15 October 2009,
    http://www.garanteprivacy.it/garante/doc.jsp?ID=1664257
13. The Italian data protection authority, Processing of biometric data for the purpose of verification of the presence of employees and access to particular areas of production, document n. 1306551 of 15 June 2006,
    http://www.garanteprivacy.it/garante/doc.jsp?ID=1306551
14. The Italian data protection authority, RFID tags: the Italian data protection authority identifies the guarantees for their use, document n. 1109493 of 9 March 2005,
    http://www.garanteprivacy.it/garante/doc.jsp?ID=1109493
15. The European Union has already pronounced a Recommendation on RFID issues, but it's focalized especially on consumer protection over retail distribution. The Recommendations 2009/387/CE, http://eur-lex.europa.eu/LexUriServ/
    LexUriServ.do?uri=OJ:L:2009:122:0047:0051:EN:PDF
16. Cardarelli, F., Sica, S., Zeno-Zenchovic, V.: Il codice dei dati personali. Temi e problemi, Giuffrè, Milano (2004)
17. The Italian data protection authority, Video surveillance, document n. 1734653 of 8 April 2010, http://www.garanteprivacy.it/garante/
    doc.jsp?ID=1712680#3.4

Evaluating and Benchmarking the Interactions between a Humanoid Robot and a Virtual Human for a Real-World Social Task

S.M. Mizanoor Rahman

Dept. of Mechanical Engineering, Vrije Universiteit Brussel (VUB), Pleinlaan 2,
1050 Brussels, Belgium
mizansm@hotmail.com

Abstract. We developed two social agents (a virtual human and a humanoid robot) with various similar functionalities, interaction modalities, intelligence, autonomy etc. and integrated them through a common communication platform based on a novel control algorithm to assist each other in a real-world social task (searching for a hidden object).We also studied human's interactions with those social agents and with some other allied agents for that task to benchmark the interactions. We developed the standards of the performances as well as the performance measurement methods for the agents for the task. We also adopted several hypotheses regarding the attributes and performances of the agents for their interactions for the task.We evaluated the attributes and performances of the robot and the virtual human in their interactions for the task, analyzed them and compared them with the standards. The results showed that both the robot and the virtual human performed satisfactorily in their social interactions though the performances varied slightly.We also found a trade-off between the attributes and the performances of the agents. The results will help develop intelligent social agents of different realities to assist humans in various real-world social tasks, or to get the real-world social tasks done in cooperation between artificial social agents of different realities.

Keywords: Virtual human, humanoid robot, social robot, social task, human-computer interaction, human-robot interaction, benchmarking, system integration.

1 Introduction

1.1 Virtual Humans and Social Robots

The virtual humans are the software generated human-like animated characters. They can be enriched with many social functions and attributes for their interactions with humans such as they can show human-like actions, motions, gestures, emotions, facial expressions, intelligence etc.,communicate and interact with humans, memorize the facts and retrieve them according to the dynamic context, and show reasoning and decision making abilities about what they perceive etc [1]-[2].

B. Papasratorn et al. (Eds.): IAIT 2013, CCIS 409, pp. 184–197, 2013.

On the other hand, ideally,social robots are human-like robots, they take inspiration from humans, are enriched with human-like communication capabilities, capable of understanding human's affective states, expressions, intentions, actions etc., can interpret them based on contextual information and act based on situations [3]-[4].

1.2   Accomplishing Real-World Tasks by Virtual Humans and Social Robots

The virtual humans (VHs) are presently used to perform many tasks such as serving as the virtual tutor, student or trainee, patient, advertiser etc. They have increasing contributions towards the anatomy education, psychotherapy and biomedical research [5]-[9]. However, the VHs still could not come beyond the virtual environments. Their contributions could be augmented if they could perform real-world social tasks for humans or could cooperate with humans to peform the social tasks. However, such contributions are still not available. On the other hand, the social robots (SRs) are proposed for various social activities and interactions with humans such as therapy for abnormal social development, autism etc [10]-[13]. However, their applications in accomplishing social tasks in cooperation with humans are still limited. In most cases, either they do not look like the human [11], [13], or they look like the human, but cannot act like the human [14]-[15], which reduces their social acceptance.

1.3   Cooperation between Virtual Human and Social Robot in Real-World Tasks

We think that the autonomous SRs and VHs have a lot in common in their objectives and performances though there is a difference that the SRs exist physically while the VHs are software-based visual agents.We also think that the SRs and the VHs may separately cooperate with the humans and also with each other to perform the real-world tasks. However, such cooperation is usually not seen. It is true that a few initiatives have been taken to stage the cooperation between the VHs and the SRs [16]-[17]. However, these attempts are still in the concept design phases, and no real characters and the cooperation methods have been proposed to justify the initiatives.

1.4   Performances Evaluation of the Social Agents

We think that there should have well-defined evaluation methods and standards for evaluating and benchmarking the performances of the social agents in their various social interactions with each other and with the humans, which might help improve their performances as well as their social acceptance and impacts. However, such suitable evaluation techniques are still not available.Of course, a few researchers are addressing the evaluation and bechmarking of the social agents, but their efforts are still limited in scope and applications [18]-[19].

1.5   Objective of the Paper

Hence, the objective of the paper was to present social interactions between a virtual human and a social robot for a real-world social task (searching for a hidden object). Human's interactions with some allied agents were also studied to benchmark the interactions.

2   Requirements for the Integration between Social Robot and Virtual Human

The effective integration of the social robot with the virtual human for a specific real-world task needs to satisfy a set of requirements. The robots need to have attributes for social interactions such as interactivity, intelligence, autonomy, perception, bilateral communication and interactions, social functions etc. [3]-[4], [10]-[15].Similarly, the virtual humans should have intelligent decision technologies, autonomy, interaction modalities, personality, natural interactivity etc. [20]-[21]. Kapadia *et al.* identified several key limitations in the existing representation, control, locomotion, multimodal perception and authoring of the autonomous virtual humans that must be addressed to stage successful interactions between the virtual human and the social robot [22]. Other requirements for creating interactive virtual humans for interactions with social robots are presented in [23]. Emotion, memory, remembering, recognition etc. for the social robots and the virtual humans also seem to be important for their integration for multimodal social interactions for many cases [24]-[26].

The required interaction modes for the selected task might be vision, audition (speech), demonstration, recognition, gesture, locomotion etc. It means that, the social agents may need to see and recognize each other, the object and the environment, to speak and listen the counterpart for verbal instructions by the agents about the search path for the hidden object, to show gesture and understand/recognize the counterpart's gesture that may be used by the agents to demonstrate/understand the search path for the hidden object. They may also need to show movements to search for the object etc. They need to be enriched with the required technologies, control methods and algorithms, interfaces, sensors, common communication platform etc. They should also be as human-like in appearances and performances as possible.

3   Development of the Social Agents

3.1   The Virtual Human

We developed a realistic autonomous intelligent 3D virtual human (VH) with a western woman face. We used Smartbody (http://smartbody.ict.usc.edu/) for her control and animation. We created the model based on the joints and skeleton requirements of Smartbody and exported it to the software Autodesk Maya 3D (http://www.autodesk.com/). We determined the anthropomorphic data (walking velocity, joint angles, body dimensions etc.) for the VH by being inspired by that for the human. We used Ogre (http://www.ogre3d.org/) for graphical rendering.

The software package included Application Programming Interfaces (APIs) for various functions (actions, emotions, expressions etc.). The VH could be displayed in a screen as in Fig.1 (a). The VH was enriched with many social functionalities and attributes such as speech (from text to speech), locomotion (walk to a position), manipulation, gaze, nonverbal behaviours, facial expressions, emotions, actions, communications with human, turn head, look at a position, point at something etc.

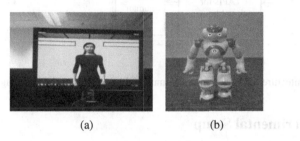

(a)   (b)

Fig. 1. The intelligent autonomous social agents, (a) the virtual human, (b) the social robot

3.2   The Social Robot

We used a NAO robot (http://www.aldebaran-robotics.com/en/) as shown in Fig.1 (b) as the social robot (SR). We developed various functions and attributes for the robot to make it intelligent, autonomous and social such as stand up, sit down, walk, shake hand, wave hand, grab and release object, look at a position, point at something, speech (text to speech) etc. Like the VH, it could perceive the environment through sensors such as video, audio etc. It could make decision based on some adaptive rules and stored information and react by moving, talking or showing internal emotions. The software package included the APIs for the functions.

3.3   Development of Common Communication System for the Social Agents

Animation of each function for each character was commanded from a common command script (client), which was networked with the control server through the I2P (Integrated Interaction Platform) Thrift interface. The I2P was our in-house platform, which could be used to animate both the SR and the VH using the same command script (client) through specifying the character. However, each character had its own APIs for the functions called in the client script. The similar functions between the VH and the SR generated similar behaviours. Architecture of the common communication scheme for the social agents through the I2P is illustrated in Fig.2.

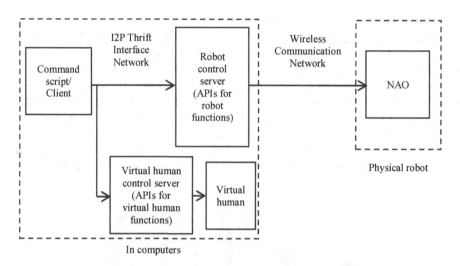

Fig. 2. Architecture of the common communication system for the social agents through I2P

4   Experimental Setup

As shown in Fig.3, we had three rooms. In Room 1, we put the computers to control the SR, the VH and other hardwares. In Room 2, we put 10   rectangular boxes of identical dimensions and appearance (black). Five boxes were put randomly on a table in the left side of the room, while the remaining   five boxes were put randomly on sofas in the right side. An object was hidden in any of the 10 boxes by the experimenter. One agent needed assistance (called the assisted agent) from another agent (called the assistant agent) to search for the hidden object. Usually, the assisted agent stood at point P1, and the assistant agent stood at point P2 (the assistant agents who existed physically e.g. social robot) or appeared at the screen (the assistant agents who were physically non-existed e.g. virtual human, assistance through video etc.). There was a sound system near point P2 and the voice of the assistant agent could be played through it. Laptop 2 was used for Skype connection with Laptop 1 if any real human served as the assistant agent but he/she did not appear physically, instead appeared in the screen through Skype. In addition, kinect cameras were put in Room 2, and other devices required for gesture, action and speech recognition were put.

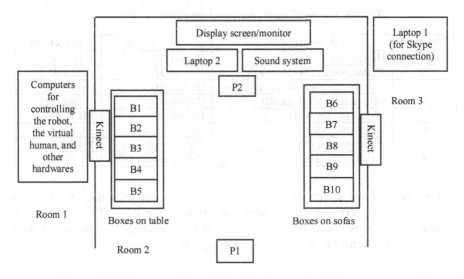

Fig. 3. Layout diagram of the experimental setup

5   Experiment Design

5.1   Experiment Protocols

We considered eight experiment protocols to evaluate the interactions between different social agents for searching for the object (Table 1). In the protocols from 1 to 6, the human was the assisted agent and received assistance from various assistant agents such as another human (protocol #1), voice of another human (protocol #2), video with voice of another human (protocol #3), a human appeared through Skype (protocol #4), the virtual human (protocol #5), the social robot   (protocol #6) etc. for searching for the hidden object. In protocols #7 & 8, the VH and the SR assisted each other for searching for the hidden object. We considerd the protocols from 1 to 6 to benchmark the interactions between the VH and the SR.

The VH had human-like functionalities, but it was artificial, screen-based and did not appear physically in front of the assisted agent. Similarly, the telepresented Skyped-human also did not appear physically in front of the assisted agent, it was screen-based, but it was natural. We thought the Skyped-human to be the physically non-appeared real human with the highest intelligence and autonomy. Hence, we considered the Skyped-human as the standard for the VH. On the other hand, the SR was physically embodied and existed like the real human, it had human-like appearance, but it was artificial. The human is the physically embodied and physically existed natural agent with the highest intelligence and autonomy. Hence, we considered the human as the standard for the SR. Human voice was non-embodied. Human video with voice did not physically exist. These two agents were

Table 1. The social agents and their interactions (as acronyms)

Protocol#	Assistant agent	Assisted agent	Interactions
1	Human (H)	Human (H)	H-H
2	Human voice only (Hvoice)	Human (H)	Hvoice-H
3	Human video with voice (Hvideo)	Human (H)	Hvideo-H
4	Skyped human (SkypedH)	Human (H)	SkypedH-H
5	Virtual human (VH)	Human (H)	VH-H
6	Social robot (SR)	Human (H)	SR-H
7	Virtual human (VH)	Social robot (SR)	VH-SR
8	Social robot (SR)	Virtual human (VH)	SR-VH

used to measure the effects of sound, vision and physical existance on the agent performances. The VH and the SR were both artificial, but they differed in physical existance. The two protocols (#7 & 8) were used to understand the social interactions between the VH and the SR, which was our primary goal.

5.2   Subjects

One hundred forty two (142) human subjects were selected to participate in the experiments for different protocols (1 assistant human and 20 assisted humans for protocol 1, 1 assistant human appeared through Skype and 20 assisted humans for protocol 4, 20 assisted humans for each of the protocol 2, 3, 5 and 6, and 20 human subjects to evaluate the VH-SR and SR-VH interactions for protocols 7 & 8). 115 subjects were male, 27 were female and they were aged between 21 and 35 years. All the subjects were right-handed and they reported to be physically and mentally healthy with sound functionalities of their eyes and ears.

5.3   Hypotheses

We adopted few hypotheses (research questions as well) to justify the interactions between the agents. The hypotheses were as the following: (i) whether or not the performances of the assistant agents were satisfactory for the task (for protocols#1-8), (ii) whether or not there were variations in the performances of the assistant agents for the same assisted   agent (protocols#1-6), (iii) especially, between the VH and the SR in protocols 5 and 6, whose performances were the better in assisting the human, (iv) whose performances were the better when the VH and the SR assisted each other for searching for the object (protocols#7 & 8), (v) whether or not the agent attributes could affect the agent performances, etc.

6   The Experiments

Protocol#1: The assistant agent (human) stood at P2 as in Fig.3 keeping the face towards point P1.The experimenter kept the object hidden in any of the 10 boxes (say, it was hidden inside box B1) in presence of the assistant agent. Then, the assisted agent stood at P1 keeping his/her face towards P2.Then, the assistant agent instructed (once only) the assisted agent how to find the object.The instructions included-

Speech: the assistant agent told "hello! I will help you find the object. The box containing the object is lying on the table. It is not on top of another box. Closest to the screen".

Gesture, facial expressions, emotions and actions: the assistant agent also turned towards the box where the object was hidden, looked at the box, pointed at it with the hand, made some facial expressions matching the gesture and actions etc.

Then, the assisted agent identified the correct box based on the instructions he/she received from the assistant agent. He/she moved to the box, pointed it, touched it, grabbed it, told "the object is here" and released it. The experimenter then opened the box and checked whether or not the object was inside the box. Then, the assisted agent subjectively evaluated the attributes and performances of the assistant agent in his/her assistance for the assisted agent in searching for the object. The evaluation was administered by the experimenter, and was done using a rating scale following a set of predefined criteria. The evaluation criteria for the agent attributes were (i) anthropomorphism- how human-like the assistant agent was in appearance and performances, (ii) embodiments-how embodied or physically existed the assistant agent was, (iii) gesture and action-match between gesture and action of the assistant agent, (iv) stability-how competent the assistant agent was in avoiding any disturbance, noise etc. The performance criteria for the assistant agents were (i) cooperation- how cooperative the assistant agent was in assisting the assisted agent, (ii) clarity of instructions-how clearly the assisted agent could understand the instructions of the assistant agent, (iii) effectiveness-how effective the instructions of the assistant agent were for the assisted agent in finding the object, (iv) cognitive load- how much cognitive load the assisted agent felt for finding the hidden object, the least cognitive load was to be the best, and (v) companionship- whether or not the assisted agent desired to establish a social companionship with the assistant agent based on the assistance. In the rating scale, (+1) was for the worst and (+5) was for the best evaluation for the assistant agent.The experimenter also objectively evaluated the peformances of the assistant agent based on two criteria: (i) time-time taken by the assisted agent to find the correct box. The performance of the assistant agent would be the best if the assisted agent could find the correct box within the least possible time, (ii) accuracy-whether or not the assisted agent could find the correct box.

Then, the assisted agent was replaced by another subject, (but, the assistant agent was unchanged) and the whole procedures as described above were repeated for the second subject (assisted agent). In this way, 20 subjects separately acted as the assisted agent. The subjects, who participated in this protocol, did not participate in any other protocols. Figure 4 (a) illustrates the procedures for this protocol.

Protocol#2: the recorded instructions of the assistant agent of protocol#1 were played for audio only in the sound system. The recorded voice of the previous assistant agent served as the assistant agent for this protocol. Then, the same procedures as employed for protocol#1 were employed.

Protocol#3: The recorded video with sound of the assistant agent of protocol#1 was displayed in the screen. The video with sound served as the assistant agent for this protocol. Then, the same procedures as employed for protocol#1 were employed.

Protocol#4: A real human standing at Room 3 appeared at the screen of Room 2 through the Skype. The Skyped-human served as the assistant agent. Then, the same procedures as employed for protocol#1 were employed as in Fig 4 (b).

Protocol#5: The VH appeared at the screen and served as the assistant agent. Then, the same procedures as employed for protocol#1 were employed as in Fig. 4 (c).

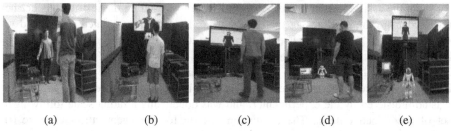

| (a) | (b) | (c) | (d) | (e) |

Fig. 4. The human receiving assistance from (a) another human, (b) the Skyped-human, (c) the VH, and (d) the SR for searching for the object. In (e), the SR and the VH are assisting each other for searching for the object. The object is hidden inside any of the 10 black boxes as seen.

Protocol#6: The SR stood at P2 and served as the assistant agent. Then, the same procedures as employed for protocol#1 were employed as shown in Fig. 4 (d).

Protocol#7: In this case, 10 relevant instruction methods for 10 locations of the 10 boxes were set (called) for the VH in the programming script (client). The VH could instruct the SR about the correct location of the box where the object was hidden if the object was hidden in any of the 10 boxes of 10 locations. However, the VH was needed to be taught the correct location of the box through the programming script. For example, in an experiment trial, the object was hidden in a box closest to the screen (B1). The program was run and the VH instructed the SR to find the object based on the instruction methods set for that location. The instruction methods for B1 location included-

Speech: same as used in protocol#1
Gesture, emotions, expressions and actions: the VH also showed emotions, facial expressions, gesture and actions matching her speech. For example, the VH turned towards the box where the object was hidden, smiled, looked at the box, moved towards the box (within the screen), pointed at it with the hand, told "the object is there", then stopped and expressed happiness.

In the same programming script (client) as used for the VH, the required functions, gestures, expressions, emotions, speech, actions etc. for 10 different destinations (locations for 10 boxes) were set (called) for the SR. The SR could recognize the gesture, actions and speech of the VH and immediately determine the correct location of the box where the object was hidden, then turned towards the location, moved to that location, looked at the box, pointed at the box, took an attempt to grab the box (but, it could not grab due to its small fingers), then released the grab, then told "the object is inside this box" and then stopped working.Then, the experimenter opened the box and checked whether or not the hidden object was found there. This trial was repeated for 20 times and each of the 20 subjects evaluated the attributes and performances of the assistant agent based on the same criteria and methods employed for protocol#1. The experimenter also recorded the time and accuracy data for each trial. Figure 4 (e) illustrates the procedures for this protocol.

Protocol#8: the opposite of protocol#7 happened when the SR assisted the VH in searching for the object. The SR was taught the correct location of the hidden object through the programming script. The instruction methods for the SR were same as that for the VH. The VH could recognize the gesture, actions and speech of the SR and immediately determine the correct location of the box where the object was hidden, then turned towards the box, moved towards that location (up to screen limit), looked at and pointed at the box, then told "the object is inside that box". Then, the experimenter opened the pointed box and checked whether or not the hidden object was found there. This trial was repeated for 20 times and the same evaluation procedure as employed in protocol#7 was conducted.

7   Experiment Results and Analyses

Figure 5 shows the mean evaluation scores for the performances of the assistant agents for interactions between different assistant and assisted agents. The figure shows that the human, Skyped-human, human-video, SR, VH, and the human-voice secured the 1st, 2nd, 3rd, 4th, 5th and 6th position respectively for their performances when serving as the assistant agents for the assisted agents (human).The performances of the assistant agents (except human voice) were satisfactory for the task, which justifies the hypothesis (i) of section 5.3. However, there are variations in the performances of the assistant agents for the same assisted agent, which justifies the hypothesis (ii). The Skyped-human performed better than the human-video because the assisted agent (human) could communicate with the Skyped-human, which was not possible for the human-video. However, both the human-video and the Skyped-human performed better than the VH. The reason may be that the VH was artificial, but the Skyped-human and the human-video were the agents with natural origin. The results also show that the SR performed better than the VH probably due to the reason that the SR had physical existence, but the VH lacked it. This finding justifies the hypothesis (iii). Analyses of Variances (ANOVAs) showed, for each criterion in each interaction, variations in the evaluation scores due to variation in assisted agents (evaluators) were not significant ($p>0.05$ at each case). The figure also shows that for VH-SR and SR-VH interactions where the VH and the SR assisted each other, the SR   performed better than the VH, which justifies the hypothesis (iv). This might happen probably due to the reason that the SR had physical existence, but the VH lacked it. Again, the performances of the SR and the VH as the assistant agents were evaluated for two conditions (protocols 5 & 7 for the VH, and protocols 6 & 8 for the SR). ANOVAs showed that the variations in performances for each of the two agents between these two conditions were not statistically significant ($p>0.05$ at each case). It indicates that the VH and the SR exhibit similar performances in their assistance for natural (human) and artificial (VH or SR) assisted agents. It proves that the VH and the SR may be employed to assist each other in a remote or unmanned environment or in any social environment where human is not the performer but the beneficiary.

Figure 6 shows the mean evaluation scores for the attributes of the agents. The human voice lacked most of the attributes except the stability. The stability for the assistant agents (except in protocol#1) was also low. The reasons may be that these agents were slightly vulnerable to the external disturbances such as sound and noise. The SR was also affected by floor properties and obstacles (if any). As Fig.6 shows, the assistant agents i.e. the human, Skyped-human, human-video, SR, VH, and the human-voice secured the 1st, 2nd, 3rd, 4th, 5th and 6th position respectively in terms of their attributes. The order for the agent attributes exactly matches that for the agent performancs in Fig.5. In addition, the relationships for the attributes among (i) human-video, Skyped-human, and VH, and (ii) VH and SR for different conditions were exactly same as that for the agent performances (Fig.5). These findings indicate that agent attributes affect agent performances [27], which justifies the hypothesis (v).

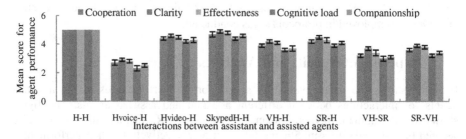

Fig. 5. Mean (n=20) evaluation scores for the performances of the assistant agents for interactions between different assistant and assisted agents

Figure 7(a) shows the mean times required by the assisted agents to find the box for interactions between various assistant and assisted agents. As Fig.7(a) shows, the assistant agents in the interactions H-H, SR-VH, SkypedH-H, Hvideo-H, SR-H, VH-H, VH-SR and Hvoice-H secured the 1st, 2nd, 3rd, 4th, 5th, 6th, 7th and 8th position respectively for their performance for this criterion. This order (excluding SR-VH) matches the orders of the performances and the attributes of the assistant agents in figures 5 and 6 respectively. In SR-VH, the VH found the box based on the assistance of the SR. However, this interaction was software-controlled for the fixed speed of the VH (same speed as the assisted human of protocol#1 as we were inspired by the human while developing the VH). This is why, the time required by the VH was almost same as that required by the assisted human in protocol#1. Again, we see that there is no error bars for the SR-VH interaction, because there was no variation in the time required by the VH as it was controlled by the software for fixed speed. In VH-SR interaction, the input speed of the SR was the same as that of the assisted human of protocol#1(as we were also inspired by the human while developing the SR) and the interaction was software-controlled. Hence, the time required by the SR was also supposed to be the same as that required by the assisted human in protocol#1. However, the SR took the time which was longer than that the assisted human took in protocol#1, and its time-based performance was ranked as the 7th. We also see that there are some small error bars for the VH-SR interaction. The reason may be that eventhough the SR was controlled for the fixed speed, it was affected by the disturbance (e.g. floor properties) in the physical environment. This also reflects in the lower stability of the SR (Fig.6). The Hvoice-H took the longest time due to its low attributes (Fig.6). In general, the required time was related to the agent attributes, which justifies the hypothesis (v). ANOVAs show that the variations in time between the assisted agents were not significant ($p>0.05$ at each case).

Accuracy of the assisted agents is shown in Fig.7(b). The results show that all the assisted agents in all interactions (except in Hvoice-H) could accurately find the box. This relationship also matches the relationships between the interactions in terms of performances, attributes and time in Figures 5, 6 and 7(a) respectively. The failure of Hvoice-H is due to the lack of attributes of the assistant agent (Fig.6).

The VH in VH-H and VH-SR interactions was very close to the Skyped-human in SkypedH-H interaction, and the SR in the SR-H and SR-VH interactions was close to the human (assistant agent) in the H-H interaction in terms of attributes. Similarly, in terms of peformances, the VH was able to achieve about 80% and 77% performances of the Skyped-human (standard for the VH) in the VH-H and VH-SR interactions respectively, and the SR was able to achieve about 76% and 74% performances of the human (standard for the SR) in the SR-H and SR-VH interactions respectively. However, the human's performance was better than the Skyped-human's performance as the assistant agent. Hence, the SR performed better than the VH.

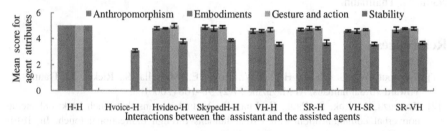

Fig. 6. Mean ($n=20$) evaluation scores for the attributes of the assistant agents for interactions between different assistant and assisted agents

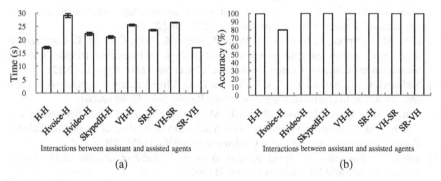

Fig. 7. (a) Mean ($n=20$) times (with standard deviations) required by the assisted agents to find the box, (b) Accuracy (%) in finding the box by the assisted agents for interactions between the assistant and the assisted agents

8   Conclusions and Future Works

We developed a social robot and a virtual human to assist each other in a real-world social task based on a control algorithm through a common communication platform.We evaluated the interactions between them and also benchmarked the interactions with some other allied interactions. The results showed that the performances of the interactions between the robot and the virtual human were satisfactory, which indicates that the integration betweeen the agents were successful. Again, their performances varied from each other and were affected by their attributes. The integration between social robot and virtual human for real-world task, evaluation and benchmarking of social agents of different realities, communication for social agents of different realities through a common platform etc. that we proposed here are the most novel and have excellent prospects and applications. Thus, the findings will help develop   social robots and virtual humans to assist the humans in real-world tasks, and also to assist each other in the social environment. In future, we will improve the attributes, functionalities and capabilities of the social agents, and employ them in the tasks with more complex social interactions.

Acknowledgements. The author acknowledges the supports that he received from his past colleagues of the Institute for Media Innovation, Nanyang Technological University, 50 Nanyang Drive, Singapore 637553 especially the supports from Prof. Nadia M. Thalmann.

References

[1] Swartout, W., Gratch, J., Hill, R.W., Hovy, E., Marsella, S., Rickel, J., Traum, D.: Toward virtual humans. AI Magazine 27(2), 96–108 (2006)

[2] Kotranza, A., Lok, B., Pugh, C., Lind, D.: Virtual humans that touch back: enhancing nonverbal communication with virtual humans through bidirectional touch. In: IEEE Virtual Reality Conference, pp. 175–178 (2009)

[3] Castellano, G., Peters, C.: Socially perceptive robots: challenges and concerns. Interaction Studies 11(2), 201–207 (2010)

[4] Leite, I., Martinho, C., Paiva, A.: Social robots for long-term interaction: a survey. International Journal of Social Robotics 5(2), 291–308 (2013)

[5] Hays, M., Campbell, J., Trimmer, M., Poore, J., Webb, A., Stark, C., King, T.: Can role-play with virtual humans teach interpersonal skills? In: Proc. of Interservice/Industry Training, Simulation and Education Conference (I/ITSEC), Paper No. 12318, Pages 12 (2012)

[6] SikLanyi, C., Geiszt, Z., Karolyi, P., Magyar1, A.: Virtual reality in special needs early education. The International Journal of Virtual Reality 5(4), 55–68 (2006)

[7] Campbell, J., Hays, M., Core, M., Birch, M., Bosack, M., Clark, R.: Interpersonal and leadership skills: using virtual humans to teach new officers. In: Proc. of Interservice/Industry Training, Simulation, and Education Conference, Paper No. 11358 (2011)

[8] Saleh, N.: The value of virtual patients in medical education. Annals of Behavioral Science and Medical Education 16(2), 29–31 (2010)

[9] Lawford, P., Narracott, A., McCormack, K., Bisbal, J., Martin, C., Brook, B., Zachariou, M., Kohl, P., Fletcher, K., Diaz-Zucczrini, V.: Virtual physiological human: training challenges. Phil. Trans. R. Soc. A 368(1921), 2841–2851 (2010)

[10] Scassellati, B.: Using social robots to study abnormal social development. In: Proceedings of the Fifth International Workshop on Epigenetic Robotics: Modeling Cognitive Development in Robotic Systems, pp. 11–14 (2005)

[11] Dautenhahn, K., Werry, I.: Towards interactive robots in autism therapy-background, motivation and challenges. Pragmatics & Cognition 12(1), 1–35 (2004)

[12] Scassellati, B., Admoni, H., Mataric, M.: Robots for use in autism research. Annu. Rev. Biomed. Eng. 14, 275–294 (2012)

[13] Fischer, L., Alexander, E., Yan, X., Su, H., Harrington, K., Fischer, G.: An affordable compact humanoid robot for autism spectrum disorder interventions in children. In: Proc. of 33rd Annual Int. Conf. of the IEEE EMBS, Boston, USA, pp. 5319–5322 (2011)

[14] Nishio, S., Ishiguro, H., Hagita, N.: Geminoid: teleoperated android of an existing person. In: Filho, A. (ed.) Humanoid Robots: New Developments, ch. 20. InTech (2007)

[15] Kaneko, K., Kanehiro, F., Morisawa, M., Miura, K., Nakaoka, S., Kajita, S.: Cybernetic human hrp-4c. In: Proc. of IEEE-RAS Int. Conf. on Humanoid Robots, pp. 7–14 (2009)

[16] Dragone, M., Duffy, B., O'Hare, G.: Social interaction between robots, avatars & humans. In: Proc. of IEEE Int. Workshop on Robot and Human Interactive Communication, pp. 24–29 (2005)

[17] Forland, E., Russa, G.: Virtual humans vs. anthropomorphic robots for education: how can they work together? In: Proc. of ASEE/IEEE Frontiers in Education Conference, pp. S3G (2005)

[18] Kipp, M., Kipp, K.H., Ndiaye, A., Gebhard, P.: Evaluating the tangible interface and virtual characters in the interactive COHIBIT exhibit. In: Gratch, J., Young, M., Aylett, R.S., Ballin, D., Olivier, P. (eds.) IVA 2006. LNCS (LNAI), vol. 4133, pp. 434–444. Springer, Heidelberg (2006)

[19] Nabe, S., Cowley, S., Kanda, T., Hiraki, K., Ishiguro, H., Hagita, N.: Robots as social mediators: coding for engineers. In: Proc. of the 15th IEEE International Symposium on Robot and Human Interactive Communication, pp. 384–390 (2006)

[20] Kasap, Z., Thalmann, N.: Intelligent virtual humans with autonomy and personality: state-of-the-art. Intelligent Decision Technologies 1, 3–15 (2007)

[21] Kang, Y., Subagdja, B., Tan, A., Ong, Y., Miao, C.: Virtual characters in agent-augmented co-space. In: Conitzer, Winikoff, Padgham, van der Hoek (eds.) Proc. of the 11th Int. Conference on Autonomous Agents and Multiagent Systems (AAMAS 2012), Valencia, Spain, June 4-8 (2012)

[22] Kapadia, M., Shoulson, A., Boatright, C.D., Huang, P., Durupinar, F., Badler, N.I.: What's next? the new era of autonomous virtual humans. In: Kallmann, M., Bekris, K. (eds.) MIG 2012. LNCS, vol. 7660, pp. 170–181. Springer, Heidelberg (2012)

[23] Gratch, J., Rickel, J., Andre, E., Badler, N., Cassell, J., Petajan, E.: Creating interactive virtual humans: some assembly required. IEEE Intelligent Systems, 2–11 (July/August 2002)

[24] Kasap, Z., Moussa, M., Chaudhuri, P., Thalmann, N.: Making them remember-emotional virtual characters with memory. IEEE Computer Graphics and Applications 29(2), 20–29 (2009)

[25] Kasap, Z., Thalmann, N.: Building long-term relationships with virtual and robotic characters: the role of remembering. The Visual Computer 28(1), 87–97 (2012)

[26] Zhao, W., Xie, X., Yang, X.: Control virtual human with speech recognition and gesture recognition technology. Advances in Intelligent and Soft Computing 139, 441–446 (2012)

[27] Wainer, J., Feil-Seifer, D., Shell, D., Mataric, M.: The role of physical embodiment in human-robot interaction. In: Proc. of the 15th IEEE International Symposium on Robot and Human Interactive Communication, pp. 117–122 (2006)

Assessing the Differential Effect of Web Usability Dimensions on Perceived Usefulness of a B2C E-Commerce Website

Geetanjali Sahi[1] and Sushila Madan[2]

[1] Lal Bahadur Shastri Institute of Management, Delhi, India
geetanjali@lbsim.ac.in
[2] University of Delhi, Delhi, India
sushila_lsr@yahoo.com

Abstract. The current invigorated wave of E-commerce initiatives, post the initial boom and dot com bubble burst is definitely more prudent. Therefore, business community is looking to academe for understanding of how usability can be increased to reap the numerous benefits of E-commerce. This study has been undertaken in context of B2C E-commerce websites and its main purpose is to analyze the differential impact of web usability dimensions on perceived usefulness. This is done by studying customers' responses regarding B2C E-commerce websites with respect to four usability dimensions. A questionnaire survey is used to collect data from select respondents (N=415) and analysis is performed using structural equation modelling (SEM). Findings suggest that although all four dimensions significantly impact perceived usefulness, system quality followed by trust are the two most important factors. The study has important implications for website designers, developers and researchers.

Keywords: B2C E-commerce, web usability, system quality, trust, content quality, support quality, perceived usefulness, technology acceptance model (TAM).

1   Introduction

Accelerated advancements in information technology domain have enabled businesses to break traditional barriers and explore new opportunities in the sphere of E-commerce. E-commerce encompasses all business activities carried on with the use of electronic media, i.e. the computer network. One of the most common models in E-commerce is Business-To-Consumer (B2C) model in which, businesses sell products and services through electronic channels directly to the customer. B2C E-commerce has grown both in diversity and transacted money value in recent years and the trend is expected to be the same in future. A report released by IAMAI and IMRB International in 2013 [15] suggests that the E-commerce market which was valued at

B. Papasratorn et al. (Eds.): IAIT 2013, CCIS 409, pp. 198–211, 2013.

Rs 47,349 Cr. in December 2012 is expected to grow by 33 percent to reach Rs 62,967 Cr. by the end of 2013. A study by Forrester Research Inc. [8] on Online Retail 2011 to 2016 reveals that India's E-commerce market has shown an explosive growth of 400 percent in last five years and is expected to grow more than five-fold by 2016.

Due to phenomenal increase in B2C E-commerce sales and the hyper competitive nature of E-commerce market, it is imperative to understand the factors in a B2C website that prospective buyers perceive as relatively more useful than others. In B2C environment, customers have access to numerous websites offering similar products and services, so, if a website is not usable, users would simply access any other site that meets their needs in a more efficient and effective manner. As an organization's website is a gateway to its information, products and services, it must be usable so that customers use and transact through it. Hence website usability is an important area for research in order to understand factors customers consider important in a B2C E-commerce website.

Numerous researchers and web development practitioners have proposed various factors for measuring usability. However, not much research has been conducted that investigates the differential impact of web usability dimensions on visitor's perception of website's usefulness. In fact, no known literature addresses this issue in Indian context. Investigating the relationship between specific usability factors and perceived usefulness with B2C E-commerce website will provide developers and designers of these sites with a tool for improving the website's likelihood of success.

2   Literature Review

Researchers have suggested many definitions of website usability, for instance, Palmer [28] defines usability using download delay, navigability, content, interactivity and responsiveness. Nielsen [26] defines usability in terms of learnability, efficiency, memorability, error recovery and satisfaction. Shneiderman [33] suggests that usability can act as a balancing factor wherein inadequate functionality will render the application useless and complexity and clutter can make the interface difficult to use. ISO 9241-11 defines usability as, the extent to which a product can be used by specified users to achieve specified goals with effectiveness, efficiency and satisfaction in a specified context of use.

Agarwal and Venkatesh [1] highlight five factors viz. content, ease of use, promotion, made for the medium and emotion and aver that importance of content is highest. Ranganathan and Ganapathy [30] focused their research on website design parameters and suggested that security is the best predictor of online purchase intent. Tarafdar and Zhang [34] investigated the impact of individual traits such as gender, innovativeness, computer anxiety, computer self-efficacy on website usability and found significant demographic differences. Further, Palmer [28] identified metrics namely frequency of use, likelihood of return, and user satisfaction that could be used to identify the elements of successful website design.

DeLone and McLean [5] proposed a model for conceptualizing IS success and identified six factors viz. System Quality, Information Quality, Use, User Satisfaction, Individual Impact and Organizational Impact. Basing their study on above, Molla and Licker [25] extended their model by defining a dependent variable called Customer E-commerce Satisfaction and added two dimensions namely trust and service quality. DeLone and McLean [6] updated their model by including service quality and aver that their updated model applies to the E-commerce environment [7]. Jahng et al. [16] proposed a theory of congruence for E-commerce environments and state that a "fit" between E-commerce system, product and user characteristics leads to favorable user outcomes. Liu and Arnett [20] ascertained factors critical to website success and found quality of information, service, system use, playfulness and design of the website to be the key.

It can be concluded from the discussion above that researchers have examined numerous website attributes, and there is no unified model or framework to classify them. Therefore this study attempts to fill this gap by linking website usability dimensions to perceived usefulness and identifying their relative importance.

2.1   Review of Constructs Used in the Study

For the present research five constructs have been studied comprising of four independent variables viz. system quality, trust, information quality and support quality jointly called as web usability dimensions and one dependent variable i.e. perceived usefulness. Web usability dimensions refer to the factors that directly impact perceived usefulness with a B2C website and are very briefly described in the following paragraphs.

System quality refers to the desired characteristics of an E-commerce system. According to Grover et al. [12], it is concerned with performance characteristics of the information system (IS) being studied. System quality research in the E-commerce literature has focused mainly on aspects such as navigability [23],[28]; response time [6],[18]; availability[7],[23]; reliability[7],[36]; security[18],[36]; consistency[28], [30] and customization [18],[28]. The second dimension *Trust* refers to the level of security present in the website to prevent customer details from being accessed illegally and securing web transactions. Trust is therefore a critical factor for the success of any E-commerce venture as trust determines the level of security user feels in divulging personal information over internet. The role of trust in E-commerce has received attention from many IS researchers [11], [19], [24], [29].

In B2C E-commerce scenario, where there is no face to face contact, web vendor's website serves as an interface between vendor and customer [28] hence the importance of content on the website becomes significant. *Content quality* is defined as the degree to which content displayed on the B2C E-commerce website is proper in terms of is relevance, completeness, timeliness, accuracy, depth and breadth [23], [27] The fourth independent variable in this study is *Support Quality* which can be defined as the overall support delivered by the website such as tracking order, comparing products, feedback, reviews, search capabilities etc. Zeithaml et al. [38] define e-SQ as the extent to which a website facilitates efficient and effective shopping, purchasing and delivery of products and services.

In B2C E-commerce, the only interface between customer and retailer is the website, and it is therefore a primary influence on user perceptions and affects customer's perceived usefulness which is the dependent variable in this study. *Perceived Usefulness* is defined as the degree to which the prospective user believes that using a particular system would be free of effort, easy to be understood and used thus increasing users' job performance [4]. If user perceives the website as useful it is more likely that user will initiate the act of transacting with it and continue doing so in future as well. So in a sense perceived usefulness can be seen as one of the basic factors determining the success of a B2C website thereby reflecting its overall excellence. Liao et.al. [19], following [4] define perceived usefulness as the degree to which a consumer believes that using a particular website will increase performance in purchasing and information searching.

Perceived usefulness of a website is thus a very important part of the store's overall image as it is the usefulness of the website that initially attracts the user and can greatly influence online shopping behavior. Nielsen [26] argues that users experience usability of a site before they have committed to using it and before they have spent any money on potential purchases. So perceived usefulness can be seen as a critical success measure of a website as it is only if the users perceive the website to be useful will they interact, be satisfied and finally purchase and indulge in re-purchase behavior with it. This study patterns the system quality construct used in [5],[18],[28]; trust construct using [11],[24]; content quality after [1],[3],[20]; support quality from [1],[38] and perceived usefulness from [3],[4],[23] by adapting it to suit the present context.

3   Development of Hypotheses

In order to ascertain the differential importance of website usability dimensions on perceived usefulness, a hypothesis linking each usability dimension to perceived usefulness has been formulated in this section. Relating system quality and perceived usefulness, Seddon [32] explained that system quality has a positive impact on perceived usefulness of a website. According to [21],[26], poor E-commerce system quality has been found to have a negative influence on the perceptions of usefulness of the website in the mind of customers. Thus, the hypothesis suggested is:

Hypothesis 1 (H₁): System Quality dimension of B2C E-commerce website has a positive impact on Perceived Usefulness.

Pavlou [29] in relating trust to perceived usefulness asserts that trust becomes a predictor of perceived usefulness of a website because it enhances shopping comfort and reduces the perception that e-vendors' websites will engage in harmful and opportunistic behaviors. McCord and Ratnasingam [22] apply TAM to study the impact of trust on perceived usefulness of the website and verify that a consumer that trusts a website will perceive it as more useful. Prior empirical evidence introduces trust as an antecedent of perceived usefulness [11],[29], it can therefore be hypothesized that:

Hypothesis 2 (H₂): Trust dimension of B2C E-commerce website has a positive impact on Perceived Usefulness.

Content quality deals with attributes relating to the characteristics of content on the website. Researchers aver that quality of content and usefulness of a system are closely related with each other and that users will perceive a web site to be of greater usefulness if it provides higher quality of information [5],[30],[32]. So it can be hypothesized that:

Hypothesis 3 (H₃): Content Quality dimension of B2C E-commerce website has a positive impact on Perceived Usefulness.

Ranganathan and Ganpathy [30] relate Support quality and Perceived Usefulness by suggesting that provision of features such as product samples; movie clippings, demonstrations and product reviews increase the usability of the B2C website. According to McKinney et al. [23] and Zeithaml et al. [38], service/support quality positively influences perceived usefulness. There is therefore support for the following hypothesis:

Hypothesis 4 (H₄): Support Quality dimension of B2C E-commerce website has a positive impact on Perceived Usefulness.

4   Research Methodology

Data for the present study has been collected from both primary and secondary sources. Primary data has been collected from respondents for the purpose of the present study using questionnaire survey method. Secondary data from printed and online articles and research reports offering statistical information also forms an integral part of the study.

The questionnaire for the present study has been developed after reviewing similar studies undertaken by various researchers e.g. [1],[4],[5],[24] and adapting them to suit present context. It is aimed at taking responses of people visiting B2C E-commerce websites regarding website usability dimensions and perceived usefulness (No of items = 27) using a 5 point likert scale where 5 indicates a response of strongly agree and 1 indicates a response of strongly disagree. A pilot survey with a sample of 50 respondents was conducted based on which, wordings of three sub-parts of three questions were slightly modified to make it clearer. Thereafter, final revised questionnaire was designed using googledocs and web link of the survey, was sent to prospective respondents. Respondents for the study were selected using *judgmental sampling* on the basis of following criteria; a) more than 20 years of age; b) minimum 2-5 hours of internet usage per week; and c) purchased some product or service online in last six months. The questionnaire was administered to 620 prospective respondents and produced 450 returned responses. Of these, 35 questionnaires have been eliminated because they either appeared unreliable or were incomplete. Finally a total of 415 usable surveys provide the data for analysis.

5   Data Analysis and Findings

This section discusses findings of the analysis done using SPSS and AMOS software. After testing the reliability and validity of each construct, hypothesis formulated in the previous section are tested and finally the relative importance of website usability dimensions in determining perceived usefulness is analyzed.

5.1   Construct Reliability and Validity

Reliability is an important property of measurement and can be defined as the ratio of true variance to total variance. One of the important measures of reliability is Cronbach alpha, which measures how closely related a set of items are as a group. A "high" value of alpha i.e. more than 0.7 or above [27] is often used as evidence that the items measure an underlying (or latent) construct. The various constructs considered in the research study along with their measured variables are shown in table 1. Table 1 also depicts the mean, standard deviation and cronbach alpha statistics for various constructs. With regard to the measurement of the constructs' reliability and validity, Hair et al. [13] and Fornell and Larcker [9] suggest that composite reliability (CR) and average variance extracted (AVE) should be applied. Fornell and Larcker, [9] suggest that value of CR greater than 0.7 and value of AVE more than 0.5 indicate high reliability of the constructs measured. As shown in Table 1, all values of CR, AVE and Cronbach alpha exceed their benchmark thereby indicating high level of reliability.

Table 1. Mean, Standard Deviation, Cronbach alpha, AVE and CR values of constructs used in the study

Construct	Included Measured Variables	Mean	S.D	Cronbach Alpha	AVE	CR
System Quality (SQ)	SQ1- Availability	4.13	0.82	0.94	0.71	0.94
	SQ2- Download Delay	3.73	0.88			
	SQ3- Progressive Rendering	3.88	0.86			
	SQ4- Too Much Information	3.62	0.93			
	SQ5- Common Layout	3.74	0.94			
	SQ6- No Broken Links	3.83	0.95			
	SQ7- Navigation	3.97	0.85			
Trust (T)	T1- User Authentication	4.05	0.93	0.91	0.64	0.91
	T2- Customer Well being	3.47	1.01			
	T3- Vendor Commitment	4.08	0.86			
	T4- Having Security Certificate	3.63	0.86			
	T5- Terms & Conditions	3.75	1.00			
	T6- Chatting with Expert	3.88	0.93			

Table 1. (*Continued.*)

Construct	Included Measured Variables	Mean	S.D	Cronbach Alpha	AVE	CR
Content Quality (CQ)	CQ1- Relevant Content	3.82	0.85	0.91	0.67	0.91
	CQ2- Use of Multimedia	3.96	0.85			
	CQ3- Content depth breadth	4.01	0.79			
	CQ4- Current Information	3.69	0.88			
	CQ5- Word Clarity	3.70	0.85			
Support Quality (SuQ)	SuQ1- Product Comparison	4.09	0.88	0.92	0.71	0.92
	SuQ2- Track Order	4.09	0.88			
	SuQ3- Free Service	3.89	0.91			
	SuQ4- Customer Review	4.14	0.80			
	SuQ5- Mobile, SMS, E-mail Alert	4.16	0.84			
Perceived Usefulness (PU)	PU1- Easy to use	4.12	0.74	0.86	0.57	0.85
	PU2- Convenient	4.31	0.69			
	PU3- Makes shopping easy	4.16	0.63			
	PU4-Increases productivity	4.26	0.70			

5.2   Confirmatory Factor Analysis (CFA) Results for the Proposed Constructs

After testing individual constructs, it is important to test how well the factor structure of measured variables represent the latent constructs hence CFA is performed using AMOS software. The output of CFA is shown in figure 1. Correlation Statistics of CFA performed on constructs of the study are shown in table 2 which indicate that all constructs are valid and explain the related measured variables significantly. CFI of the model is 0.943 which is above the threshold value of 0.9[14] and RMSEA of the model is 0.06 which is below 0.08[14], indicating a good model fit.

5.3   Hypotheses Testing

Hypotheses formulated in previous section have been tested using SEM. Results are shown in table 3 along with statistics such as like unstandardized (URC) and standardized regression coefficient (SRC), squared multiple correlation (SMC) and critical ratio (CR). Result of hypothesis testing shows that system quality positively influences users' perceived usefulness. In fact it is the most significant predictor (0.86, p<0.001) of perceived usefulness and explains 74.3 percent variance in it. An explanation for this can be that, the more navigable and available a website is, the more the user is likely to find it easy to use and convenient and therefore is more likely to perceive it as useful. Findings of [18],[21],[32] concur with above finding.

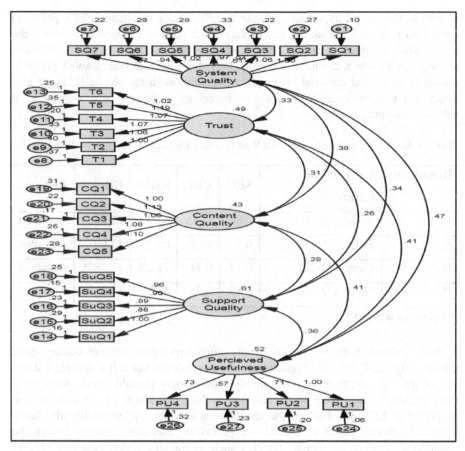

Fig. 1. Confirmatory Factor Analysis of constructs used in study

Table 2. Correlation Statistics of constructs used in study

Constructs	Pearson Correlation				
	SQ	T	CQ	SuQ	PU
System Quality (SQ)	1	0.61 **	0.74**	0.56**	0.84**
Trust (T)		1	0.67**	0.48**	0.81**
Content Quality (CQ)			1	0.56**	0.76**
Support Quality (SuQ)				1	0.64**
Perceived Usefulness (PU)					1

** Significant at p<0.01

Results of the second hypothesis indicate that trust has a significant (0.70, p<0.001) impact on perceived usefulness and explains 69.3 percent variance in it, hence the hypothesis is accepted. It can thus be inferred that customers perceive those websites as more useful which are more secure as they don't have to bother about probable misuse of their vital personal information. Agreeing with the above, [22],[29] also assert that trust becomes a predictor of perceived usefulness of a website as it enhances shopping comfort.

Table 3. Regression Statistics- Impact of Web Usability Dimensions on Perceived Usefulness

Hypothesis	Independent Construct	SRC	URC	SMC	CR	Remark
H_1	System Quality	0.86	0. 85	74.3%	22.69*	Accepted
H_2	Trust	0.7	0.65	69.3%	15.69*	Accepted
H_3	Content Quality	0.74	0.71	71.2%	17.283*	Accepted
H_4	Support Quality	0.65	0.56	42.5%	13.31*	Accepted

* Significant at p<0.001

As is evident from the results of the third hypothesis, content quality quite significantly (0.74, p<0.001) impacts perceived usefulness, hence it is accepted. It can be said that the more clear, relevant, timely is the content available on the website the more customers are likely to perceive it useful. The above observation is also supported by [27],[30]. Further, the results point out that support quality also has a significant (0.65, p<0.001) impact on perceived usefulness, hence it can be understood presence of support features such as tracking order, customer review, mobile alerts etc. have a positive influence on customers' perceptions of the website, a view which is also shared by previous researchers [30],[38]. As indicated by the results above, all web usability dimensions have a significant but differential impact on perceived usefulness; hence all four hypotheses are accepted.

6   Assessing Relative Importance of Web Usability Dimensions in Determining Perceived Usefulness

The primary objective of this study is to understand relative importance of website usability dimensions in determining perceived usefulness from customers' perspective so that website designers can give due importance to the dimensions highlighted. As can be gathered from the previous section that all hypotheses have been accepted, therefore the next logical step is to understand their relative importance in ascertaining perceived usefulness. To achieve this objective, Structural Equation Modelling is applied considering System Quality, Trust, Content Quality and Support Quality as exogenous variables and Perceived Usefulness (PU) as endogenous variable and is depicted by figure 2. The results indicate that in determining perceived usefulness of a B2C website, most important factor is system quality (0.52, p<0.001), closely followed by trust (0.516, p<0.001) and content quality (0.47, p<0.001). Though the relationship between support quality and perceived usefulness as shown in table 4 is high (0.65, p<0.001) but in presence of other constructs becomes very weak (0.19, p<0.001) as shown in table 4. It can further be observed that the impact of all dimensions though significant has also reduced such as in the case of system quality from 0.86 to 0.52.

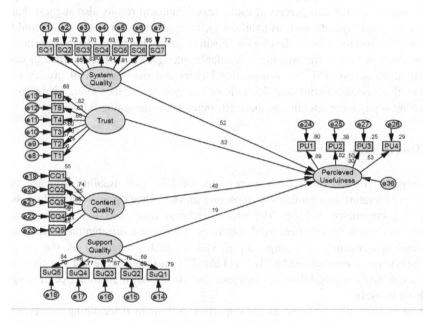

Fig. 2. Relative importance of Web Usability Dimensions according to Perceived Usefulness

Table 4. Regression statistics of Web Usability Dimensions according to Perceived Usefulness

Independent Construct	Standardized Regression Estimates	Unstandardized Regression Estimates	S.E.	C.R.	Squared Multiple Correlation
System Quality	0.52	0.33	0.02	14.59*	
Trust	0.516	0.37	0.03	12.39*	
Support Quality	0.19	0.12	0.02	5.59*	0.80
Content Quality	0.477	0.37	0.03	11.64*	

* Significant at p<0.001

This behaviour can be explained with the help of **'Moderation Effect'**. Baron and Kenny [2], state that a moderator is a variable that alters the direction or strength of the relation between a predictor and an outcome. Researchers such as [2],[10] posit that moderation effects are important to study for understanding the comparative importance of independent variables for predicting the dependent variable. As can be inferred from the above explanation and figure 2, individual impact of support quality construct on perceived usefulness which was high (0.65, $p<0.001$), has reduced significantly (0.19, $p<0.001$) as a result of dominance of other three constructs. Hence it can be said that system quality, trust and content quality moderate the relationship between support quality and perceived usefulness. Empirical results also suggest that attributes of system quality such as availability, navigability, download delay, could play a very important role in developing positive perceptions regarding websites' usability. As it is only if the website is available, navigable and has less download time, will it be accessed by the prospective buyers and the question of quality of content or the amount of trust that the website can generate comes later. Therefore, designers must pay more attention to these attributes while designing B2C websites.

7   Discussion

This study investigated the relative importance of four web usability dimensions suggested in literature as significantly impacting an individual's perceived usefulness of a B2C E-commerce website. The results indicate that these four criteria are relatively good predictors of perceived usefulness but have a differential impact on the dependent construct. Not surprisingly, system quality emerged as the most important criteria, a view shared by [3],[21],[26],[32] who have suggested that factors such as availability, navigability etc. increase the likelihood of customer perceiving the website as useful.

Content quality also surfaced as an important feature in determining perceived usefulness. Content of the B2C website is extremely important as it forms organization's core business and contains all information about products to be sold. The results of the present study are in agreement with [1],[3],[25] who endorse that as in E-commerce, customers cannot physically see, touch or feel a product, therefore there is a need to provide as much detail as possible to help them make a sound purchase decision. As the customers of a B2C website act in real time, it is imperative that information content on the website be current, clear, relevant and timely thereby helping the users to take correct and efficient decisions.

Trust plays a very important role in almost any commerce comprising of monetary transactions. As endorsed by [11],[17],[22],[29], in the present study as well Trust emerged as an important predictor of perceived usefulness. Uncertainty regarding the reliability of services, products, or providers is high in an E-commerce environment. In such a scenario, the decision regarding who to trust and with whom to do business becomes even more difficult and falls on the shoulders of individuals. Therefore, web vendors need to create an environment in which a consumer can be confident about any online transaction [37].

Interestingly, contrary to the findings of [23],[30], the construct support quality came out as a significant but a very weak predictor of perceived usefulness. This behaviour can be attributed to two reasons, first being the moderation effect of other three constructs on perceived usefulness. The second reason can be that the importance of support quality can be felt more after the prospective buyer has already had an initial feel of the website and therefore support quality is more likely to influence satisfaction with the website and the buyer's intent to purchase online than perceived usefulness.

Findings of the research have important implications for online retailers of India that desire to establish a successful web presence as it is necessary for them to ensure that their E-commerce website is, first and foremost, perceived as useful. It is only after this that the chances of the customer purchasing, returning recommending it increase. The usability dimensions and their relative importance in determining perceived usefulness can aid website designers and vendors in creating more successful and useful websites and help the vendors in providing an enriching online shopping experience to the customers. For researchers, the results suggest that each of the five constructs used in the study are reliable both in terms of internal consistency, convergent validity and construct validity. High amount of variance explained by usability dimensions implies that these factors are possibly among the most important antecedents of perceived usefulness. Thus the study forms a sound base both for researchers and practitioners.

8   Limitations and Conclusion

This research attempted to identify the differential impact of web usability dimensions on perceived usefulness. Although the findings of the present research provide meaningful implications thus advancing the understanding of Website usability, this study is not without limitations. Firstly, the present study was limited only to studying the functional aspects of the B2C websites. However, non-functional aspects of the website such as enjoyment, playfulness, fun and emotional satisfaction may also be important and contribute significantly to perceived usefulness as is highlighted by[31],[35]. Secondly the present study did not focus on specific type of products as proposed by [16] who posit that product type and its characteristics can be one of the key drivers of the website design. The study examined website usability in context to E-commerce websites only limiting its external validity to same type of websites. In addition, this study is limited by the sample set used in the analyses, the method employed in acquiring the sample set, and by the source providing the sample.

In conclusion, this study has advanced research in the area of B2C E-commerce website usability by (1) providing evidence of the reliability and validity of constructs to determine the usability of B2C E-commerce websites; (2) identifying the relative importance of website usability dimensions in determining perceived usefulness thus providing practical results that can be used immediately by practitioners in the real world, and by researchers in further analysis.

References

1. Agarwal, R., Venkatesh, V.: Assessing a firm's Web presence: A heuristic evaluation procedure for the measurement of usability. Information Systems Research 13(2), 168–186 (2002)
2. Baron, R.M., Kenny, D.A.: The moderator-mediator variable distinction in social psychological research: Conceptual, strategic, and statistical considerations. Journal of Personality and Social Psychology 51, 1173–1182 (1986)
3. Brown, I., Jayakody, R.: B2C E-commerce Success: A Test and Validation of a Revised Conceptual Model. The Electronic Journal Information Systems Evaluation 12(2), 129–148 (2009)
4. Davis, F.: Perceived Usefulness, Perceived Ease of Use, and User Acceptance of Information Technology. MIS Quarterly 13(3), 319–340 (1989)
5. DeLone, W., McLean, E.: The Quest for the Dependent Variable. Information Systems Research 3(1), 60–65 (1992)
6. DeLone, W., McLean, E.: The DeLone and McLean Model of Information Systems Success – A 10 Year Update. Journal of Management Information Systems 19(4), 9–30 (2003)
7. DeLone, W., McLean, E.: Measuring e-Commerce Success: Applying the DeLone and McLean Information Systems Success Model. International Journal of Electronic Commerce 9(1), 31–47 (2004)
8. Forrester Research, Asia Pacific Online Retail Forecast, 2011 To 2016- A Look At Growth In Five Markets With A Focus On China, Japan, And Australia (2010), http://www.forrester.com (retrieved April 16, 2012)
9. Fornell, C., Larcker, D.: Evaluating Structural Equation Models, Unobservable Variables and Measurement Error. Journal of Marketing Research 18(1), 39–50 (1981)
10. Frazier, P., Tix, A., Barnett, C.L.: The relational context of social support. Personality and Social Psychology Bulletin 29, 1113–1146 (2003)
11. Gefen, D., Straub, D.: Managing user trust in B2G e-services. eService Journal 2(2), 7–25 (2003)
12. Grover, V., Purvis, R., Coffey, J.: System quality: measures of the information processing system itself (2005), http://business.clemson.edu/ISE/html/system_quality.html (accessed on September 10, 2012)
13. Hair, J.F., Black, W.C., Babin, B.J., Anderson, R.E., Tatham, R.L.: Multivariate Data Analysis, 6th edn. Pearson Prentice Hall, Upper Saddle River (2006)
14. Hu, L., Bentler, P.M.: Cutoff criteria for fit indexes in covariance structure analysis: Conventional criteria versus new alternatives. Structural Equation Modeling 6, 1–55 (1999)
15. Internet and Mobile Association of India, Digital Commerce (2013), http://www.indiadigitalreview.com/news/ ecommerce-market-may-touch-rs-62-967-cr-2013-iamai (retrieved July 20, 2013)
16. Jahng, J., Jain, H., Ramamurthy, K.: Effective Design of Electronic Commerce Environments: Proposed Theory of Congruence and an Illustration. IEEE Transactions on Systems, Man, and Cybernetics 30(4), 453–471 (2000)
17. Kim, D.J., Ferrin, L.D., Rao, H.R.: Trust and Satisfaction, Two Stepping Stones for Successful E-Commerce Relationships: A Longitudinal Exploration. Information Systems Research 20(2), 237–257 (2009)

18. Lee, Y., Kozar, K.A.: Investigating the effect of website quality on e- business success: an analytic hierarchy process (AHP) approach. Decision Support Systems 42(3), 1383–1401 (2006)
19. Liao, C., Palvia, P., Lin, H.N.: The Roles of Habit and Web Site Quality in E-Commerce. International Journal of Information Management 26(6), 469–483 (2006)
20. Liu, C., Arnett, K.P.: Exploring the factors associated with website success in the context of e-commerce. Information and Management 38, 23–33 (2000)
21. Lohse, G.L., Spiller, P.: Internet retail store design: how the user interface influences traffic and sales. Journal of Computer Mediated Communication 5(2), 1–20 (1999)
22. McCord, M., Ratnasingam, P.: The Impact of Trust on the Technology Acceptance Model in Business to Consumer E-Commerce. In: Information Resources Management Association International Conference, Innovation through IT, New Orleans, pp. 921–924 (2004)
23. McKinney, V., Yoon, K., Zahedi, F.: The Measurement of Web-Customer Satisfaction: An Expectation and Disconfirmation Approach. Information Systems Research 13(3), 296–315 (2002)
24. McKnight, D.H., Choudhury, V., Kacmar, C.: Developing and Validating Trust Measures for E-commerce: An Integrative Typology. Information Systems Research 13(3), 334–359 (2002)
25. Molla, A., Licker, P.: E-Commerce Systems Success: An Attempt to Extend and Re-specify the DeLone and McLean Model of Information Systems Success. Journal of Electronic Commerce Research 2(4), 1–11 (2001)
26. Nielsen, J.: Usability 101: Introduction to Usability (2003), http://www.useit.com/alertbox/20030825.html (accessed on May 30, 2013)
27. Nunnally, J.C.: Psychometric Theory. McGraw-Hill, New York (1978)
28. Palmer, J.: Website Usability, Design, and Performance Metrics. Information Systems Research 13(2), 151–167 (2002)
29. Pavlou, P.A.: Consumer acceptance of electronic commerce-integrating trust and risk with the technology acceptance model. International Journal of Electronic Commerce 7(3), 69–103 (2003)
30. Ranganathan, C., Ganapathy, S.: Key dimensions of business-to- consumer websites. Information and Management 39, 457–465 (2002)
31. Schenkman, B.N., Jonsson, F.U.: Aesthetics and preferences of web pages. Behaviour & Information Technology 19(5), 367–377 (2000)
32. Seddon, P.: A Re-specification and Extension of the DeLone and Mclean Model of IS Success. Information Systems Research 8(3), 240–253 (1997)
33. Shneiderman, B.: Designing the User Interface, 4th edn. Pearson-Addison Wesley, New York (2005)
34. Tarafdar, M., Zhang, J.: Analysis of Critical Website Characteristics: A Cross-Category Study of Successful Websites. Journal of Computer Information Systems 46(2), 14–24 (2005)
35. Venkatesh, V., Brown, S.A.: A Longitudinal Investigation of Personal Computers in Homes: Adoption Determinants and Emerging Challenges. MIS Quarterly 25(1), 71–102 (2001)
36. Whitworth, B., Fjermestad, J., Mahinda, E.: The web of system performance. Communications of the ACM 49(5), 93–99 (2005)
37. Wu, F., Mahajan, V., Balasubramanian, S.: An analysis of e-business adoption and its impact on business performance. Journal of the Academy of Marketing Science 31(4), 425–447 (2003)
38. Zeithaml, V., Parasuraman, A., Malhotra, A.: Service quality delivery through web sites: A critical review of extant knowledge. Journal of the Academy of Marketing Science 30(4), 362–375 (2002)

Modified Deformable Parts Model for Side Profile Facial Feature Detection

Pisal Setthawong and Vajirasak Vanijja

School of Information Technology, King Mongkut's University of Technology Thonburi, Thailand
51500701@st.sit.kmutt.ac.th, vajirasak@sit.kmutt.ac.th

Abstract. Deformable Parts Model(DPM) is a facial feature detection approach. Though the approach is accurate, robust, and works well for a wide range of facial profiles, when faced with a side profile, the typical approach produces less than satisfactory results. This paper discusses about issues faced when attempting to detect facial features on the side profile and proposes modifications to the DPM approach so that it works with detection facial features on side profiles.

Keywords: Deformable Parts Model, Facial Feature Detection, Side Profile Facial Feature Detection, Image Processing.

1 Introduction

Facial Feature Detection is an important image processing task in which important facial features are detected and marked for later use. Systems such as facial recognition systems [1] and certain face pose estimation systems[14] rely on the facial feature system to provide an accurate estimate of key facial features which would provide an ideal starting point for later facial analysis. If the initial facial feature detection process has not provided accurate facial feature positions, the accuracy from the later processing would be severely degraded or simply would not work.

There had been many facial feature detection approaches that have been developed over the years, and one of the popular approaches is Deformable Parts Model (DPM). DPM is not the fastest approach proposed, but the approach provides robust and accurate results in facial feature detection over a wide variety of facial profiles. Though typical DPM approach in facial feature detection can detect many profiles accurately, at certain side profiles, the detection of features is less than ideal. This paper will illustrate why typical DPM approaches for facial feature is not ideal when detecting features for in a side profile, propose suggestions on how to improve the detection rates for side profiles, and provide a side by side comparison between the an open-source implementation of DPM and the proposed modified approach in detecting facial features in side profile.

2 Background

This section explains about the DPM approach in facial feature detection and issues that are present when attempting to detect facial features on side profiles.

B. Papasratorn et al. (Eds.): IAIT 2013, CCIS 409, pp. 212–220, 2013.

2.1   Facial Feature Detection Approaches

One of the first approaches in detecting facial feature is to create independently trained detectors of each individual facial feature [16]. Detectors are trained for the eyes, nose, mouth, face regions, and etc. The AdaBoost based detectors [15] and Haar's Classifier are popular approaches in this area. Though the independent trained detectors can detect facial features, one of the major weakness of this approach is that it detects many false positive facial features. The extreme local nature of the approach is a contributor to the high false positive rate as illustrated in Figure 1. To deal with the high false positive rates, providing a geometric configuration can help lower the rates. The detection is done with the independent individual detectors in which are set as candidate features in which would later be scored based on the geometric bias of the features to select the most likely positions for the features.

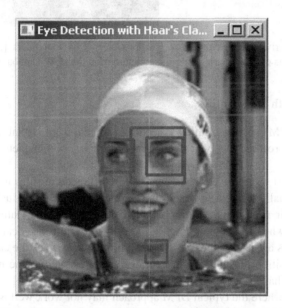

Fig. 1. The detection of the Eye Region with Haar's Classifier Independently usually returns many false positive results

The DPM approach [2] changes from the two stepped independent detectors and geometric configuration into merging both the processes into a single model. The DPM is defined where there features and their set of connections between pairs of features much like an undirected graph where vertices are the features and the edge are the connection between the pairs of features. The DPM detector then estimates the feature positions by using a single scoring function consisting of the local feature model and the deformation cost using an optimization function. Due to the accurate results of DPM, the approach has been used in many successful facial feature detection systems [4,8,10] and one of the results are illustrated in Figure 2.

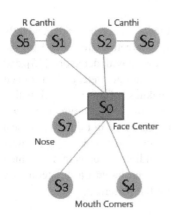
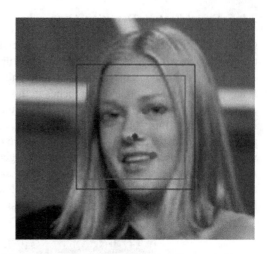

Fig. 2. Left: Underlying Graph of Facial Feature Detected by Flandmark [6], a variation of DPM Right: Results of Flandmark on a sample picture from the LFW Database[7]

2.2   Issues with Side Profiles

Though the DPM approach allows accurate detection of facial features, when used with side profiles, the typical DPM approach is not satisfactory in a number of cases.

One of the first issues faced when using DPM with side profiles is that the feature detectors are usually trained on frontal-like poses. Though individual feature detectors are surprising robust in detection of candidate positions, the features are less stable in its form when the subject is at a wider angler from the ideal frontal profile. Once the features are less stable, the detection process may miss the candidate feature or report the position that may be inaccurate. Features such as the nose and mouth region generally have issues due the form change at wider angles [9].

Another area where the typical DPM approach may not work well is that the underlining graph topology of the facial features and their geometric relationship does not work well with side profiles. In side profiles, there is a possibility that certain features such as one of the eyes may be hidden due to a wide face angle. As in the example when one of the eyes is hidden, the underlying graph is not suitable as a feature is missing and the relationship between should be changed accordingly. In this case, the original approach still attempts to fit the model to the input picture which results in a model over fitting case in which the feature detected are generally inaccurate. The issues discussed with DPM on side profiles are depicted in Figure 3.

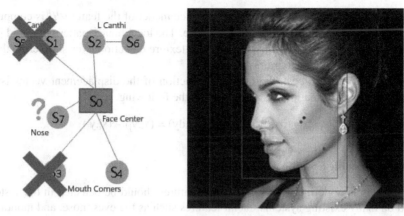

Fig. 3. With a side profile, certain features may be obscured or may change in form. This causes inconsistencies with the default assumptions and causes the model to detect incorrect features due to over-fitting.

3   Proposed System

This section contains details of the proposed system that is implemented. The first subsection contains details of general DPM approaches [4,13] that are selected and utilized in the system, and the second subsection discusses about the variations to DPM approach that are implemented.

3.1   General DPM Approaches

This section describes some of the general DPM approaches that have been selected to use in the proposed system. Assuming picture inputs that are grayscale and of a certain width and height, the system aims to detect the facial features. For the DPM, The configuration of the graph topology is defined by the a graph $G = (V,E)$ where V consists of N features and E is the connection between neighboring features. Each feature is assigned a position s_i in which is the position of the ith feature in the image I. The quality of the feature configuration is then defined by the local feature appearance model based on the match of the feature on position s and the input image, and the deformation cost evaluating the positions related with the neighboring landmarks which is defined by the following equation respectively.

$$F(I,s) = \sum_{i \in V} q_i (I,s_i) + \sum_{(i,j) \in E} g_{ij} (s_i, s_j) \qquad (1)$$

The values of q_i and g_{ij} are the combination of of predefined maps and parameter vectors that are learnt from examples which are defined as

$$q_i (I,s_i) = (w_i^q, \Psi_i^q (I, s_i)) \qquad (2)$$

$$g_{ij} (s_i, s_j) = (w_{ij}^g, \Psi_{ij}^g (s_i, s_j)) \qquad (3)$$

The feature descriptor of the local appearance model of the feature Ψ_i^A is computed using the local binary pattern pyramid structure. The local binary pattern pyramid [11] is selected as it provides good performance in texture detection over simpler methods as intensity values and histograms.

For the deformation cost, the quadratic function of the displacement vector is selected [5]. The deformation cost is defined as the following.

$$\Psi_{ij}^{\theta}(s_i,s_j) = (dx,dy,dx^2,dy^2),\ (dx,dy) = (x_j,y_j) - (x_i,y_i) \tag{4}$$

3.2   Side Profile Specific Modifications

The first step is to define what set of facial features should be detected in the system. Based on many existing systems, facial features such as the eyes, nose, and mouth are important features to detect. For side profiles, some of the usual features cannot be detected directly. For the proposed system, the selection of the near-eye canthi, nose position, and mouth corner position is selected. The nose position is a vital feature and is important in facial detection. For the eye position, the canthi or the corner of the eyes are important positions. For the canthi, the far canthi are potentially obscured at higher side angles so the near-eye canthi is selected as the feature to be detected. For the mouth corner, the far mouth corner can be difficult to detect when the mouth is open. This is because the far mouth corner is hidden, and the lips form two possible positions for the corner. Based on the features that are selected, it is evident that the typical geometric model and graph topology of a typical DPM approach has to be modified which is displayed in Figure 4.

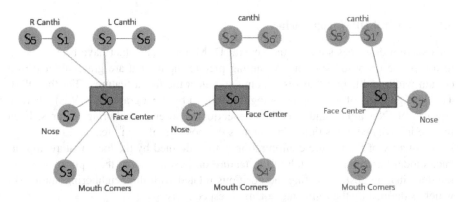

Fig. 4. Left: An example graph topology used in DPM for frontal facial feature detection Middle: A modified topology for side profiles in which subjects are facing to their right Right: A modified/symmetric topology for side profiles in which subjects facing to their left

Another modification is the relaxation of the search space of the feature positions. The typical approach utilizes an AABB bounding box to define a constraint on potential position of the individual features to provide a limited search space and to early prune false positives. The search space is usually constrained to the normal y-axis, and is symmetric in a vertical nature for corresponding feature sets such as the eye canthi. However in side profiles and at certain angles, the features may not be aligned vertically and the y-axis constraints will not be suitable, and a relaxation of the constraint y-axis is permitted to allow a wider range of cascading windows for test in which we allow slight x-axis variation in the search space.

Another modification from the typical approach is the usage of a new face detection approach. Typical approaches utilize Haar's like classifier before enlarging the detected face region for usage. However as commonly available face classifier are trained on frontal images, the approach does not work well with side images. Our proposed system utilizes a HSV color blob model [12] to detect the face region. This works well with a wider range of face region, but has more false positive cases. In our experiment, we select only the positive detections.

Fig. 5. Sample Results from the Proposed System

4   Results and Conclusions

The test cases are built from the complete list of side profile pictures from the Labeled Faces in the Wild (LWF) database [7]. As the number of side profiles in the LFW is small, there has been an additional number of side profile pictures that have been downloaded to increase the test case size. A total of 54 side profiles from the LFW database were selected and an additional 46 side profiles used for the test case. All the selected facial feature of the side profile pictures are marked by human experts.

To compare the results of the proposed system, a popular open source implementation of DPM called Flandmark [6,13] is used for comparison. The proposed system and Flandmark will be used to detect the same facial features that consist of the canthi, nose, and mouth corner. As Flandmark utilizes a frontal haar's classifier to detect the face region which does not detect the side profile well, the face region is manually defined when the detector fails to detect the face region. Also due to difference in features sets, the selection of the closer canthi would be used when comparing the canthi accuracy. To calculate the accuracy, the displacements between the detected and the position have to be calculated. However the pixel Euclidean distance is dependent on the original image size, the normalized coordinate system based on the face region is used instead for both the detected and marked features.

The first calculation done is the feature average mean normalized deviation (F_{AMND}) which is used as an indicator of how accurate each of the feature are which is defined by the following equation

$$F_{AMND} = \frac{1}{M} \sum_{i=0}^{M-1} \quad \| F_i - F'_i \|$$ (5)

Where $F = \{F_0,..., F_{M-1}\}$ are the normalized position which is manually marked of each individual feature, $F' = \{F'_0,..., F'_{M-1}\}$ are the positions of each individual feature that are detected by the approach, and M is the total number of test cases.

The second calculation is the average mean normalized deviation (R_{AMND}) which finds the average displacement of all the features in each set. The mean of the deviation of the number of features detected which is defined by F_{no} is calculated first before averaging out the displacement which is defined by the following equation:

$$R_{AMND} = \frac{1}{M} \sum_{j=0}^{M-1} \quad (\frac{1}{F_{no}} \sum_{i=0}^{F_{no}-1} \quad \| F_{ij} - F'_{ij} \|)$$ (6)

The last calculation is the average maximum normalized deviation ($R_{MAX-AND}$) in which selects the feature with the maximum error from each set to figure out what is the potential largest error of each set. $S = \{S_0,..., S_{M-1}\}$ and $S' = \{S'_0,..., S'_{M-1}\}$ contains the set of all the features that are detected, and the maximum deviation is selected from each set before being averaged.

$$R_{MAX-AND} = \frac{1}{M} MAX(\| S_i - S'_i \|)$$ (7)

The results are compiled, summarized, and are compared side by side in the tables below.

Table 1. Comparing the R_{AMND} and $R_{MAX-AND}$ between the proposed system and Flandmark

	R_{AMND} [%]	SD R_{AMND} [%]	$R_{MAX-AND}$ [%]	SD $R_{MAX-AND}$ [%]
Flandmark	16.6777	10.1151	27.1126	17.2479
Proposed System	3.9029	1.8461	7.3318	4.6764

Table 2. Comparing the F_{AMND} between the proposed system and Flandmark

	Flandmark		Proposed System	
	F_{AMND} [%]	SD F_{AMND} [%]	F_{AMND} [%]	SD R_{AMND} [%]
Canthus1	2.6999	1.4053	12.0171	10.8920
Canthus2	3.8472	2.8434	17.8346	12.5205
Nose	6.3705	5.1268	22.9311	17.4813
Mouth Corner	2.6938	1.9636	13.9280	9.4210

The results of the proposed modified DPM shows improvement in area of the detection of features in side profiles. There is an improvement in the detection of all the facial features when compared with the original system. The improvements are especially evident in the area of the nose position as the features deviates highly from frontal to side profiles. Another cause why the nose position may show a high error rate is potentially from the marked nose position which may fluctuate between test cases which can lead to a higher displacement. One of the interesting results from the system is that the values of Canthus1 and Canthus2, which are the two corners of the eyes, are significantly different. The accuracy of Canthus2 which is the farther eye corner from the camera shows a higher error rate. Though the canthi detection is satisfactory in accuracy, the difference in accuracy points to conclusion that it would be better to train a separate near and far canthus detector in the future work to improve accuracy.

Though the results are satisfactory, the approach focuses detects facial feature on a side profile, and is not a general purpose facial feature detection approach. Currently the authors are working on a general purpose DPM approach that would work seamlessly along a wide range of profiles from frontal to side. Explorations of utilizing techniques such as conditional forest [3] or cascading techniques are currently being explored in which could help solve the issue at hand. Once there is additional progress in the research has been validated, an update to the research is planned.

References

1. Amarapur, B., Patil, N.: The Facial Features Extraction for Face Recognition Based on Geometrical Approach. In: Canadian Conference on Electrical and Computer Engineering, pp. 1936–1939. IEEE (2006)
2. Crandall, D., Felzenszwalb, P., Huttenlocher, D.: Spatial priors for part-based recognition using statistical models. In: CVPR, pp. 10–17 (2005)
3. Dantone, M., Gall, J., Fanelli, G., Gool, L.V.: Real-time facial feature detection using Conditional Regression Forests. In: CVPR (2012)
4. Everingham, M., Sivic, J., Zisserman, A.: Hello! My name is...Buffy" – automatic naming of characters in TV video. In: Proceedings of the British Machine Vision Conference (2006)
5. Felzenszwalb, P.F., Girshick, R.B., McAllester, D., Ramanan, D.: Object detection with discriminatively trained parts based models. IEEE Transactions on Pattern Analysis and Machine Intelligence 99(1) (2009)

6. Flandmark Open-source implementation of facial landmark detector, http://cmp.felk.cvut.cz/~uricamic/flandmark/

7. Huang, G.B., Ramesh, M., Berg, T., Learned-Miller, E.: Labeled Faces in the Wild: A Database for Studying Face Recognition in Unconstrained Environments. University of Massachusetts, Amherst, Technical Report 07-49 (October 2007)

8. OKAO Vision Facial Feature Extraction API, http://www.omron.com

9. Setthawong, P., Vannija, V.: Head pose estimation on eyeglasses using line detection and classification approach. In: Papasratorn, B., Lavangnananda, K., Chutimaskul, W., Vanijja, V. (eds.) IAIT 2010. CCIS, vol. 114, pp. 126–136. Springer, Heidelberg (2010)

10. Sivic, J., Everingham, M., Zisserman, A.: Who are you? – learning person specific classifiers from video. In: Proceedings of the IEEE Conference on Computer Vision and Pattern Recognition (2009)

11. Sonnenburg, S., Franc, V.: COFFIN: A Computational Framework for Linear SVMs. In: Proceedings of ICML (2010)

12. Tathe, S.V., Narote, S.P.: Face detection using color models. World Journal of Science and Technology 2(4) (2012)

13. Uřičář, M., Franc, V., Hlaváč, V.: Facial landmarks detector learned by the structured output SVM. In: Csurka, G., Kraus, M., Laramee, R.S., Richard, P., Braz, J. (eds.) VISIGRAPP 2012. CCIS, vol. 359, pp. 383–398. Springer, Heidelberg (2013)

14. Vatahska, T., Bennewitz, M., Behnke, S.: Feature-based head pose estimation from images. In: 7th IEEE-RAS International Conference on Human Humanoid Robots, pp. 330–335. IEEE (2007)

15. Viola, P., Jones, M.: Fast and Robust Classification using Asymmetric AdaBoost and a Detector Cascade. Neural Information Processing Systems 14, 1311–1318 (2002)

16. Viola, P., Jones, M.: Robust real-time face detection. International Journal of Computer Vision 57(2), 137–154 (2004)

Design of Disease Management System for Chronic Heart Failure: A Case Study from Advanced Heart Failure Clinic at King Chulalongkorn Memorial Hospital

Chaiyawut Sookpalng and Vajirasak Vanijja

School of Information Technology, King Mongkut's University of Technology Thonburi,
Bangkok, Thailand
chaiyawut.so@gmail.com, vv@sit.kmutt.ac.th

Abstract. Nowadays, chronic diseases are one of the most challenging health problems in many healthcare organizations. A disease management system was designed to improve the treatment for chronic patients by facilitating the patients to report their condition to the care specialists at the hospital. However, achieving this goal demands the study of introducing the disease management system to the CHF patients.

A disease management system called EasyCare was developed to match with the requirements from the care specialists at Advanced Heart Failure Clinic at King Chulalongkorn Memorial Hospital. The EasyCare system consists of three parts; short message service (SMS), web portal, and interactive voice response (IVR). A significant amount of time and effort had been used in the system design phase to make sure that majority of the CHF patients can use the EasyCare system with at least only one single telephone device.

This study aims to obtain knowledge from evaluating performance and technology acceptance of the EasyCare system. A group of thirteen CHF patients and one care specialist had participated in the study. A survey was performed to the participants to get feedbacks and suggestions. However, this EasyCare system doesn't intend to support large group of patients. It only developed for study purpose to show the possibility of using the disease management system to support health care in the future.

Keywords: eHealth,, health informatics, telemedicine, home monitoring, disease management, chronic disease, heart failure, elderly, aging society, treatment compliance.

1 Introduction

In 2005, chronic diseases had represented around 60 % of all deaths worldwide [1]. Cardiovascular diseases owned the largest group (30 %), following by cancer (13 %), chronic respiratory diseases (7 %), and diabetes (2 %). The most common cause of mortality is Ischemic heart disease (reduced oxygen supply to the heart) which caused as many deaths as all types of cancer together [2]. In USA and Canada, chronic diseases accounted for 88 % of all deaths; CVD 38 %, cancer 23 %, respiratory diseases

B. Papasratorn et al. (Eds.): IAIT 2013, CCIS 409, pp. 221–231, 2013.
© Springer International Publishing Switzerland 2013

8 %, and diabetes 3 % [2]. In European region, chronic diseases accounted for 86 % of all deaths; CVD 51 %, cancer 19 %, respiratory diseases 4 %, and diabetes 1 % [2]. In fact, these patterns are similar to most regions of the world, except for poverty where communicable diseases, maternal and perinatal conditions, and nutritional deficiencies are the major cause of death instead [1].

Elderly people were highly affected by the chronic diseases. As 77 % of all deaths from chronic diseases worldwide occurred in the age group 60 year old and older [1]. In USA in 2007, 80 % of their population over 65 years old had one or more chronic diseases [3]. More than 60 % had two or more [4]. In Thailand, chronic diseases are one of the primary causes of death for the elderly, and also trending to become more vital in the future. In 2009, Ministry of Public Health had reported that 39 million people of the total population in Thailand were currently at risk to chronic diseases [5].

Chronic diseases are associated with high expenditure on health care. People with chronic diseases represent five times higher expense than normal [6]. In USA in 2005, about 80 % of total health care costs were related to the chronic diseases [4] [6]. A total cost due to morbidity and mortality for CVD alone was $394 billion [6], cancer was $210 billion, and diabetes was $132 billion [6]. In Europe, a total cost for CVD in EU was e169 billion. In Germany and UK was e54 billion and e37 billion respectively [7]. In Sweden had estimated e5 billion in the total costs on CVD, almost e3 billion were health care costs, representing 11.6 % of the total health care expenditures [7].

2   Related Concepts

According to the World Health Organization (WHO), a cardiovascular disease (CVD) is the number one cause of mortality in the world [2]. Chronic heart failure (CHF), or congestive heart failure or heart failure, is considered as a paradigm of CVD. In 2006, five million people in the USA (estimated 2% of total population) [8] suffered from CHF [9]. The recent studies showed that the treatment compliance of the CHF patients was very low [10-12]. This brings the opportunity to improve the treatment compliance with the disease management system.

2.1   Physiology and Pathology of CHF

The heart and its circulatory system are responsible for distributing blood to flow throughout the body. A deoxygenized blood flows into a right ventricle by passing a superior vena cava and a right atrium. The right ventricle then pushed the blood through a pulmonary artery into the lungs. From the lungs, where oxygen is collected, the oxygenized blood enters to a left ventricle through a pulmonary veins and a left atrium. The left ventricle then finally pushes the blood to flow throughout the human body.

There are two types of CHF, diastolic and systolic dysfunctions. In diastolic dysfunction refers to a compliance reduction of the ventricles, so it needs a higher filling pressure to be able to meet body's metabolic needs. In the severe case, this process can lower a stroke volume and a cardiac output which result in less blood being pumped out into the body at each stroke. In systolic dysfunction refers to an impairment of ventricular contractibility of the heart due to a damage of cells or muscle weakening. In this case, the heart is unable to pump all the blood from a ventricle which results in lowered stroke volume and cardiac output as well.

As described above, both diastolic and systolic dysfunctions result in lowered stroke volume. The body tries to compensate this condition by increasing heart rate, blood pressure, and swelling (edema). The edema that affected from the right side of the heart will occur in a peripheral system; leading to swelling of limbs e.g. legs and feet. While the edema that affected from the left side of the heart will occur in a pulmonary system; leading to accumulate water in lungs. Therefore, CHF will force the heart to work harder and could lead to a completely loss of cardiac function.

The CHF patients can be classified into one of the four classes of New York Heart Association (NYHA) where class I is the least severe case and NYHA class IV is the most severe case respectively, see Table 1.

Table 1. A classification of heart failure according to the New York Heart Association [13]

Class	Symptoms
I	No symptoms and no limitation in ordinary physical activity.
II	Mild symptoms and slight limitation during ordinary activity. Comfortable at rest.
III	Marked limitation in activity due to symptoms, even during less-than-ordinary activity. Comfortable only at rest.
IV	Severe limitations. Experiences symptoms even while at rest.

The most common symptoms of heart failure are breathlessness at rest or on exercise, fatigue, tiredness, and ankle swelling. The common signs of heart failure are tachycardia, tachypnea, pulmonary rales, pleural effusion, raised jugular venous pressure, peripheral edema, and hepatomegaly.

2.2   Treatment of CHF

More than 80% of the CHF patients are treated from the underlying causes with non-pharmacological and pharmacological treatments. A non-pharmacological treatment will monitor changes in the physical signs and heart failure symptoms. For example, sudden weight gain could lead to a fluid retention or body fluid buildup, while sudden weight loss could lead to a reduction in total body fat and lean body mass. The non-pharmacological techniques will only effective only if the patients are on diet, regularly exercise, reducing alcohol intake, and stop smoking. For many worsen cases will require a pharmacological treatment, which has several drugs involved. The diuretics, angiotensin-converting enzyme (ACE) inhibitors, angiotensin receptor blockers, beta-blockers, aldosterone antagonists and cardiac glycosides. A care specialist must closely monitor patient physical signs and heart failure symptoms to administrate new drug or changing its dose.

About 10% of CHF patients will require surgical treatment. This includes mitral valve surgery and implantable devices such as pacemakers and defibrillators (ICD). And less than 5 % of CHF patients will require heart transplantation. The heart replacement surgery can increase quality of life greatly. However, it will only apply to the patient at the end stage of CHF due to the risks of procedure like organ rejection and infection. The lack of donor hearts is also a major issue.

3   System Description

The important issue for developing the disease management system for chronic patients is the introduction and the technology acceptance among users. This section described the design rationale and the system overview of the EasyCare system that was used in this study in Thai public health care sector.

3.1   System Design Rationale

A close study with heart failure clinic brought an opportunity to obtain the knowledge from the real clinical environment. This study can get the constructive feedbacks from the real care specialists and accessed to the real CHF patients. In this study, we involved all participates from Advanced Heart Failure Clinic at King Chulalongkorn Memorial Hospital. A disease management system called EasyCare was developed to use among them. A significant amount of time and effort had been put into the system design to make sure that the majority of the CHF patients can use it.

At the beginning, a prototype of the EasyCare system was developed from the most desirable features among the care specialists. The prototype started from a few features and continuously added a new one once the current version had been reviewed by the care specialists. The design phase of an EasyCare system opened up a chance to remove the features or concepts that were non-beneficial.

3.2   System Overview

An EasyCare system used in this study consisted of three parts which are short message service (SMS), web portal, and interactive voice response (IVR), see Fig. 1. A single telephony device e.g. telephone, mobile phone or computer with internet access is required to use with the EasyCare system.

Patient can use Short Message Service (SMS) via mobile phone. The design was taken to those whose have a moderate level of mobile experience, familiar with the numeric pad, and have ability to send and receive text message. There are about 30 percent of Thai elderly has been using mobile phone (both feature phone and smart phone) [14] since 2009, so patients who had a mobile phone should be able to use the service.

Fig. 1. A schematic illustration of disease management system called EasyCare

Patient can use Interactive Voice Response (IVR) via telephone or mobile phone. The design was taken to patients with low experience on technology especially for the elderly. These patients are hardly to accept an EasyCare system from the beginning. Therefore, the concept of IVR is simple and easy to understand. Any devices that can make a phone call e.g. telephone, mobile phone, can be used with the IVR. A phone call is costly but it is simple and straightforward to guarantee the reachability of the EasyCare system from anyone, anytime and anywhere.

Patients and care specialists can use the web portal via any computer with internet access or smart phone. The web portal consisted of two parts; patient and care specialist parts. A patient part of the web portal provided a form for patients to report their conditions to heart failure clinic over the internet. A care specialist part of the web portal provided a management tool for viewing the patient's conditions, giving advices, and communicating with CHF patients over SMS or email.

4   System Evaluation

To evaluate the EasyCare system, a field trial was begun in February-April of 2013 for serving three proposes; first is to see if the EasyCare system is usable among users in the real environment, second is to see if the EasyCare system can help to improve healthiness of the CHF patients, and third is to see if the EasyCare system can help to maintain patient self-caring at home. A healthiness of each patient will be evaluated into one of the following groups; worse, stable, or better, see Table 2. This study was mainly done at early stage as an introduction of the EasyCare system to provide knowledge for larger studies in the future with more patient involved, more controlled, and longer duration.

Table 2. A group for classifying the CHF patients in the field trial

Group		Criteria
Worse	-	Body weight increases more than 2kg over a day
	-	More amount of Lasix consumption
	-	Interval visit less than or equal to 2 weeks
Stable	-	Body weight increases more than 2kg over a month
	-	Same amount of Lasix consumption
	-	Interval visit higher than 1 month
Better	-	Maintain body weight
	-	Reduce the amount of Lasix consumption
	-	Interval visit higher than 1 month

The field trial was started by forming a group of thirteen CHF patients and one care specialist at Advanced Heart Failure Clinic. Patients were randomly chosen among group of NYHA class I and II. The care specialist was responsible for taking care of the thirteen patients by monitoring patients' health via web portal and giving the daily advises. The EasyCare system was demonstrated to the CHF patients at an initial meeting. The instruction of the system was presented in both oral and giveaway pamphlet. During the presentation, patients were free to ask questions regarding to technical or functional issues about the EasyCare system. At the end, thirteen patients were ready to use the EasyCare system from their mobile phone with a great intention to use.

4.1   Result from Field Trial

Over three months of the field trial, the result showed that CHF patients, especially the elderly, had hard time to change their behavior towards the new solution. At the end, only three out of thirteen patients was using the EasyCare system and another ten had neglected. This result was due to the difficulties from using SMS and IVR. Many elderly couldn't use the IVR because they owned the bad mobile phone. By letting patients use their own mobile phone, which mostly cheap, we're facing problems such as the keypad was too small, the IVR voice was hard to hear, the automated process was hard to follow when switching back and forth to listen and answer. The elderly couldn't use the SMS because the syntax was too complicated. They also complained about the cost from using both SMS and IVR services. From this reason, patients agreed that both IVR and SMS were too difficult to use and handle well in practice. The IVR service should be simpler, take no cost and take less time to complete the task and the SMS service will need more time to learn and understand.

Beside from the ineffective result, three patients had been regularly using the web portal of the EasyCare system for over three months with no difficulties. Therefore, we can evaluate the EasyCare system from those patients. Starting from their backgrounds, see Table 3. They are over 60 years of age (P1=64, P2=67 and P3=62). Patient P1 and Patient P2 have children who can help with the technical issues. Patient P1 has no children but he can use the computer and internet.

Table 3. A summary of patient's who participated in the study

Patient	Sex	Age	Living with family	Currently Using	Intend to use
P1	Female	64	Yes	Mobile Phone	Yes
P2	Female	67	Yes	Mobile Phone	Yes
P3	Male	62	No	Email, Mobile, Phone	Yes

Three patients agreed that using the web portal was easy and understandable. A common error such as missing parameters or entering an incorrect value will be handled by an error message and the instruction to correct the mistake. For this reason, the body weight, blood pressure, and vital signs of heart failure were continuously received from patients during the trial period. This was due to the advantages from using the web portal. However, the web portal faced a problem once due to the absent of internet connection. While the web portal was closed for maintenance, patients were asked to use SMS and IVR instead for a short period of time. The solution had minimized an impact of the failure.

Table 4. A comparison between an average usage of an EasyCare system and the frequency of Lasix's dose adjustment in one month

Patient	System Usage (times/month)	Dose Adjusted (times/month)
P1	16	11
P2	9	0 (Disused)
P3	19	0 (Disused)

When compare an average usage of the EasyCare system and the frequency of Lasix's dose adjustment in one month, see Table 4. The result showed that patients had used the EasyCare system regardless to the condition of their health. Patient P1 used the EasyCare system for 16 times in one month, and 11 times were for adjusting Lasix's dose. Patient P2 and Patient P3 have used the EasyCare system for 9 times and 19 times respectively while they already disused the Lasix consumption. So, the EasyCare system can be used to maintain the present of CHF patients with no additional cost. It can help care specialist to monitor patient's health and increase a chance to detect the early signs and symptoms of heart failure. On the one hand, if no Easy-Care system, CHF patients will neglect to the traditional heart failure treatment when they have a good health. They will stay absent from heart failure clinic until the case start getting worse. And by that time, care specialist will have a hard time to diagnose the early signs and symptoms of heart failure.

A summary of each patient was analyzed by the care specialist after the field trial has ended, see Table 5. Three participants were classified in a "better" group because they can maintain the body weight while continuing to reduce the amount of Lasix consumption during the field trial. Patient P1 and Patient P2 had improved the NYHA score to class I (the least severe case). All patients can lengthen their interval visit while using the EasyCare system to maintain self-caring at home.

Table 5. A summary of each patient over three months

Patient	Period of use	NYHA (class)	Body Weight (kg)	Diuretic Dose (mg)	Interval Visit (times per month)	Heart Failure Group
P1	Pre	II	48.4±0.86	300±90	2	Stable
	Post	I	47.3±1.16	190±75	4	Better
P2	Pre	II	52.3±0.62	20	2	Stable
	Post	I	51.7±0.5	Disused	4	Better
P3	Pre	I	74.7±0.48	20	3	Stable
	Post	I	72.3±0.67	Disused	5	Better

The graphs below show the summary of body weights and the amount of Lasix consumptions of patient P1 during the trial period. The blue line represents the values before patients have used the EasyCare system, following by the red line which represents the values after the patient have used the EasyCare system.

While Patient P1 was using the EasyCare system, she can maintain her body weight over three months, see Fig. 2.

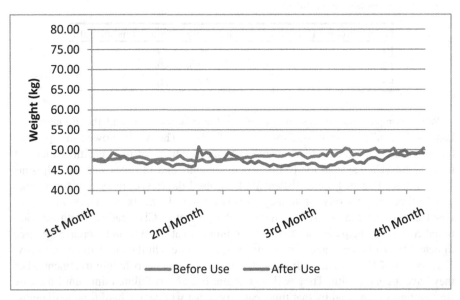

Fig. 2. A summary of weights of Patient P1 over three months (in kilogram)

While Patient P1 was using the EasyCare system, she can reduce the amount of Lasix consumption from 500 mg per day to 100 mg per day over three months, see Fig. 3.

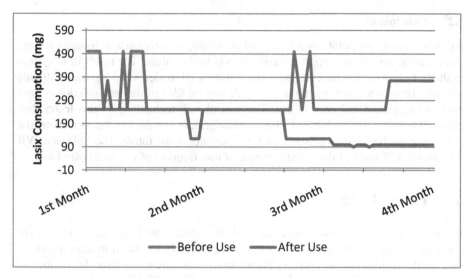

Fig. 3. A summary Lasix consumption of Patient P1 over three months (in milligram)

Therefore, Patient P1 was classified in a "better" group because she can maintain her body weight while continuing to reduce the amount of Lasix consumption.

5   Discussion and Conclusion

5.1   Discussion

In this study, the result from field trial showed that technology acceptance among CHF patients was very low since only three out of thirteen patients were using the EasyCare system on their daily basis. The ease of use had failed after one week of the field trial when ten patients faced the difficulties and an inability to use SMS and IVR at home. The frequent of use had failed when patients cannot use the EasyCare system at least three times a week - It was inconvenient for them since they usually contact their care specialist only once a month or less. The cost of use had failed when the elderly had to pay for making a phone call or sending an SMS for themselves. Most elderly considered to save this cost and neglected to the EasyCare system instead.

On the other hand, a web portal part of the EasyCare system gained the technology acceptance among CHF patients during the field trial. Three patients had been regularly using the EasyCare system with the web portal and the result showed that they were healthier over three months. They gained confident living with the disease while maintained self-caring at home with the EasyCare system. Therefore, there is a sign that the disease management system can improve the quality of life of CHF patients if the adequate supports were provided.

5.2   Conclusion

All these arguments point towards a good possibility to develop a web-based disease management system to support chronic patients in the future. The result from system evaluation showed that the care specialist and the CHF patients had a positive attitude towards the web technology in the future. A general idea of the web solution is very easy to understand and easy to use. The cost of web technology is also lesser than others. Therefore, the web-based disease management system has the most potential to become the health care solution for CHF patients in the future. The SMS and IVR approaches will need a future study on ease of use, frequent of use, and cost of use.

6   Future Work

In this thesis, the field trial was conducted to evaluate the EasyCare system in the home environment. However, the work was considerably too small to draw a conclusion on the technology acceptance. Future study can follow the User Acceptance of Information Technology: Toward a Unified View (UTAUT) [15] for deeper analysis about the user acceptance model. The UTAUT model requires at least 30 participants in one study to get the statistically result. Therefore, there is a good opportunity to conduct new study with various chronic conditions e.g. diabetes, high blood pressure, lupus, multiple sclerosis and sleep apnea. For suggestion, the first step to achieve this goal is to find the large amount of participants. The study must plan to easily collect the conditions from all patients. This can be done by developing the embedded toolkits, the system that let patients enter bunches of conditions at once, the social network apps, or smart phone apps.

Acknowledgements. The author gratefully acknowledged financial support from National Research Universities (NRU), Thailand. The fund had covered instruments, books, conference pass, and monthly expenses. Author feels thankful to doctor and care specialists at Advanced Heart Failure Clinic at King Chulalongkorn Memorial Hospital who gave knowledge about the heart failure and the treatment concepts. Thank you for the CHF patients for being well participated in the field trial. Author is also grateful for the use of computing facilities at School of Information Technology (SIT), King Mongkut's University of Technology Thonburi (KMUTT).

References

1. World Health Organization, Preventing chronic diseases: a vital investment, Geneva (2005)
2. World Health Organization, Causes of death, http://www.who.int/entity/ healthinfo/statistics/bodgbddeathdalyestimates.xls (accessed 2002)
3. Centers for Disease Control and Prevention, and The Merck Company Foundation, The state of aging and health in america 2007 (2007)

4. Anderson, G., Horvath, J.: The growing burden of chronic disease in america. Public Health Reports 119(3), 263–270 (2004)
5. ค. อ. เดือนตรานนท์, "นวัตกรรมการแพทย์ยุค 2.0. INNOMag, pp. 45-48 (2011)
6. Council of State Governments (CSG), Healthy states - costs of chronic diseases: What are states facing? (2006)
7. Leal, J., Luengo-Fernandez, R., Gray, A., Petersen, S., Rayner, M.: Economic burden of cardiovascular diseases in the enlarged european union. European Heart Journal Advance (2006)
8. Thom, E.T.: Heart disease and stroke statistics–2006 update: A report from the american heart association statistics committee and stroke statistics subcommittee (2006)
9. National Board of Health and Welfare (Socialstyrelsen), Socialstyrelsens riktlinjer for hjartsjukvården. Det medicinska faktadokumentet, Stockholm, Sweden (2004)
10. Swedberg, K., Writing, C., Cleland, J., Dargie, H., Drexler, H., Follath, F., Komajda, M., Tavazzi, L., Smiseth, O.A., Gavazzi, A., Haverich, A., Hoes, A., Jaarsma, T., Korewicki, J., Levy, S.: Guidelines for the diagnosis and treatment of chronic heart failure: executive summary (update 2005). The Task Force for the Diagnosis and Treatment of Chronic Heart Failure of the European Society of Cardiology 26(11), 1115–1140 (2005)
11. Ekman, I., Andersson, G., Boman, K., Charlesworth, A., Cleland, J.G.F., Poole-Wilson, P., Swedberg, K.: Adherence and perception of medication in patients with chronic heart failure during a five-year randomised trial. Patient Education and Counseling 61(3), 348–353 (2006)
12. Cline, C.M.J., Björck-Linn, A.K., Israelsson, B.Y.A., Willenheimer, R.B.: Non-compliance and knowledge of prescribed medication in elderly patients with heart failure. European Journal of Heart Failure 1(2), 145–149 (1999)
13. American Heart Association, Diagnosing Heart Disease (March 21, 2008), http://www.americanheart.org/presenter.jhtml?identifier=330 (accessed March 19, 2013)
14. สำนักงานสถิติแห่งชาติ, "จำนวนและสัดส่วนผู้ใช้โทรศัพท์มือถืออายุ 60 ปีขึ้นไป (2009), http://social.nesdb.go.th/SocialStat/StatReport_Final.aspx?reportid=366&template=2R2C&yeartype=M&subcatid=25 (accessed March 19, 2013)
15. Venkatesh, V., Morris, Davis: User Acceptance of Information Technology: Toward a Unified View. MIS Quarterly 27(3), 425–478 (2003)

Effect of Codec Bit Rate and Packet Loss
on Thai Speech Recognition over IP

Tuul Triyason and Prasert Kanthamanon

School of Information Technology, King Mongkut's University of Technology Thonburi,
Pracha-utid Road, Bangmod, Toongkru, Bangkok, Thailand
`tuul.tri@st.sit.kmutt.ac.th, prasert@sit.kmutt.ac.th`

Abstract. Nowadays, VoIP has become the core communications on the internet. One of the crucial applications on VoIP is the automated IVR system that interacts with the user automatically. Speech recognition plays an important role behind this kind of system. This paper studies the effect of codec bit rate and network packet loss on Thai speech recognition systems over an IP network. We encoded the speech samples of male, female and artificial voice with various bit rates of Speex codec. The speech sample was sent by RTP through the IP network with packet loss simulation. The speech quality was measured by PESQ and compared to word error rate of speech recognition. The results show that the codec bit rate and level of packet loss have a significant impact on the performance of speech recognition over IP.

Keywords: VoIP, QoS, PESQ, Thai language, speech recognition.

1   Introduction

Today, speech and speaker recognition gain more popularity in a wide variety of technologies. Speech recognition systems can be found in many mobile devices. In various kinds of recognition system, speech signals have to travel through a different type of network before processed by a recognition engine at the end point. VoIP or IP-Telephony is one of the popular methods for voice communication in next generation network. It decreases the communication cost from the PSTN operator. One of the crucial applications on VoIP are the automated IVR systems. This kind of IVR interacts with the user through speech communication automatically. Speech recognition over IP plays an important role in this kind of system. However, IP is an unreliable and best effort network. The speech quality of VoIP can be affected by many parameters such as delays, packet loss and low bit rate coding [1]. Static delay does not affect a speech quality directly but affects the conversational quality. Low bit rate coding may result in lower bandwidth consumption but a speech signals will lose some spectral characteristics. Packet loss on an IP network can be the cause of voice clipping which directly affects speech listening quality [2]. Recent studies show that speech quality in VoIP correlates significantly to the performance of speech recognition [3-4]. However, most of the evaluation has been based on English or other

B. Papasratorn et al. (Eds.): IAIT 2013, CCIS 409, pp. 232–241, 2013.

Western languages (e.g. French). In linguistic theory, tone can be used to distinguish language into two main categories, tonal languages and non-tonal languages [5]. Most of the western languages are non-tonal languages while many East Asian languages are tonal such as, the Chinese language, Vietnamese and the Tai-Kadai family of languages in South-East Asia. Our previous work shows that the speech quality of tonal language was different between a tone in Thai and Chinese [6]. However, there is very little research between the correlation between a speech quality and a performance of tonal speech recognition over IP.

The objective of this research is to study the effect of bit rate and packet loss in the performance of tonal speech recognition over IP. The speech quality degradations were objectively measured using the Perceptual Evaluation of Speech Quality method (PESQ) [7]. The results show the relation between PESQ MOS and word error rate of speech recognition. Moreover, it also indicated that MOS from objective speech quality measurement could be used as a prediction for speech recognition performance.

2   Background

2.1   Thai Language

Thai language is one of the tonal languages in Asia. It is used as an official language by over 60 million people in Thailand [8]. The Thai language is one of the subsections in the Tai-Kadai group of languages. Tai-Kadai is a language family of highly tonal languages found mostly in southern China and Southeast Asia [9]. They include Thai, Lao and some parts of Vietnam. Unlike the Chinese Mandarin language which has four contrastive lexical tones [10], The Thai language has five contrastive lexical tones on syllables which can be distinguish into mid, low, falling, high and rising tone [11].

A Tonal language, pitch is used as a part of speech, in order to change the meaning of a word. Previous research on the fundamental frequency (F0) contour using Fujisaki's model shows that the F0 and other characteristics of Thai female voices are significantly higher than male voices [12]. Figure 1 shows the pitch track and narrow band spectrogram of the following Thai in words, *khaa (mid)* to be stuck, *khaa (low)* a kind of spice, *khaa (falling)* to kill, *khaa (high)* to engage in trade, *khaa (rising)* a leg.

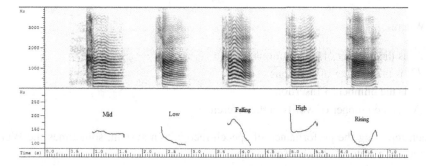

Fig. 1. Pitch track and narrow band spectrogram of Thai word *khaa* from a man speech

2.2   Speech Quality Evaluation

Perceptual Evaluation of Speech Quality (PESQ) is the objective speech quality evaluation method as described in the ITU-T recommendation P.862 [7]. PESQ can be used to measure speech quality in narrow band and wide band communication networks. It works by comparing the original signal X(t), with the degraded signal Y(t). When Y(t) is the result of the passing signal X(t) through a communication network. PESQ generated perceptual of signal Y(t) as evaluated by subjective testing.

Speech quality is rated by a Mean Opinion Score (MOS) [13]. The MOS from PESQ ranges from -0.5-4.5, with the higher scores indicating better speech quality. PESQ was later complemented with ITU-T recommendation P.862.1 which is used for mapping PESQ scores to a subjective MOS scale (Table 1) [14]. MOS obtained from this mapping results in the Listening Objective Mean Opinion Scores (MOS-LQO).

Table 1. MOS scale

MOS	Quality
5	Excellent
4	Good
3	Fair
2	Poor
1	Bad

2.3   Speech Recognition Performance Evaluation

Word Error Rate (WER) is a common evaluation method for speech recognition systems. WER is derived from the Levenshtein distance, or edit distance. The edit distance between two strings is the minimum number (or weighted sum) of insertions, deletions and substitutions required to transform one string into the other [15]. %WER is defined as

$$\%WER = \frac{S+D+I}{N} \times 100 \qquad (1)$$

Where

- S is the number of substitutions
- D is the number of deletions
- I is the number of Insertions
- N is the number of words in the reference

When reporting the performance of speech recognition system, sometimes the Word Recognition Rate (WRR) is used instead.

$$\%WRR = (1 - WER) \times 100 \tag{2}$$

Where, WRR shows the rate of correctly recognized words.

3   Experimental Description

3.1   Speech Samples

In order to study the performance of speech recognition on artificial voice, speech samples were prepared into two sets. The first set of speech samples was recorded by four males and females in a soundproof environment. All of the speakers were Thai native speakers with standard Thai pronunciation. The second sets of samples are generated from the text-to-speech software Vaja 6.0. Vaja is able to synthesize all Thai words since it has a text analysis module which can generate the pronunciation of every word even the ones not found in a dictionary [16]. All of the speech samples are recorded with a 8 kHz sampling rate and 16 bits PCM format.

3.2   Thai Speech Recognition

The speech recognition software is iSpeech-W 1.5. It works by extracting Mel-frequency cepstrum (MFCC) features from a speech and uses the Viterbi algorithm to compare with reference to the Hidden Markov Model (HMM) recognition network [17]. The acoustic model of iSpeech-W is trained from a LOTUS speech corpus which contains 70 hours of speech from 48 speakers (24 males/24females) in a clean and office environment [18].

3.3   Impairment Parameter

Bit Rate

In digital multimedia, the bit rate often refers to the number of bits used per unit of playback time to represent a continuous medium such as audio or video after source coding (data compression). In real time applications such as VoIP, the codec with a higher bit rate mode refers to higher in a speech quality. However, the higher bit rate codec may lead to high bandwidth consumption. According to VoIP traffic's behavior, the low bit rate codec is more suitable for VoIP applications [19]. The Speex codec that used in the experiment is set to 8 kHz sampling (Narrowband). In Speex CBR mode, there are 7 different narrowband bit-rates defined, ranging from 2.15 kbps to 24.6 kbps as shown in Table 2. However, the modes below 5.9 kbps should not be used for speech [20].

Table 2. Speex quality mode versus bit rate

Mode	Quality Mode	Bit Rate (bps)
1	0	2,150
8	1	3,950
2	2	5,950
3	3-4	8,000
4	5-6	11,000
5	7-8	15,000
6	9	18,200
7	10	24,600

Packet Loss

The cause of packet loss in IP network transmission may come from a bad quality link, the excessive delay in a network, or saturation of a network device buffer. The Gilbert model, shows that the probability of packet loss may depend on the previous packet (dependent loss) or not depend on the previous packet (independent loss) [4]. In this experiment, an independent loss characteristic is used in the network simulation. The loss rate is adjusted using the following values 0%, 1%, 2%, 4%, 6%, 8%, and 10%. The packetization time of the RTP is set to 20 ms (default value).

3.4   Evaluation Framework

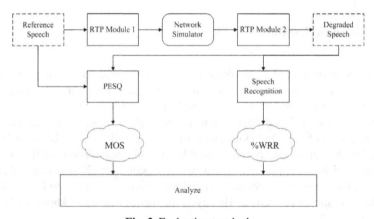

Fig. 2. Evaluation test-bed

The speech quality test-bed with speech recognition and PESQ method used in our experiment framework is shown in Figure 2. The reference speech samples are input to the RTP module 1 which, is operated using RTP ToolBox software [21]. The RTP ToolBox can manually create and terminate RTP sessions independent of call-signaling protocols like SIP. After the RTP sessions, the reference speech samples are coded using a Speex codec with various bit rates. The voice packets are streamed from RTP module 1 through network simulator. IPNetSIM works as a network simulator in this experiment [22]. The delay in the network is set to a 50 ms static delay and packet loss is varies from 0-10%. The network bandwidth is set to full Ethernet with no background traffic flow in the network. The RTP ToolBox in RTP module 2 works as a speech decoder. The degraded speech measures quality by PESQ methods (compared with reference speech) and recognized with speech recognition. The speech quality MOS is calculated using the PESQ method and compared with the %WER from speech recognition performance.

4   Results

4.1   Effect of Bit Rate Results

Figure 3, 4 and 5 shows the results for the performance of speech recognition compared to speech quality. It is clear that the lower bit rate mode of the Speex codec results in lower speech quality and performance of word recognition rate. However, in case of human speech, the female word recognition performance is better than male in the first three bit rate modes as show in Figure 3 and 4. PESQ scores do not show any significant difference between male and female speech at the same bit rate. WRR is converged to a stable state performance when the bit rate starts at 11.0 kbps which is the default bit rate of the Speex codec (quality mode 5). In case of artificial speech, the WRR shows better performance than human speech even in the case of lowest bit rate mode (Figure 5). With Speex quality mode 2, the bit rate of codec is only 5.95 kbps but yields WRR performance at 67%. However, PESQ shows the speech quality of artificial voice is lower than human speech. At the best speech quality bit rate, the WRR of artificial speech shows a correct recognition rate of almost 90% which is better than human speech at 15%.

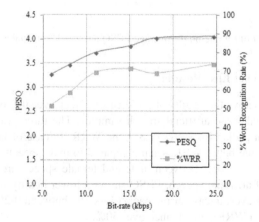

Fig. 3. The effect of bit rate on the average PESQ and WRR for Thai male speech

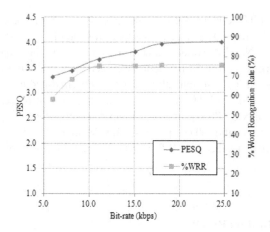

Fig. 4. The effect of bit rate on the average PESQ and WRR for Thai female speech

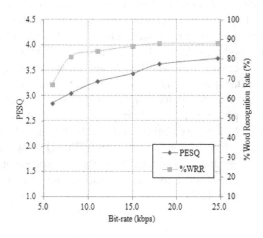

Fig. 5. The effect of bit rate on the average PESQ and WRR for Thai artificial speech

4.2 Effect of Packet Loss Results

Figure 6, 7, and 8 shows the results of packet loss effect over the average PESQ and WRR of male, female, and artificial speech samples. The three graphs show a good correlation between packet loss rate, PESQ and WRR. In case of human speech, female speech shows the better WRR when compared to male speech as observed in bit rate effect. The PESQ scores between male and female speech are not significantly different. In case of artificial speech, PESQ shows a lower quality when compared to human speech. However, in case of the packet loss rate between 0-2%, the three types of speech still have a WRR performance over 50%.

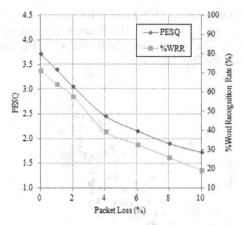

Fig. 6. The effect of packet loss on the average PESQ and WRR for Thai male speech

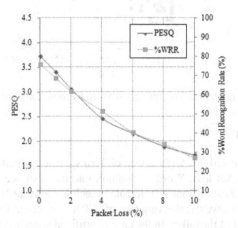

Fig. 7. The effect of packet loss on the average PESQ and WRR for Thai female speech

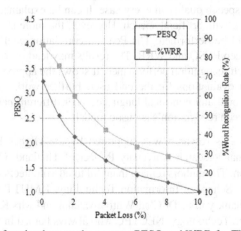

Fig. 8. The effect of packet loss on the average PESQ and WRR for Thai artificial speech

To find the correlation between PESQ and WRR, the scatter diagram of two parameters is created as shown in Figure 9. The Pearson correlation coefficient of the two parameters is 0.70. The correlation coefficient shows a good correspondence among PESQ and WRR for Thai language.

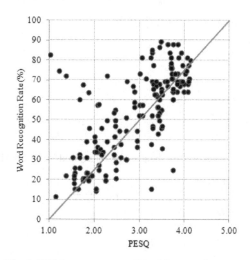

Fig. 9. PESQ scores versus Word Recognition Rate

5   Conclusion

In this paper, we evaluated the performance of Thai speech recognition over variation of codec bit rate and packet loss. Word recognition rate has also been compared with the PESQ score. The results show that Thai female speech has a better WRR when compared to Thai male speech. However, the variation of WRR may come from the difference in talking style and speed of the talker. In the case of artificial speech, it shows a better WRR when compared to human speech. Moreover, PESQ also shows that artificial speech quality is less than human speech quality in every case. It can be explained that PESQ has not been created for testing with artificial speech. However, the more study about PESQ and artificial speech should be performed. The Pearson correlation coefficient also shows a good correlation between PESQ and WRR. The results may lead us to use PESQ scores as the prediction of speech recognition performance. It shows the approach to lower the costs of speech recognition evaluations for the end user. Further work should be studied on comparison between tonal and non-tonal language under different network environments and more complex speech recognition's acoustic model.

Acknowledgements. This research was supported by the Higher Education Research Promotion and National Research University Project of Thailand, Office of the Higher Education Commission. The authors remain thankful to all volunteers from B.Sc. IT17, 18 and M.Sc.ITw23 from School of Information Technology, KMUTT who are the owners of speech samples. Thank you to Dr.Chai Wutiwiwatchai and Mrs.Kwanchiwa Tangthai from Human Language Technology, NECTEC who always helped in any speech recognition problem. Finally, thank you to Mr. John Lawry for editing.

References

1. Holub, J., Slavata, O.: Impact of IP channel parameters on the final quality of the transferred voice. In: Wireless Telecommunications Symposium (WTS), pp. 1–5 (2012)
2. Karapantazis, S., Pavlidou, F.-N.: VoIP: A comprehensive survey on a promising technology. Computer Networks 53, 2050–2090 (2009)
3. Blatnik, R., Kandus, G., Šef, T.: Influence of the speech quality in telephony on the automated speaker recognition. In: Proceedings of the 5th WSEAS International Conference on Circuits, Systems, Signal and Telecommunications, pp. 115–120. World Scientific and Engineering Academy and Society (WSEAS), Stevens Point (2011)
4. Mayorga, P., Besacier, L., Lamy, R., Serignat, J.-F.: Audio packet loss over IP and speech recognition. In: 2003 IEEE Workshop on Automatic Speech Recognition and Understanding, ASRU 2003, pp. 607–612 (2003)
5. Yip, M.: Tone. Cambridge University Press (2002)
6. Triyason, T., Kanthamanon, P.: Perceptual Evaluation of Speech Quality Measurement on Speex Codec VoIP with Tonal Language Thai. In: Papasratorn, B., Charoenkitkarn, N., Lavangnananda, K., Chutimaskul, W., Vanijja, V. (eds.) IAIT 2012. CCIS, vol. 344, pp. 181–190. Springer, Heidelberg (2012)
7. ITU-T P.862: Perceptual evaluation of speech quality (PESQ), an ojective method for end-to-end speech quality assessment of narrowband telephone networks and speech codecs (2001)
8. Daengsi, T., Wutiwiwatchai, C., Preechayasomboon, A., Sukparungsee, S.: A study of VoIP quality evaluation: User perception of voice quality from G.729, G.711 and G.722. In: 2012 IEEE Consumer Communications and Networking Conference (CCNC), pp. 342–345 (2012)
9. Diller, A.V.N.: The Tai-Kadai languages. Routledge, London (2012)
10. Chong, F.L., McLoughlin, I.V., Pawlikowski, K.: A Methodology for Improving PESQ accuracy for Chinese Speech. TENCON 2005 IEEE Region 10, 1–6 (2005)
11. Cooke, J.R., Abramson, A.S.: The Vowels and Tones of Standard Thai: Acoustical Measurements and Experiments. American Anthropologist. 65, 1406–1407 (1963)
12. Chomphan: Fujisaki's Model of Fundamental Frequency Contours for Thai Dialects. Journal of Computer Science 6, 1263–1271 (2010)
13. ITU-T P.800: Methods for subjective determination of transmission quality (1996)
14. ITU-T P.862.1: Mapping function for transforming P.862 raw result scores to MOS-LQO (2003)
15. Anusuya, M.A., Katti, S.K.: Speech Recognition by Machine. A Review (2010)
16. Vaja 6.0, http://vaja.nectec.or.th/
17. Ispeech-W 1.5, http://tvis.nectec.or.th/speech/index.php
18. Patcharikra, C., Treepop, S., Sawit, K., Nattanun, T., Chai, W.: LOTUS: Large vocabulary Thai continuous Speech Recognition Corpus. In: NSTDA Annual Conference S&T in Thailand: Towards the Molecular Economy (2005)
19. Chitode, J.S.: Principles Of Communication. Technical Publications (2008)
20. Valin, J.M.: The Speex codec manual (version 1.2 Beta 3) (2007)
21. RTPToolBox: RTP Packet Testing & Simulation Tools, http://www.gl.com/rtptoolbox.html
22. IPNetSim-(IPNetwork/WANEmulator - 100Mbps, 1Gbps, 4x1Gbps), http://www.gl.com/ipnetsim.html

A Comparative Study of VoIP Quality Measurement from G.711 and G.729 Using PESQ and Thai Speech

Kiattisak Yochanang[1], Therdpong Daengsi[2], Tuul Triyason[3],
and Pongpisit Wuttidittachotti[1]

[1] Faculty of Information Technology, KMUTNB, Bangkok, Thailand
{kiattisaky,pongpisitw}@kmutnb.ac.th
[2] Enterprise Services, JADS Comm Limited, Bangkok, Thailand
Therdpong1@yahoo.com
[3] School of Information Technology, KMUTT, Bangkok, Thailand
51501701@st.sit.kmutt.ac.th

Abstract. This paper presents the study of VoIP quality measurements from two popular codecs, G.711 and G.729, using the methods of Perceptual Evaluation of Speech Quality (PESQ) and Thai speech. In this study, from four lists of Thai speech, it has been found that G.711 provides better voice quality than G.729 in every condition of packet loss. Also, it has been found that Objective Listening Quality - Mean Opinion Score (MOS-LQO) of male speech is slightly higher than MOS-LQO of female speech, whereas MOS of child speech is the lowest. Then, MOS-LQO values from four Thai speech lists have been compared. Next, MOS-LQO from PESQ of male and female speech at the best condition have been compared with the Subjective Listening Quality Mean Opinion Score (MOS-LQS) from ACR listening tests in another laboratory. Lastly, referring to packet loss effects, objective MOS from PESQ have been compared with subjective MOS from conversation tests. It has been found that there is no significant difference among MOS-LQO from the four Thai speech lists, but it has been found that there is a significant difference between subjective MOS and objective MOS from each codec in each condition. Therefore, one can say that this is evidence that PESQ requires intensive study with Thai speech to modify PESQ for VoIP quality measurement in Thai environments confidently.

1 Introduction

VoIP quality measurement is one of the interesting issues referring to VoIP technology. Particularly, research on VoIP quality measurement based on Thai speech is very interesting because Thai is a tonal language, which is unique. At this moment, it still requires deep investigation, although some issues with the Thai language have been studied already, for example, subjective MOS studies with G-family codecs using subjective tests and Speex using PESQ [1-2].

Therefore, this study has been conducted in order to investigate VoIP quality measurement using PESQ with Thai speech, which has been applied to the Thai

B. Papasratorn et al. (Eds.): IAIT 2013, CCIS 409, pp. 242–255, 2013.
© Springer International Publishing Switzerland 2013

Speech Set for Telephonometry (TSST) [3], with unofficial collaboration between Faculty of Information Technology, KMUTNB, and School of Information Technology, KMUTT.

2   Background

VoIP quality measurement methods have been mainly classified into subjective methods and objective methods [4] [5]. Some of those are presented as follows:

2.1   Subjective Methods

Subjective result of voice quality is an important issue because it is necessary to be benchmarked for objective measurement tool calibration. It has been stated in [2] that, in general, it is agreed that subjective result of voice quality evaluation gives better reliability that the result from objective measurement.

Conceptually, subjective testing seems a very simple idea to obtain Mean Opinion Score (MOS), which is a key quality indicator for speech communication that is standardized by ITU-T [6]. MOS is the average of scores, using a 5-point scale (5=Excellent, 4=Good, 3=fair, 2=poor, 1=bad) from individual scores. However, for reliability of MOS, it requires 16 subjects or more, requiring controlled conditions (e.g., packet loss effects) in a quiet environment, such as a soundproof room [7].

Absolute Category Rating (ACR) testing is one of the better known subjective methods. This method has been issued by ITU-T; its result is a MOS of listening quality, which refers to how subjects rate what they hear during a call or speech sample [6-7]. It is used to obtain the absolute quality of the voice sample, through the direct hearing of the speech sample, without a reference speech sample [7].   Of course, ACR testing requires standard speech files; otherwise, variability in scores might be high. That means the MOS result might suffer from unreliability. Nevertheless, for its limitation, some effects such as delay effects cannot be tested using this method.

Therefore, conversation testing can be an alternative, particularly to evaluate conversational quality, which refers to how subjects rate the overall quality of a call impacted by, for example, echo and/or delay effects, thus it is the most realistic atmosphere recommended by ITU-T because this method can reach the same standard of realism [5] [7] [8]. Moreover, this method does not require speech files, while each round of testing can provide two scores. Therefore, with the same numbers of subjects, it should be able to decrease time of 50% to gather scores.

2.2   Objective Methods

Even though there is no objective measurement method that can replace subjective measurement method perfectly, objective measurement method has several advantages, such as, shorter time consumption, no collaboration with a lot of subjects and fewer endeavors [2, 9].

There are several objective measurement methods for speech communications, However, the major methods are PESQ for intrusive methods and E-model for non-intrusive methods, which have been confirmed by the search results from IEEE*Xplore*®, as shown in Table 1 [10] [11]. In that table, it can be seen from the search that the results of PESQ are higher than results of the E-model.

Table 1. Research directions using PESQ and E-model in last five years

Objective Method	Result	Remark
PESQ	41	Jan 2009 – Aug 2013
E-model	37	

For PESQ, which has been used in this study, it has been surveyed from [5] [12] [13] [14] [15] [16] and summarized in [17] as follows:

- PESQ is state-of-the-art in terms of objective voice quality measurement and has been claimed to have very high correlation with the subjective voice quality measurement methods

- it is the most common and popular method of intrusive measurement methods, including the original version, P.862 that supports narrow-band telephone networks and speech codecs, and P.862.2 which supports wideband telephone networks and speech codecs

- the original ITU-T P.862 PESQ supports only narrow-band telephone networks, whereas its new version was extended to support wideband telephone networks

- it uses the strength of both Perceptual Speech Quality Measurement (PSQM) and Perceptual Analysis Measurement System (PAMS), which are psycho-acoustic and cognitive models, and a time alignment algorithm respectively

- it is recommended to evaluate the impact of a codec to voice quality and to test the networks before operation

- it can be applied to evaluate several factors, such as transmission errors, codec errors, noise in the system, packet loss and time clipping

- it works as the model that compares the degraded signals to the original signals, instead of subjective evaluation

- this model permits the discovery of time jitter and identification of frames involved and which frames are affected by the delay and erased in order to prevent a bad score

- the average correlation between PESQ scores and the subjective scores was 0.935, reported in [14], whereas, it is claimed in [16] that the correlation is up to 0.95.

2.3   Thai Language and Thai Sound System

The Thai language is a tonal language used as the official language in Thailand that has population of over 65 million people. There are 44 Thai consonants that are classified into three groups known as High, Middle and Low class consonants.

The phoneme of Thai consists of 21 initial consonants, 11 cluster consonants, 9 final consonants, 21 vowels (consisting of short vowel, long vowel and diphthong) [18]. Particularly, there is a tonal feature that is very important for the Thai sound system, due to different tones of Thai speech which change the meaning of Thai words [18]. There are five tones shown in Table 2.

Moreover, from the research on neuroscience, it has been reported in [20] that from the study using Electroencephalogram technique and Low-Resolution Brain Electromagnetic Tomography (LORETA) with the Mismatch Negativity (MMN), with 9 Thai native listeners who do not have Chinese knowledge, that only the left hemisphere (LH) of Thai native speakers were activated significantly when listening to the condition with Thai speech which is their mother language, whereas, their right hemisphere (RH) were activated when listening to the condition with Chinese speech. Besides, it has been reported in [21] that the part of LH was predominant in the perception of the prosody of Thai speech sound, while the prosody of Chinese speech sound was dominated by part of the RH. That means only the left hemisphere can significantly respond to native speech sounds.

For speech samples that are necessary for the listening tests and different kinds of objective voice quality tests, ITU-T recommended that the speech samples must be meaningful and easy to understand [5], therefore, the 'Harvard sentences' that have been used widely cannot be used for voice or speech quality measurement in Thailand, due to those sentences are only in English [22].

Instead of using a set of Thai speech from the 'Multi-lingual speech database for telephonometry 1994' that's provided by NTT-AT with expensive costs [22], local Thai speech sets have been considered. However, instead of following [2] using the well-known Thai speech corpus 'LOTUS', which has been noted that many sentences are not simple when compared with the Thai Speech Set for Telephonometry (TSST) [3] [4]. TSST has therefore been considered for application, following [23] for further investigation. Some parts of speech sentences of TSST are shown in Table 3.

2.4   Related Works

In 2002, it was reported that results from the study with English and Dutch speech with loss effects using PESQ in [24] that the voice quality from male speech is higher than the voice quality from female speech.

Table 2. An example of Thai words with five tones

	Thai Tone				
	Mid	Low	Falling	High	Rising
Word	เลา	เหล่า	เล่า/เหล้า	เล้า	เหลา
Phonetic Symbol	lā	là	lâ	lá	lǎ
Meaning	noun classifier of a flute	set or group	to tell/alcohol	a (pig or duck) pen	to sharpen (a pencil)

Several years later in 2008, there was one research work from the same laboratory that is consistent with [24]. It presented voice quality with the GSM codec, English speech and six conditions [12]. It has been found that the voice quality from male speech using PESQ is higher than the voice quality from female speech. While it is inconsistent with [24], when using 3SQM, it was found that the voice quality from female speech is higher than the voice quality from male speech.

Similar to [25], the study with G.711 and G.729 using PESQ, it has been observed that the results from the experiment with delay effects of the voice quality from English female speech is slightly higher than the voice quality from English male speech. However, it has been observed from the same article that it is inconsistent with Chinese speech because the voice quality of Chinese male speech is slightly higher than the voice quality of Chinese female speech. Nevertheless, with loss effects, it has not been observed clearly from the experiment with G.711 about the differences of the voice quality from English male speech and English female speech, while the result of Chinese speech is consistent with the result of the experiment with delay effects.

For the study with Thai, both male and female speech, with Speex codec using PESQ [2], the result from the experiment with Thai speech is consistent with [24], and [12] that used PESQ tests. It has been observed that the voice quality from Thai male speech is higher than the voice quality from Thai female speech.

However, all above were mainly from objective tests using PESQ, the results are inconsistent with the result from the subjective tests, because it has been shown in [26] from interview tests, the voice quality from the female interviewer is slightly higher than the voice quality from the male interviewer. Besides, it has been compared between G.711 and G.729 referring to loss effects in [8] using conversation tests but it did not analyze type or gender of speech.

Therefore, it is still necessary to investigate and analyze Thai speech, both male and female.

3   Methodology

From Table 3, the speech lists have been adopted from [23], which follows [27] that recommended to have the length of each speech sample around 8-30 s, as shown in Table 4, as follows:

1)   List2: there are three forms of speech samples (A, B and C). Each speech sample, with the length of 8 s, consists of two speech sentences. For each form, there are 2 child speech samples (a boy and a girl), 4 female speech samples and 4 male speech samples; therefore, totally there are 30 speech samples for this speech list.

2)   List3: there are three forms of speech samples (A, B and C). Each speech sample, with the length of 8 s, consists of three speech sentences. Similar to List2, for each form, there are 2 child speech samples (a boy and a girl), 4 female speech samples and 4 male speech samples; therefore, totally there are 30 speech samples for this speech list.

3)   List4: there are three forms of speech samples (A, B and C). Each speech sample, with the length of 10-12 s, consists of four speech sentences. Similar to List2, for each form, there are 2 child speech samples (a boy and a girl), 4 female speech samples and 4 male speech samples; therefore, totally there are 30 speech samples for this speech list.

Table 3. Selected Speech Samples for creating Subgroups of TSST as a Small Size Approach

Speech Group No.	Thai Sentences (or Phrases) with English Meaning
G1-1	สวัสดีครับ/ค่ะ (Hello.)
G2-1	หมายเลขที่ท่านเรียกไม่สามารถติดต่อได้ในขณะนี้ (The number you've tried to reach cannot be connected.)
G2-2	คิดถึงนะ (Miss you.)
G4-1	สอบถามข้อมูลอื่นเพิ่มเติมอีกไหมครับ/คะ (Would you like to ask for more information?)
G5-1	ต่อไปเป็นข่าวในพระราชสำนัก (Next, it is the royal news.)
G5-2	Where have you been? (ไปไหนมาเหรอ)
G6-1	กรุณาถือสายรอสักครู่ครับ/ค่ะ (Please hold on one moment.)
G6-2	ยินดีต้อนรับครับ/ค่ะ (Welcome.)
G7-1	วันนี้จะไปเที่ยวที่ไหนดี (Where are we going today?)
G7-2	ไม่ได้เจอกันตั้งนาน (Long time no see.)
G8-1	กำลังจะไปไหน (Where are you going?)
G8-2	ขอรบกวนเวลาสักครู่นะครับ/คะ (Please give me sometime.)
G9-1	วันนี้ไปกินข้าวที่ไหนกันดี (Where will we go to eat today?)
G9-2	จะกลับเมื่อไหร่ (When will you come back?)
G11-1	ดูแลรักษาสุขภาพด้วยนะ (Take care of your health.)
G11-2	ตกลงนะครับ/คะ (Are you ok?)
G12-1	กรุณาติดต่อกลับมาใหม่ (Please contact again.)
G12-2	กลับถึงบ้านหรือยัง (Have you reached home?)
G13-1	วันนี้เรียนวิชาอะไร (What subject are you going to study today? or What subject have you studied today?)
G13-2	จะกลับถึงบ้านกี่โมง (When will you reach home?)
G14-1	กำลังทำอะไรอยู่เหรอ (What are you doing now?)
G14-2	วันนี้รถติดมากเลย (Traffic is/was bad today.)
G15-1	ขณะนี้เวลาแปดนาฬิกา (Now, the time is eight a.m.)
G15-2	ขอโทษนะครับ/คะ (I'm sorry.)
G17-2	ยุ่งอยู่หรือเปล่า (Are you busy now?)
G18-2	ตื่นนอนหรือยัง (Have you woken up yet?)
G20-1	วันนี้อากาศร้อนมาก (Today is very hot.)
G22-2	กินข้าวหรือยัง (Have you eaten food?)
G23-1	ขอบคุณมากครับ/ค่ะ (Thank you very much.)
G24-1	นอนหลับหรือยัง (Have you slept yet?)
G25-2	แค่นี้ก่อนนะครับ/คะ (Ok, I have to hang-up now.)

Table 4. Lists of TSST that were created and selected for this study

Subset of TSST	Item	Length (s)	Speech group no.
List2	A	8	G12-2
			G20-1
	B	8	G6-1
			Subset of TSST
	C	8	G4-1
			G8-2
List3	A	8	G2-2
			G10-2
			G22-2
	B	8	G13-2
			G15-2
			G18-2
	C	8	G14-2
			G17-2
			G24-1
List4	A	10	G2-2
			G14-2
			G22-2
			G23-1
	B	10	G8-1
			G10-2
			G15-2
			G25-2
	C	12	G1-1
			G2-1
			G8-2
			G6-1
List10	A	30	G5-1
			G5-2
			G6-1
			G6-2
			G7-1
			G7-2
			G8-1
			G8-2
			G9-1
			G9-2
	B	30	G11-1
			G11-2
			G12-1
			G12-2
			G13-1
			G13-2
			G14-1
			G14-2
			G15-1
			G15-2

4)   List10: there are two forms of speech samples (A and B). Each speech sample, with the length of 30 s, consists of ten speech sentences. Also, for each form, there are 2 child speech samples (a boy and a girl), 4 female speech samples and 4 male speech samples; therefore, totally there are 20 speech samples for this speech list.

Then, all speech lists, which consist of 110 speech samples, were tested using the PESQ tool and the network simulator in VoIP Lab, KMUTT with G.711 (A-law) and G.729, referring to packet loss effects (0%, 2%, 6% and 10%). Totally, there are 8 under test conditions (2 codecs x 4 loss conditions). Each speech sample was repeated 10 times per condition; therefore, the gathered data from this study are 8,800 records totally.

4   Results and Discussion

After obtaining the data and MOS-LQO [2], only comparison between MOS-LQO provided by G.711 and G.729 but also three issues have been considered, type of speech (child, female and male) and comparison between the results from G.711 and G.729, and the comparison among the results from four lists of speech samples. Moreover, the trends of results from PESQ tests were compared with the subjective results from the other study in another laboratory. The results are shown below:

4.1   Comparison of MOS from Thai Speech of Child, Female and Male

For overall, as shown in Fig. 1 – Fig. 4, referring to packet loss effects, MOS- LQO from G.711 is higher than G.729. It is consistent with the subjective result as reported in [8]. Then the type of speech has been compared, as shown in Fig. 1 – Fig. 4, it can be seen that:

1)   At the best condition of packet loss (0%), the MOS-LQO from G.711 no significant difference among child speech, female speech and male speech was found. Whereas, it has been discovered that there is a slight difference among three of them from G.729, for male speech over female speech over child speech.

2)   For overall, it can be seen that MOS-LQO from G.711 is better than MOS-LQO from G.729 in each condition under testing.

3)   At the packet loss of 2%, 6% and 10%, the MOS-LQO from both G.711 and G.729, differences among three of them from G.729, for male speech over female speech over child speech were discovered.

4)   The results from all speech lists tend to be in the same manner that MOS-LQO from male speech is higher than female speech, whereas MOS-LQO from child speech is the worst. This might be one of the reasons that ITU-T does not provide child speech samples in [28]. For overall, the result from this study is consistent with the results from PESQ tests in [24] [12], whereas, it is inconsistent with the observed results from 3SQM tests in [12] and PESQ tests in [25].

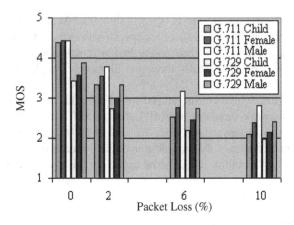

Fig. 1. Comparison of MOS among child speech, female speech and male speech from List2

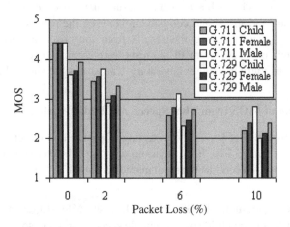

Fig. 2. Comparison of MOS among child speech, female speech and male speech from List3

Moreover, it is inconsistent with the result from [26]. It has been reported that interviewees prefer female interviewer over male interviewer, which might stem from the gender of speech.

Therefore, from the results, it can be summarized that PESQ tool responds to low speech frequency over high speech frequency because fundamental frequency of male speech is lower than female speech and child speech, as presented in [9]. This is evidence which can be used to improve objective tools when working with male and female speech. Of course, at present, child speech samples should not be used when studying objective methods (e.g. PESQ).

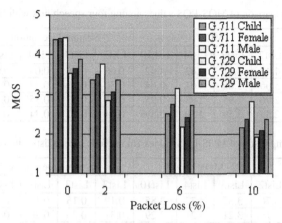

Fig. 3. Comparison of MOS among child speech, female speech and male speech from List4

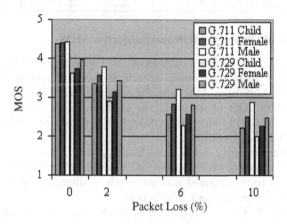

Fig. 4. Comparison of MOS among child speech, female speech and male speech from List10

4.2   Comparison of MOS from Four Speech Lists

As shown in Table 5, the results without MOS-LQO from child speech, one can see no difference of MOS-LOQ provided by G.711 from four speech lists, the maximum difference is 0.02 at packet loss of 2%, whereas MOS-LQO is exactly the same, 2.59, at packet loss rate of 10%. While, the standard deviation tends to be higher when the packet loss rate is increased.

For the results from G.729, as shown in Table 6, although there is no significant difference among the four speech lists, it can be observed that MOS-LQO values from List10 in all conditions are higher than List2 –List4, whereas, the standard deviation values from List10 are lower than the others.

Therefore, it can be summarized that each Thai speech list from TSST can be used with PESQ tool with confidence.

Table 5. Comparison of MOS-LQS values among four speech lists with G.711

Loss (%)	MOS				Standard Deviation			
	List2	List3	List4	List10	List2	List3	List4	List10
0	4.42	4.41	4.42	4.42	0.06	0.06	0.05	0.05
2	3.66	3.66	3.64	3.64	0.30	0.30	0.27	0.27
6	2.96	2.95	2.95	2.95	0.33	0.33	0.35	0.35
10	2.59	2.59	2.59	2.59	0.31	0.32	0.34	0.34

Table 6. Comparison of MOS-LQS values among four speech lists with G.729

Loss (%)	MOS				Standard Deviation			
	List2	List3	List4	List10	List2	List3	List4	List10
0	3.76	3.82	3.77	3.85	0.19	0.15	0.15	0.14
2	3.17	3.21	3.21	3.29	0.31	0.26	0.28	0.19
6	2.56	2.60	2.57	2.70	0.28	0.26	0.26	0.18
10	2.22	2.25	2.24	2.37	0.25	0.25	0.25	0.17

4.3   Comparison of Objective MOS and Subjective MOS

Similar to Section 4.2, MOS-LQO values from child speech were discarded, MOS-LQO from PESQ of male and female speech at the best condition have been compared with MOS-LQS from ACR listening tests in another laboratory [9], it has been found that MOS-LQO of 4.41-4.42, as in Table 5, is slightly higher than MOS-LQS of 4.23 for G.711, whereas MOS-LQS of 4.18 is higher than MOS-LQO of 3.76-3.85, as in Table 6, for G.729.

Without available subjective MOS from listening tests referring to packet loss effects, the result of objective MOS, MOS-LQO, from G.711 and G.729 in this study with Thai speech has been compared with the result of subjective MOS, MOS-CQS [1], from conversation tests that are available in [8].

As shown in Fig. 5, G.711, MOS-CQS is lower than MOS-LQO at the best condition of packet loss. However, MOS-CQS is higher than MOS-LQO at the other conditions, particularly packet loss of 6% and 10%.

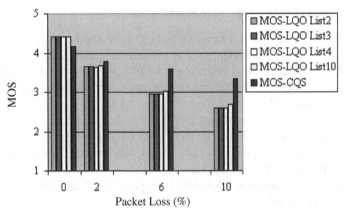

Fig. 5. Comparison of MOS-LQO and MOS-CQS from G.711

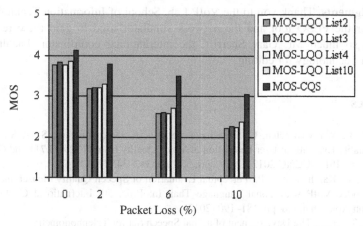

Fig. 6. Comparison of MOS-LQO and MOS-CQS from G.729

For G.729, as shown in Fig. 6, it can be seen that MOS-CQS at each condition it is higher than MOS-LQO significantly, particularly at packet loss of 2%, 6% and 10%.

However, this issue should be re-investigated and compared to MOS-LQS and MOS-LQO using Thai speech. Then, the localization-mapping factor based on Thai users should be found for PESQ calibration.

5   Conclusion and Future Work

This paper presents the comparative study of VoIP quality measurement from G.711(A-law) at 64 Kbps and G.729 at 8 Kbps using PESQ and Thai speech, referring to packet loss effects.

From this study with Thai speech, firstly, it has been found referring to packet loss that MOS-LQO from G.711 is slightly higher than MOS-LQO from G.729 in each condition. Also, it has been found that MOS-LQO from Thai male speech is higher than MOS-LQO from Thai female speech. Whereas, MOS-LQO from Thai child speech is the lowest, compared to the others. Therefore, it can be summarized that PESQ tends to give higher values of MOS-LQO for speech sample that have low fundamental frequency like male speech, due to the fundamental frequency of male speech is lower than female and child speech. Thus, PESQ should be improved to include this issue as future work.

Secondly, it has been found that there is no significant difference from this study that MOS-LQO from four speech lists (List2, List3, List4 and List10), although MOS-LQO from List10 seems slightly higher that MOS-LQO from others. Therefore, each of them can be used with confidence.

Lastly, it has been found that there are significant differences between objective MOS from PESQ and subjective MOS from conversation tests. Therefore, the MOS-LQS should be conducted using the four speech lists in this paper and then compared with MOS-LQO from this study as future work, in order to modify PESQ for Thai speech especially.

Acknowledgments. Thank you to the VoIP Lab, School of Information Technology, KMUTT for the PESQ tool and the network simulator used to gain these results. Thank you so much Mr. Gary Sherriff, the international coordinator, Faculty of Information Technology for editing.

References

1. Daengsi, T., Wutiwiwatchai, C., Preechayasomboon, A., Sukparungsee, S.: A Study of VoIP Quality Evaluation: User Perception of Voice Quality from G.729, G.711 and G.722. In: Proc. 9th IEEE-CCNC 2012, Las Vegas, NV, pp. 342–345 (2012)
2. Triyason, T., Kanthamanon, P.: Perceptual Evaluation of Speech Quality Measurement on Speex Codec VoIP with Tonal Language Thai. In: Proc. 5th International Conference IAIT, Bangkok, Thailand, pp. 181–190 (2012)
3. Daengsi, T., et al.: The Development of a Thai Speech Set for Telephonometry, http://desceco.org/O-COCOSDA2010/proceedings/paper_53.pdf (accessed November 2012)
4. Daengsi, T., Preechayasomboon, A., Sukparungsee, S., Wutiwiwatchai, C.: Thai Text Resource: A Recommended Thai Text Set for Voice Quality Measurements and Its Comparative Study. KKU Science Journal 40(4), 1114–1127 (2012)
5. ITU-T Recommendation P.800 (Methods for subjective determination of transmission quality), http://www.itu.int/rec/T-REC-P.800-199608-I/en (accessed November 2012)
6. Telchemy. Voice Quality Measurement (Application Note), http://www.telchemy.com/appnotes/ TelchemyVoiceQualityMeasurement.pdf (accessed August 2013)
7. Rango, F.D., et al.: Overview on VoIP: Subjective and Objective Measurement Methods. IJCSNC 6, 140–153 (2006)
8. Daengsi, T., Sukparungsee, S., Wutiwiwatchai, C., Preechayasomboon, A.: Comparison of Perceptual Voice Quality of VoIP Provided by G.711 and G.729 Using Conversation-Opinion Tests. IJCIM 20(1), 21–26 (2012)
9. Daengsi, T., Wutiwiwatchai, C., Preechayasomboon, A., Sukparungsee, S.: VoIP Quality Measurement: Insignificant Voice Quality of G.711 and G.729 Codecs in Listening-Opinion Tests by Thai Users. Information Technology Journal 8(1), 77–82 (2012)
10. http://ieeexplore.ieee.org/search/searchresult.jsp?queryText %3DVoIP+Quality+E-model&addRange=2009_2013_Publication_ Year&pageNumber=1&resultAction=REFINE (accessed August 2013)
11. http://ieeexplore.ieee.org/search/searchresult.jsp?queryText %3DVoIP+Quality+PESQ&addRange=2009_2013_Publication_ Year&pageNumber=1&resultAction=REFINE (accessed August 2013)
12. Goudarzi, M., Sun, L.: Performance analysis and comparison of PESQ and 3SQM in live 3G mobile networks, http://www.tech.plym.ac.uk/spmc/staff/ mgoudarzi/Performance%20analysis%20and%20comparison%20of% 20PESQ%20and%203SQM.pdf (accessed August 2013)
13. ITU-T Recommendation P.862. Perceptual evaluation of speech quality (PESQ): An objective method for end-to-end speech quality assessment of narrow-band telephone (2001)
14. ITU-T Recommendation P.862.2. Wideband extension to Recommendation P.862 for the assessment of wideband telephone networks and speech codecs (November 2007)

15. Karapantazis, S., Pavlidou, F.-N.: Voip: A comprehensive survey on a promising technology. Computer Networks 53, 2050–2090 (2009)
16. Ditech Networls. Limitations of PESQ for Measuring Voice Quality in Mobile and VoIP Networks, https://www.google.co.th/url?sa=t&rct=j&q=&esrc=s& source=web&cd=1&ved=0CDEQFjAA&url=http%3A%2F %2Fwww.packagingdigest.com%2Ffile%2F4534-white_paper_ on_the_limitations_of_PESQ.pdf%3Fforce%3Dtrue&ei=NTdFUoXmHIH QrQfU2oHoDw&usg=AFQjCNGKfvZ5aWrk_kD2wr8IkamNfku5zw&bvm=bv.53 217764,d.bmk (accessed September 2013)
17. Daengsi, T.: VoIP Quality Measurement: Recommendation of MOS and Enhance Objective Measurement Method for Standard Spoken Thai Language. Ph.D. Thesis, Faculty of Information Technology, King Mongkut's University of Technology North Bangkok (November 2012)
18. Sodanil, M., Nitsuwat, S., Haruechaiyasak, C.: Thai Word Recognition Using Hybrid MLP-HMM. IJCSNS 10(3), 103–110 (2010)
19. Wutiwiwatchai, C., Furui, S.: Thai speech processing technology: A review. Speech Communication 49, 8–27 (2007)
20. Sittiprapaporn, W., Chindaduangratn, C., Kotchabhakdi, N.: Brain electric activity during the preattentive perception of speech sounds in tonal languages. SJST 26, 439–445 (2004)
21. Sittiprapaporn, W., Chindaduangratn, C., Kotchabhakdi, N.: Functional Specialization of the Human Auditory Cortex in Processing of Speech Prosody: A Low Resolution Electromagnetic Tomography (LORETA) Study, http://anchan.lib.ku.ac.th/ kukr/bitstream/003/17786/1/KC4205011.pdf (accessed December 2012)
22. IEEE. Recommended practice for speech quality measurements. IEEE Trans. on Audio Electroacoust. 17(3), 225–246 (1969)
23. Suayroop, K., et al.: A VoIP Quality Measurement Study with Thai Speech Sets Using PESQ and G.711A-law. In: Proc. 34th Electricall Engineering Conference (EECON-34), Chonburi, Thailand (2011)
24. Sun, L., Ifeachor, E.: Perceived Speech Quality Prediction for Voice over IP-based Networks. In: Proc. IEEE Int. Conf. Communications 2002 (ICC 2002), New York, NY, pp. 2573–2577 (2002)
25. Ren, J., Zhang, H., Zhu, Y., Goa, C.: Assessment of effects of different language in VOIP. In: Proc. Int. Conf. Audio, Language and Image Processing (ICALIP 2008), Shanghai, China, pp. 1624–1628 (2008)
26. Daengsi, T., Wutiwiwatchai, C., Preechayasomboon, A., Sukparungsee, S.: Speech Quality Assessment of VoIP: G.711 VS G.722 Based on Interview Tests with Thai Users. IJITCS 4(2), 19–25 (2012)
27. ITU-T Recommendation P.862.3 (Application guide for objective quality measurement base on Recommendations P.862, P.862.1 and P.862.2) (November 2007)
28. Annex B Speech files, ITU-T Recommendation P.501, http://www.itu.int/ net/itu-/sigdb/genaudio/AudioForm-.aspx?val=10000501 (accessed August 2013)

A New Multi-sensor Track Association Approach Based on Intuitionistic Fuzzy Clustering

Zhao Lingling, Dong Xianglei, Ma Peijun, Su Xiaohong, and Shi Chunmei

Harbin Institute of Technology, Harbin, China
hit.zhaolingling@gmail.com

Abstract. To extend some multi-target trackers to a multi-sensor scenario for improving their accuracy and dependable, an efficient track association and fusion algorithm is necessary. This paper proposes a new track association approach which imports the intuitionistic fuzzy set into track association. The proposed method firstly transforms the extracted target states into intuitionistic fuzzy sets, then makes use of the clustering intuitionistic fuzzy sets to obtain an equivalent association matrix, and finally associates and fuses the states from different sensors with the equivalent matrix. The numerical simulation results show that this method can significantly control the time cost and performs better compared with the association algorithm with fuzzy clustering.

Keywords: multi-target tracking, multi-sensor, track association, intuitionistic fuzzy sets.

1 Introduction

The probability hypothesis density (PHD) filter [1,2] and the cardinalized PHD (CPHD) filter [3] can handle with a time-varying and unknown number of target tracking problem and become practical in the field of multi-target tracking. But when these filters are extended to a multi-sensor system, some additional means have to be used to distinguish which target these tracks from multiple sensors belong to. In this case, a multi-sensor track association and fusion algorithm is essential.

Multi-sensor track association is to combine tracks obtained from the filters of diverse sensors, sensing multiple objects to yield improved accuracy and more inferences than in a single sensor system. Up to now, different methods have been introduced into multi-sensor track association, including fuzzy clustering [4,5], NN algorithm [6], neural network [7], equivalent innovations [8], K-Medoids clustering [9] and particle cloud [10], etc. These methods improved the accuracy and efficiency of multi-sensor fusion to some extent. Nevertheless, they do not consider the uncertain correlative ingredient which exists among tracks in the process of track association.

Thankfully, the uncertainty can be dealt with by Intuitionistic fuzzy sets (IFS)[11]. IFS was proposed by Atanassov, as a generalization of Zadeh's fuzzy set, characterized by a membership function and a non-membership function. In comparison with fuzzy sets, IFS show better suitability for expressing a degree of hesitation of a

B. Papasratorn et al. (Eds.): IAIT 2013, CCIS 409, pp. 256–266, 2013.

decision process. Relying on the unique advantage of IFS in performance of uncertainty or hesitation of associated information among tracks, this paper takes the concept of IFS into account and proposes a computationally efficient and cost effective multi-sensor track association method combined with intuitionistic fuzzy clustering algorithm, Results from Monte Carlo simulations show that the proposed method performs track association and fusion better compared with the method employing fuzzy clustering.

The remainder of this paper is organized as follows. A brief problem description is addressed in section 2. In section 3, we review the definition of IFS and introduce the steps of transformation from target states to IFSs. The multi-sensor track association approach based on intuitionistic fuzzy clustering is presented in section 4. The results of simulation are provided in section 5 while the conclusion is in section 6.

2   Track Association in Multi-sensor Multi-target Systems

2.1   Track Association Description

In this section, the problems of track association and fusion in a multi-sensor multi-target situation are formulated using the following tracking example.

Assume there are M sensors in an overlapping coverage scenario, represented by $S_1, S_2, \ldots, S_M$, each of which observes a set of targets whose number is unknown time-varying. In general track association problem, most researchers focus on the correlation among whole tracks, but here we only talk about associating and fusing the tracks from one frame at time k, then the track association shrinks to state association. Suppose that N_1 target states are estimated from S_1, N_2 target states from S_2, ... , and N_M target states from S_M, these target states are sequentially denoted by

$$x_1, \ldots, x_{N_1}, \ldots, x_{N_1+N_2}, \ldots, x_{N_1+N_2+N_3}, \ldots, x_{N_1+\cdots+N_M} \tag{1}$$

where each target state is composed of L attributes

$$x_i = \left(x_{i1}, \ldots, x_{ij}, \ldots, x_{iL} \right) \tag{2}$$

where scalar x_{ij} represents the j th attribute of target state x_i, $1 \leq j \leq L$.

The goal is to divide the $N_1 + N_2 + \ldots + N_M$ states into several groups and ensure that states in one group come from a same target. In general, states with similar attribute values are more probably from one target, so we only select those with similar attribute values to compose a group. What's more, when clustering a track group, no more than one state of a sensor can be selected because of the assumption that one sensor receives at most one observation from a target.

2.2   Intuitionistic Fuzzy Set and Clustering

Intuitionistic fuzzy set(IFS) is a generalization of fuzzy set proposed by Zadeh. Besides membership degree and non-membership degree, it extends fuzzy set with uncertainty (or hesitation) degree to describe the uncertainty or hesitation to certain statement and is defined as follows:

$$A = \{< x, \mu_A(x), v_A(x) \mid x \in X >\} \tag{3}$$

Where X is a universe of discourse, $\mu_A(x)$ is a membership degree while $v_A(x)$ is a non-membership degree. They satisfy the following conditions:

$$\mu_A(x) \in [0,1], v_A(x) \in [0,1], \mu_A(x) + v_A(x) \in [0,1] \tag{4}$$

The degree of uncertainty (or hesitation) of x to A is defined as:

$$\pi_A(x) = 1 - \mu_A(x) - v_A(x) \tag{5}$$

Obviously, $\pi_A(x) \in [0,1]$ and when $\pi_A(x) = 0$, that means uncertainty does not exist, then the IFS A is equivalent to a FS. Since IFS has more capacity to deal with vagueness and uncertainty than fuzzy set, it's a natural choice to replace FS with IFS to solve the track association problem.

3   Transformation from Target States to IFSs

We present a new track association and fusion algorithm based on IFS, the framework of which is shown as figure 1. This algorithm composes of two main stages: transformation from Target States to IFSs, and track association and fusion.

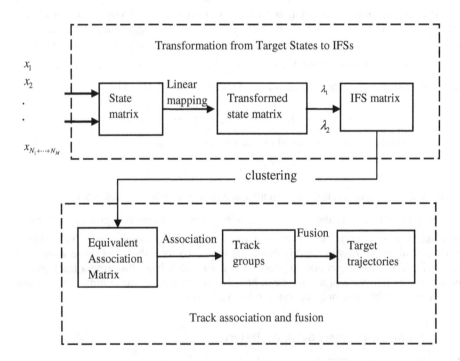

Fig. 1. The framework of track association and fusion algorithm

As mentioned above, attributes of target states suggest the possibility of state association, so we can cluster the states according to the relationships between values of their attributes. This section proposes a method to transforms the target states into IFS to express uncertainty of state relationships based on their attributes.

For simplicity, the $N_1 + N_2 + ... + N_M$ states in (1) are expressed by the following state matrix

$$X_S = \begin{bmatrix} x_{11} & x_{12} & \cdots & x_{1L} \\ \vdots & \vdots & \vdots & \vdots \\ x_{N_1 1} & x_{N_1 2} & \cdots & x_{N_1 L} \\ x_{(N_1+1)1} & x_{(N_1+1)2} & \cdots & x_{(N_1+1)L} \\ \vdots & \vdots & \vdots & \vdots \\ x_{(N_1+\cdots+N_M)1} & x_{(N_1+\cdots+N_M)2} & \cdots & x_{(N_1+\cdots+N_M)L} \end{bmatrix}$$

where each row represents one target and the first N_1 rows belong to sensor S_1, the next N_2 rows belong to sensor $S_2, \dots$, the last N_M rows belong to sensor S_M.

There may be negative elements in X_S, which can not be dealt with by IFS. So we need to make them positive using mapping which must satisfy the following properties

1)   If $x_{ij} \le x_{ik}$, $f(x_{ij}) \le f(x_{ik})$;

2)   For any x_{ij}, $f(x_{ij}) \ge 0$.

A variety of mapping strategies may be practical options, such as linear mapping and exponential mapping. For convenience, this paper selects linear mapping for an example. We can use the following linear mapping for each element in each column of X_S

$$x'_{ij} = x_{ij} - x_{j\min} \tag{6}$$

where

$$x_{j\min} = \min(x_{1j}, x_{2j}, \cdots, x_{(N_1+\cdots+N_M)j}) \tag{7}$$

then (3) is transformed into the following matrix

$$X'_S = \begin{bmatrix} x'_{11} & x'_{12} & \cdots & x'_{1L} \\ \vdots & \vdots & \vdots & \vdots \\ x'_{N_1 1} & x'_{N_1 2} & \cdots & x'_{N_1 L} \\ x'_{(N_1+1)1} & x'_{(N_1+1)2} & \cdots & x'_{(N_1+1)L} \\ \vdots & \vdots & \vdots & \vdots \\ x'_{(N_1+\cdots+N_M)1} & x'_{(N_1+\cdots+N_M)2} & \cdots & x'_{(N_1+\cdots+N_M)L} \end{bmatrix}$$

Now the IFS of each attribute in X'_S can be calculated in the following way:

1) For each element x'_{ij} in each column, select two thresholds λ_1 and λ_2, $\lambda_1 < \lambda_2$;

2) If $\left| x_{ij}' - x_{kj}' \right| \le \lambda_1, k = 1,2,\cdots, N_1 + \cdots + N_M$, x_{kj}' can be regarded as a membership of x_{ij}'. Let $x_{support} = \sum x_{kj}'$, then the membership degree of x_{ij}' can be calculated by:

$$\mu\left(x_{ij}' \right) = \frac{x_{support}}{\sum_{n=1}^{m_1+m_2} x_{nj}'} \tag{8}$$

3) If $\left| x_{ij}' - x_{lj}' \right| \ge \lambda_2$, $l = 1,2,\cdots, N_1 + \cdots + N_M$, then x_{lj}' is treated as a non-membership of x_{ij}'. Let $x_{objection} = \sum x_{lj}'$, the non-membership degree of x_{ij}' can be calculated by:

$$v\left(x_{ij}' \right) = \frac{x_{objection}}{\sum_{n=1}^{m_1+m_2} x_{nj}'} \tag{9}$$

After these steps, X_S' is converted into the following matrix

$$X_{IFS} = \begin{bmatrix} \left[\mu(x_{11}'), v(x_{11}') \right] & \left[\mu(x_{12}'), v(x_{12}') \right] & \cdots & \left[\mu(x_{1L}'), v(x_{1L}') \right] \\ \left[\mu(x_{21}'), v(x_{21}') \right] & \left[\mu(x_{22}'), v(x_{22}') \right] & \cdots & \left[\mu(x_{2L}'), v(x_{2L}') \right] \\ \vdots & \vdots & \vdots & \vdots \\ \left[\mu(x_{(N_1+\cdots+N_M)1}'), v(x_{(N_1+\cdots+N_M)1}') \right] & \left[\mu(x_{(N_1+\cdots+N_M)2}'), v(x_{(N_1+\cdots+N_M)2}') \right] & \cdots & \left[\mu(x_{(N_1+\cdots+N_M)L}'), v(x_{(N_1+\cdots+N_M)L}') \right] \end{bmatrix}$$

X_{IFS} is the IFS matrix transformed from X_S' and each row is still related to a target.

Note that the selection of λ_1 and λ_2 should be reasonable to distinguish the membership, non-membership and uncertainty degree of each attribute in the transformation. In this paper, we let

$$\text{for } x_{ij}', \quad d_{ij}^k = \left| x_{ij}' - x_{kj}' \right|, k = 1,2,\cdots, N_1 + \cdots + N_M \tag{10}$$

sort $d_{ij}^k, k = 1,2,\cdots, N_1 + \cdots + N_M$ in ascending order

$$\tilde{d}_1, \cdots, \tilde{d}_{\lfloor (N_1+\cdots+N_M)/3 \rfloor}, \cdots, \tilde{d}_{\lceil 2(N_1+\cdots+N_M)/3 \rceil}, \cdots, \tilde{d}_{N_1+\cdots+N_M} \tag{11}$$

then we define λ_1 and λ_2 as follows:

$$\lambda_1 = d_{\lfloor (N_1+\cdots+N_M)/3 \rfloor}' \tag{12}$$
$$\lambda_2 = d_{\lceil 2(N_1+\cdots+N_M)/3 \rceil}'$$

4   Association and Fusion Algorithm

Here we describe the state association and fusion steps based on intuitionistic fuzzy clustering, including calculation of association coefficients of IFSs, how to obtain an equivalent association matrix from a similar association matrix and how to use the equivalent association matrix to associate and fuse tracks.

4.1   Calculations of Association Coefficients of IFSs

Many methods have been proposed to calculate the association coefficients of IFSs [12-13]. We only consider the situation of discrete universe of discourse in this paper and select the following formula to calculate the association coefficients of two IFSs A and B

$$c(A,B)=\frac{\sum_{j=1}^{n}w_{j}\left(\mu_{A}(x_{j})\cdot\mu_{B}(x_{j})+v_{A}(x_{j})\cdot v_{B}(x_{j})+\pi_{A}(x_{j})\cdot\pi_{B}(x_{j})\right)}{\max\left(\sum_{j=1}^{n}w_{j}\left(\mu_{A}^{2}(x_{j})+v_{A}^{2}(x_{j})+\pi_{A}^{2}(x_{j})\right),\sum_{j=1}^{n}w_{j}\left(\mu_{B}^{2}(x_{j})+v_{B}^{2}(x_{j})+\pi_{B}^{2}(x_{j})\right)\right)} \quad (13)$$

where $w=(w_{1},w_{2},...,w_{n})$ is the weight vector of $x_{i}\,(i=1,2,...,n)$ with $w_{i}\geq0$ and $\sum_{i=1}^{n}w_{i}=1$.

According to (13), we can get the association coefficient of two different rows (corresponding to two targets) in X_{IFS}. In this way, $(N_{1}+N_{2}+...+N_{M})^{2}$ association coefficients can be obtained easily.

4.2   Construction of Equivalent Association Matrix

Construct a matrix for the $(N_{1}+N_{2}+...+N_{M})^{2}$ association coefficients. The matrix includes $(N_{1}+N_{2}+...+N_{M})$ rows and $(N_{1}+N_{2}+...+N_{M})$ columns.

$$C=\begin{bmatrix} c_{11} & c_{12} & \cdots & c_{1(N_{1}+\cdots+N_{M})} \\ c_{21} & c_{22} & \cdots & c_{2(N_{1}+\cdots+N_{M})} \\ \vdots & \vdots & \vdots & \vdots \\ c_{(N_{1}+\cdots+N_{M})1} & c_{(N_{1}+\cdots+N_{M})2} & \cdots & c_{(N_{1}+\cdots+N_{M})(N_{1}+\cdots+N_{M})} \end{bmatrix} \quad (14)$$

where c_{ij} represents the association coefficient of the i th target and the j th target.

C is only a similar association matrix which does not satisfy transitivity. One method is to seek for the transitive closure by composition operation to get the equivalent association matrix. we can calculate the transitive closure of C according to the clustering process proposed in [14]. Suppose that the required equivalent matrix is the following matrix

$$\bar{C}=\begin{bmatrix} \bar{c}_{11} & \bar{c}_{12} & \cdots & \bar{c}_{1(N_{1}+\cdots+N_{M})} \\ \bar{c}_{21} & \bar{c}_{22} & \cdots & \bar{c}_{2(N_{1}+\cdots+N_{M})} \\ \vdots & \vdots & \vdots & \vdots \\ \bar{c}_{(N_{1}+\cdots+N_{M})1} & \bar{c}_{(N_{1}+\cdots+N_{M})2} & \cdots & \bar{c}_{(N_{1}+\cdots+N_{M})(N_{1}+\cdots+N_{M})} \end{bmatrix} \quad (15)$$

4.3   Track Association

$\overline{C}$ can be represented as the following form:

$$S = \begin{bmatrix} S_{11} & S_{12} & \cdots & S_{1M} \\ S_{21} & S_{22} & \cdots & S_{2M} \\ \vdots & \vdots & \vdots & \vdots \\ S_{M1} & S_{M2} & \cdots & S_{MM} \end{bmatrix} \qquad (16)$$

where S_{ij} represents the equivalent association matrix between S_i and S_j,

$$S_{ij} = \begin{bmatrix} \overline{c}_{11} & \overline{c}_{12} & \cdots & \overline{c}_{1N_j} \\ \overline{c}_{21} & \overline{c}_{22} & \cdots & \overline{c}_{2N_j} \\ \vdots & \vdots & \cdots & \vdots \\ \overline{c}_{N_i1} & \overline{c}_{N_i1} & \cdots & \overline{c}_{N_iN_j} \end{bmatrix} \qquad (17)$$

Next, we introduce the track association rules between two sensors taking the case of S_{12}. we assume that the targets omitted by sensor 1 and the targets omitted by sensor 2 represent same targets. The association steps are introduced below:

1) Seek for the largest element $\overline{c}_{ij}^{\lambda}$ in S_{12}, $1 \le i \le N_1$ and $1 \le j \le N_2$;

2) Associate the i th target from sensor 1 and the j th target from sensor 2, then let all elements in the i th row or the j th column be zero;

3) Repeat step 1~2 until all element values in S_{12} are zero.

The above steps resemble greedy algorithm, and after those, $\min(N_1, N_2)$ pairs of states can be displayed.

4.4   Track Fusion

Since we have little prior knowledge about the sensors, the equal-weighted fusion method is only considered in the fusion step.

Assume that the states estimated from two sensors are all true target states, then the pairs of tracks obtained from the association step are fused as follows:

$$x_k = 0.5 * x_{1i} + 0.5 * x_{2j}, 1 \le i \le N_1, 1 \le j \le N_2, 1 \le k \le \min(N_1, N_2) \qquad (18)$$

where x_{1i} represents the i th target state from sensor 1, x_{2j} the j th target state from sensor 2 and x_k the new target state after fusion.

However, there does not always exist the condition of $N_1 = N_2$, which means there may be some states from sensor 1 or sensor 2 which are not associated in the association step. In this situation, we keep these target states without any change. Therefore, the number of the new target states is $\max(N_1, N_2)$ after fusion.

5   Simulations

Here we verify the effectiveness of the method this paper proposed in the situation of two sensors. Assume that the positions of the two sensors are $\left(x^{(1)}, y^{(1)}\right) = (-200, -200)$ and $\left(x^{(2)}, y^{(2)}\right) = (200, 200)$. Targets move in the region $[-200, 200] \times [-200, 200]$ and its number is time-varying.

The state equation is

$$X_k = \begin{pmatrix} 1 & T & 0 & 0 \\ 0 & 1 & 0 & 0 \\ 0 & 0 & 1 & T \\ 0 & 0 & 0 & 1 \end{pmatrix} X_{k-1} + \begin{pmatrix} T^2/2 & 0 \\ T & 0 \\ 0 & T^2/2 \\ 0 & T \end{pmatrix} v_{k-1} \tag{19}$$

and the measure equation is

$$r_k^{(s)} = \left\| \begin{pmatrix} 1 & 0 & 0 & 0 \\ 0 & 0 & 1 & 0 \end{pmatrix} X_k - \begin{pmatrix} x^{(s)} \\ y^{(s)} \end{pmatrix} \right\| + n_{1,k}^{(s)} \tag{20}$$

$$\theta_k^{(s)} = \arctan\left(\frac{y_k - y^{(s)}}{x_k - x^{(s)}}\right) + n_{2,k}^{(s)}, s = 1,2 \tag{21}$$

where $X_k = \left(x_k, \dot{x}_k, y_k, \dot{y}_k\right)^T$ with the weight vector in the process of calculating the coefficients of IFSs being $w = [0.3, 0.2, 0.3, 0.2]$, v_k is a 2-D zero-mean Gaussian white noise with the covariance matrix $diag[1, 0.01]$. $n_{i,k}^{(j)}$ $(i, j = 1, 2)$ are the independent zero-mean Gaussian white noise with standard deviation 2.5. $T = 1$ is the sampling period. Assume six targets appear and disappear randomly and their initial positions follow the intensity function $p_k = N(\cdot, \bar{x}, Q)$ where $\bar{x} = (0, 3, 0, -3)^T$ and $Q = diag[10, 1, 10, 1]$. The clutter number follows a Poisson distribution with the parameter r while the clutter points follow a uniform distribution in the surveillance region. We set the detection probability $P_D = 0.99$ and the frame number is 50.

We denote the track associating and fusion approach based on fuzzy clustering proposed in [4] by FS-FUSION and our method by IFS-FUSION. The four Wasserstein miss-distances displayed in the following figures show the results of sensor 1 and sensor 2 without track fusion, FS-FUSION and IFS-FUSION when r=0, r=10, and r=50, where r is the parameter of Poisson distribution clutter follows. Here we choose different r in order to evaluate the performance of the proposed algorithm in different clutter density cases, including no clutter, sparse clutter and dense clutter.

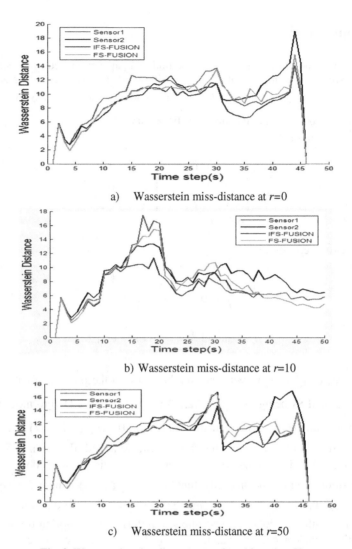

a)   Wasserstein miss-distance at *r*=0

b) Wasserstein miss-distance at *r*=10

c)   Wasserstein miss-distance at *r*=50

Fig. 2. Wasserstein miss-distance at *r*=0, *r*=10, and *r*=50

The average results over 50 Monte Carlo runs of the mean and the variance of the miss-distance error and the association time of FS-FUSION and IFS-FUSION are listed as follows.

From the figures and tables, we can get the conclusion that the proposed method in this paper improves accuracy of target tracking and performs better than FS-FUSION, especially when the number of targets increases. They also show that IFS-FUSION and FS-FUSION outperform the algorithm only using observations from one sensor. Furthermore, the average data listed in above tables display that IFS-FUSION has smaller means and variances of miss-distance than FS-FUSION with the only disadvantage of some extra time because of the transformation from target states to IFSs.

Table 1. Average results over 50 Monte Carlo runs

		Wasserstein Miss-distance		Run time(s)
		Mean	*Variance*	
r=0	IFS-FUSION	6.579	0.844	0.037
	FS-FUSION	7.431	1.413	0.020
	Sensor 1	7.369	1.618	/
	Sensor 2	7.950	1.309	/
r=10	IFS-FUSION	6.601	0.575	0.035
	FS-FUSION	7.514	0.893	0.016
	Sensor 1	7.628	3.141	/
	Sensor 2	8.395	1.226	/
r=50	IFS-FUSION	6.604	0.838	0.030
	-FUSION	7.608	0.976	0.014
	Sensor 1	7.903	2.566	/
	Sensor 2	8.298	1.804	/

6   Conclusions

In this paper, we propose a new track association method based on intuitionistic fuzzy clustering for multi-sensor multi-target tracking. The proposed method takes the uncertainty in track association into account by IFS and obtains the correlation coefficients of tracks by IFS clustering, then finds out the pairs of tracks using these coefficients and fuses them by weighted average fusion. The simulation results show that regardless of a little extra time consuming, IFS-FUSION has higher accuracy and efficiency after fusion compared with FS-FUSION.

Acknowledgment. This paper was supported by the National Natural Science Foundation of China (NSFC) under Grant 61175027 and 61305013, the Fundamental Research Funds for the Central Universities (Grant No. HIT. NSRIF. 2014071).

References

1. Mahler, R.P.: Random-set approach to data fusion. In: SPIE's International Symposium on Optical Engineering and Photonics in Aerospace Sensing, vol. 2234, pp. 287–295. International Society for Optics and Photonics, Orlando (1994)
2. Mahler, R.P.: Multi-target Bayes filtering via first-order multi-target moments. IEEE Transactions on Aerospace and Electronic Systems 39, 1152–1178 (2003)
3. Mahler, R.P.: PHD filter of higher order in target number. IEEE Transactions on Aerospace and Electronic Systems 43, 1523–1543 (2007)
4. Hang, Y.P., Zhou, Y.F., Li, L., Zhang, H.B.: Multi-sensor track association algorithm based on transitive closure clustering. Journal of Wuhan University of Technology 32, 834–837 (2008) (in Chinese)

5. Ashraf, M.A.: Fuzzy Track-to-Track Association and Track Fusion Approach in Distributed Multisensor-Multitarget Multiple-Attribute Environment. Signal Processing 87, 1474–1492 (2007)
6. Bruder, S., Johnson, R., Farooq, M.: A NN Type Multi-Sensor Tracking and Identification Algorithm. IEEE Transactions on Circuits and Systems 1, 492–495 (1993)
7. Duan, M., Liu, J.H.: Track correlation algorithm based on neural network. In: 2009 Second International Symposium on Computational Intelligence and Design, vol. 2, pp. 181–185 (2009)
8. Musicki, D., Evans, R.J.: Track fusion using equivalent innovations. In: The 10th International Conference on Information Fusion, pp. 581–588 (2007)
9. Xu, L., Ma, P.J., Su, X.H.: A multi-sensor track association algorithm based on K-Medoids clustering. Journal of Harbin Institute of Technology 44, 107–111 (2012)
10. Zhenwei, L., Lingling, Z., Xiaohong, S., Peijun, M.: A STPHD-Based Multi-sensor Fusion Method. In: Huang, T., Zeng, Z., Li, C., Leung, C.S. (eds.) ICONIP 2012, Part III. LNCS, vol. 7665, pp. 100–107. Springer, Heidelberg (2012)
11. Atanassov, K.T.: Intuitionistic fuzzy sets. Fuzzy Sets and Systems 20, 87–96 (1986)
12. Gerstenkorn, T., Mańko, J.: Correlation of intuitionistic fuzzy sets. Fuzzy Sets and Systems 44, 39–43 (1991)
13. Hong, D.H., Hwang, S.Y.: Correlation of intuitionistic fuzzy sets in probability spaces. Fuzzy Sets and Systems 75, 77–81 (1995)
14. Zhang, S., Xu, H., Chen, J., Wu, J.J.: Clustering algorithm for intuitionistic fuzzy sets. Information Sciences 178, 3775–3790 (2008)

Author Index